SCC Library

P9-DUA-898

Santiago Canyon College
Library

INTERNATIONAL
JOBS

HF
5382.7
.K62
2003

SIXTH EDITION

INTERNATIONAL
JOBS

Where They Are,
How to Get Them

NINA SEGAL

ERIC KOCHER

RESEARCH ASSISTANCE BY
Michael Kovrig

BASIC
BOOKS

A Member of the Perseus Books Group

CM69671480

Santiago Canyon College
Library

Copyright © 2003 by The Estate of Eric Kocher

Published by Basic Books, A Member of the Perseus Books Group.

All rights reserved. No part of this publication may be reproduced,
stored in a retrieval system, or transmitted, in any form or by any means,
electronic, mechanical, photocopying, recording, or otherwise, without
the prior written permission of the publisher. For information, address
Basic Books, 387 Park Avenue South, New York, NY 10016-8810. Printed
in the United States of America.

Cataloging-in-Publication Data is available from the Library of Congress.
ISBN 0-7382-0746-2

Books published by Basic Books are available at special discounts for
bulk purchases in the U.S. by corporations, institutions, and other
organizations. For more information, please contact the Special Markets
Department at the Perseus Books Group, 11 Cambridge Center,
Cambridge, MA 02142, or call (800) 255-1514 or (617) 252-5298,
or e-mail j.mccrary@perseusbooks.com.

Text design by Brent Wilcox
Set in 11.5-point Kepler MM by the Perseus Books Group

First printing, August 2003

2 3 4 5 6 7 8 9 10—06 05 04

IN MEMORIAM

Eric Kocher
1912–1999

Eric Kocher, the original author of *International Jobs,* was a Foreign Service Officer with the U.S. Department of State and Associate Dean of the School of International Affairs at Columbia University. He loved having the opportunity to provide counsel and advice to those seeking to pursue a career on the international scene and particularly enjoyed listening to and learning about their dreams and aspirations as they sought to identify their role and calling in life.

The Kocher family

Kim Rebecca Segal
1970–2002

My dearest little sister, Kimber.
My circle is ever incomplete.
I miss you.

NJS

CONTENTS

ACKNOWLEDGMENTS

As any author knows, a book is a collective effort. I am indebted to many individuals who generously gave their time, energy, and expertise.

First and foremost, my research assistant, Michael Kovrig, a Stakhanovite (smile) if there ever was one. Thank you for your energy, creativity, and fastidiousness in consistently unearthing new websites and, of course, excellent research and writing skills as we updated the several hundred organizations in this book. Michael assumed this added responsibility as a graduate student, and even though the project morphed into quite a significant job, he never complained and always met deadline. He e-mailed me bits and segments of the book from around the world, always keeping an excellent sense of humor.

I'd also like to give thanks to my editor, Ingrid Finstuen at Perseus Books, who joined me midway through the project. She jumped right in, familiarizing herself with the book and the subject matter quickly and easily. Ingrid: I appreciate your constant encouragement, reminders to me to add more and more of my own voice, and excellent editorial suggestions.

I would like to extend my gratitude to multiple friends and colleagues—old and new—experts in the field of international affairs who gave freely of their time and wisdom to provide insights into trends and new resources and to comment on the manuscript. To my stars: Christopher Abbruzesse, Timothy Bishop, Benjamin Garcia, Eric Henderson, Judith Hegedus, and Milburn Line. Thanks, too, to David Ritchie, for technical assistance when it was needed most.

It is also important to acknowledge the Kocher family, particularly Eric Kocher Jr., who graciously ceded the responsibility for another complete rewrite with absolute trust and warmth. I have worked hard to continue what your father began almost three decades ago, and I hope you are pleased with the results.

Let me end with my most important inner circle—Will, Isabel, Mom, and Dad—patient, loving, and constantly in my court.

—Nina Segal

INTRODUCTION

Rewriting a book on international careers is always a challenge, because career trends shift with political and economic changes. This edition certainly was no exception. Since the first edition of *International Jobs* was published more than twenty years ago, opportunities for global work have exploded, and more people than ever are interested in doing "something international."

For the sixth edition of *International Jobs*, it would be remiss not to acknowledge the effects of September 11. It is accurate to say that the world as most people knew it has changed dramatically, and the aftermath has forced a large segment of the public to take a closer look at international affairs. Policy institutes, government and international agencies, and the media are reallocating resources to try to understand and grapple with overwhelming questions. Certainly, concern about expatriate security has increased, causing corporations to be more cautious about sending executives abroad. However, the field of international security is growing, and as a result more measures are being implemented to attempt to ensure the safety of students, volunteers, and professionals around the world.

What hasn't changed? The rewards of working internationally remain the same—an opportunity to see the world through a different lens; learn firsthand about a new country, culture, and perhaps region; and gain the chance to acquire a second (or third) language. Overseas work experience is becoming increasingly valued as more organizations go global and as domestic organizations increasingly interact with and serve a more diversified U.S. community. Fluidity, adaptability, flexibility, and sensitivity are all characteristics that are refined overseas, and they are quite important to success in today's job market.

Overall, the changes in the world economy, the technology boom, and life in the post–September 11 era combined have created new opportunities for those interested in working globally.

Hiring has slowed recently in the private sector as consulting, business, and banks cut their numbers of new recruits after several years of a hiring surge. The emerging markets explosion that heralded the late 1990s has given way to major political and economic woes in Latin America (Argentina and Colombia, for example) and Asia (Indonesia, Thailand). New grads and midcareer individuals are still sought, but in a more competitive way.

The downturn in the private sector was somewhat balanced by certain areas of growth in the federal government. The Foreign Service is in the process of greatly expanding its ranks due to a shortage in officers. As a result, in 2002, for the first time, the State Department offered the Foreign Service Exam twice in one year instead of just once. The Central Intelligence Agency is expanding its ranks, as are other agencies that are dealing aggressively with international security and counterterrorism.

Another trend has been the rapid inclusion of technology into global career development. When the fifth edition of *International Jobs* went to press in 1999, the Internet was slowly becoming part of a job seeker's reality; today, it is almost impossible to conduct an international job search without extensively searching the web. You will see this reflected in this sixth edition—hundreds of new sites have been added, providing invaluable information about career development, the job search, global career options, and important job links.

What does all this mean for the international job seeker? Things are quite competitive, particularly in the private sector. This is nothing new for globetrotters—investing in the right education and experience and paying your dues have always been tenets of the international job world. And this sixth edition of *International Jobs* is an excellent place, we believe, to begin.

The new edition has been dramatically updated. You will find detailed information on new hiring procedures for both the federal government and the United Nations, a greatly revised international banking and consulting section, hundreds of new websites on everything from the global job search to international journalism job sites, and a chapter on nongovernmental organizations with additional information on trends in each subfield. We believe that it is *the* essential resource for the media-savvy international job seeker.

So, dust off your passport, open this book, start planning, and, as some dear friends write to me from each of their travels, "Ride Safe, Ride Far, and Ride Often. . . ."

PART
ONE

Introduction to International
Career Development

1

First Questions

INTERNATIONAL JOB OPPORTUNITIES cover a broad spectrum: federal government, business, communications, banking, nonprofit organizations and foundations, and multinational organizations such as the United Nations (UN) system.

This diversity of fields affords unparalleled opportunities for those of you who know what you want to do in the international framework and who prepare yourselves accordingly. A career decision, however, needs focus and definition if you want it to work for you. "Doing something international" is usually only the first stage in a decision. Your goals must be clearly defined to help you compete effectively with others who are also entering the international market.

Do you want to be a Foreign Service officer working in one of the embassies of the U.S. Department of State? Do you wish to be an intelligence analyst for the federal government? Or a bank manager in some remote—or cosmopolitan—part of the globe? How about a UN employee working on development issues? Or a foreign correspondent in Rome, Paris, London—or Ouagadougou or Tegucigalpa—for one of the press services?

All of these are reasonable career goals. But don't be so rigidly committed to one that everything else is excluded. If, for example, you want to work in the UN Development Programme, don't overlook similar job opportunities in nonprofit organizations or with foundations. If your aim is to be a *New York Times* correspondent in Moscow, consider also working as an overseas press officer for the federal government's United States Information Agency (USIA) or for one of the wire services.

The first question, then, is "What is it I really want to do in the international field?" Your answer must be narrower than "doing something international" but broader than "working for UNICEF in Bangladesh." If you are really lucky, you may be able to achieve a very specific objective such as the latter, but it is generally preferable to keep yourself flexible—within limits. As you go through this book, you will find that a career objective need not be nailed down to one specific job. There are related jobs that will use your background just as fully and probably give you equal satisfaction.

After you have decided what you really want to do in the international field, you will come upon other major questions needing equal attention:

How available are jobs in the field or fields I have chosen?
How do I prepare myself so that my academic credentials are strong enough to attract employers?
What limiting factors (such as location and salary) exist in my job search?
Are there special considerations—because of the international aspect—that enter into my job strategy?
How will an international career compliment my lifestyle preferences and choices?

These are some of the questions that will be discussed in this book.

WHAT EXACTLY IS AN INTERNATIONAL JOB?

International does not necessarily mean *abroad*. You can have an international career working in the international division of a corporation in New York and only occasionally travel overseas. Or you can work in the Department of State and spend your whole career moving from country to country every two to three years. The usual international career, however, consists of varying degrees of work at headquarters and in the field.

Thus, it is important to keep an open mind as you begin to explore the international arena. Do not dismiss positions that at first appear more "domestic" than "international." International positions are often among the most prestigious within an organization, and you might be expected to first pay your dues in another capacity. This is particularly true in the private sector. If you pursue a graduate degree, possess language fluency, and obtain some overseas internship experience, you will be well positioned when that international assignment becomes available.

International jobs can increasingly be found outside of the traditional bastions: New York and Washington, D.C. As states become more active in promoting trade and investment and as smaller businesses pursue strategies of global expansion, the geographic options for international work have widened tremendously. For example, the West Coast has become the gateway to Asia, and many businesses that trade with Japan, China, Malaysia, Thailand, and Central Asia have chosen San Francisco, Los Angeles, or Seattle as their base of operations. Miami has also become an important hub for trade and finance with Latin America. Chicago, with its financial center, has increased its offering of international opportunities.

CAREER EXPLORATION: HOW DO YOU FIND OUT WHAT YOU WANT TO DO?

A specific job objective (or objectives) is the foundation on which the edifice of job hunting is built. If you don't know what you're looking for, the search becomes aimless and often futile. At least one in every five students that walks into my office for career counseling has difficulty articulating exactly what it is he or she wants to do. For example, one student recently talked to me about her interest in conflict resolution (she was taking a great class in the subject). However, when we started to discuss what types of jobs and organizations she could pursue, she became silent. Not to worry, I explained; this is not at all uncommon, but it is a great place to begin.

You have to start somewhere. If you don't know what you want to do but prefer not to drift, you will be seeking two kinds of knowledge. One is self-assessment of your skills, capabilities, values, and lifestyle needs; the other is knowledge about the world of work.

Self-Assessment

Self-assessment lies beyond the scope of this book and may be explored through career counseling, aptitude and personality testing, and quiet introspection. If you take time at the outset to evaluate your skills, interests, lifestyle preferences, and work values, you can then begin to search for a position in a proactive way, rather than mold yourself into something you are not. Because you will probably make more than one career change in your life, self-assessment is an important process to learn and feel comfortable with. You will find that, though often difficult, honest self-assessment is a very empowering process that allows you to get away from the "shoulds" and "can'ts" to find the core of who you are and what you enjoy.

It is often most helpful to work on this process with a career counselor, who can provide direction, motivation, and an objective ear to keep you on track. You may also want to review some well-known books on self-assessment, including: *What Color Is Your Parachute? A Practical Manual for Job-Hunters and Career-Changers* (Richard Bolles, Ten Speed Press, 2002); *I Could Do Anything If I Only Knew What It Was* (Barbara Sher, Delacorte Press, 1996); and *Zen and the Art of Making a Living* (Laurence Boldt, Arkana Press, 1999). There are others, but these three are quite popular.

Self-assessment tools and resources are also available on the Internet. Here are two excellent sites to explore: *The Riley Guide* (www.rileyguide.com/assess.html) has links to a wealth of self-assessment resources, including several well-known instruments like the Campbell Interest and Skill Survey and the Self-Directed Search. *The Job Hunter's Bible* (www.jobhuntersbible.com) by Richard Bolles, author *of What Color Is Your Parachute?,* has a number of self-assessment tools and links on his site.

OCCUPATIONAL RESEARCH

A large part of this book is concerned with providing information on career options, but you will also want to inform yourself about various international careers in a number of other ways. Below is a brief synopsis of several different methods of researching career fields and job options.

The World Wide Web

The Internet has greatly facilitated the process of researching a particular organization or company, and so this edition of *International Jobs* has included organizational website addresses whenever possible, as well as tips on how these sites can most effectively be used. Often you can download job listings or applications, and the access to information is, of course, nearly instantaneous. Instead of calling an organization to request literature and then waiting a week for an annual report to arrive in your mailbox, you can now log on to the web and have the same information in minutes or less. This is often the best place to start your research on an organization. If you ask obvious questions over the phone or in person, you may well find yourself directed to the website for your answers. In addition, you will often find links to other websites, dramatically expanding any initial ideas you had about possible places to explore.

In some of these sites you'll find chat rooms, which allow you to share insights with other job seekers; I've also seen chat rooms where you can ask a career counselor specific questions. This obviously is not a substitute for developing an ongoing dialogue with a career counselor who knows you and can help you customize your job search, but for individuals who do not have that option, or who just have a quick question, chat rooms are a good option.

When you are communicating with a career counselor or potential employer via the information superhighway, it is important to maintain the same standards of formality and professionalism as you would if communicating by regular mail. For example, if you send a resume and cover letter via e-mail, make sure that you check for typos and don't harass people by sending multiple e-mails just as you shouldn't leave ten voicemail messages on a prospective employer's machine. Also, be sure to use e-mail only when you are sure it is appropriate. An e-mailed thank-you note to Vladivostok or Beijing is fine, but be cautious not to send a thank-you note either through e-mail that is short and informal. I still prefer a longer thank-you letter through e-mail or snail mail.

Several books have been written about how to best use the web in your job search; one very popular one is *How to Get Your Dream Job Using the Web* (Shannon Karl and Arthur Karl, Coriolos Group Books, 1997).

A few websites that have extensive information on international employment and living include:

Monster.com (http://international.monster.com/workabroad). This popular site has articles for everyone from students through midcareer professionals on a wide range of topics, including the private and public sectors, teaching abroad, and regional, cultural, and relocation information. Although the list of international jobs isn't nearly as extensive as the U.S. database, there are still thousands of postings.

EscapeArtist (www.escapeartist.com). An excellent hub of information on living and working internationally, this site offers articles and databases on living abroad, foreign investment, international real estate, individual countries, and some useful directories. Resources and job ads are usefully accessible by country or region, and the database is searchable. Escape Artist also offers a free e-mail newsletter, "Escape from America Magazine."

International Career Employment Center (www.internationaljobs.org). Has a list of "hot jobs" that anyone can browse; offers more services such as resume posting, a weekly newsletter, profiles of employers, and detailed job ads for paying members. The site focuses on international jobs in development, education, communications, foreign policy, governance, intelligence, environmental programs, commerce, engineering, computer systems, translation, health care, and internships.

OverseasJobs (www.overseasjobs.com). Part of the AboutJobs.com network, this site offers searchable job listings sorted by country and region. Many of the jobs listed here are entry-level or English teaching positions. Also offers a newsletter.

JobPilot (www.jobpilot.com). Functions as a hub for a set of regional and country-specific job sites. Stronger on Europe than other regions, this set of sites is noteworthy for its detailed search engine that lets you precisely specify countries and job sectors you're targeting, in the language of the advertisements. Also has various useful articles and an e-mail newsletter.

WetFeet (www.wetfeet.com). Although it doesn't specifically deal with international careers, this career-guidance website is a treasure trove of information on industries, companies, and careers, many of which can include international elements. A great place to start researching careers.

CareerBuilder (www.careerbuilder.com/JobSeeker/Jobs/jobfindil.asp). Offers some international postings on this dedicated page. Useful tools include searches you can save and have results e-mailed to you on a regular basis.

InterAction (www.interaction.org/jobs/index.html). Run by the American Council for Voluntary International Action, this site offers newsletters and e-mail updates on jobs at international organizations—for a fee.

Global Career Center (www.globalcareercenter.com). This international career services company's site includes a short list of foreign and U.S. jobs, resume posting, and information on work permits.

The Federation of International Trade Associations (www.fita.org/jobs/jobres.html). This page has a good list of links to international career websites; some are general-purpose, but others are specific to careers such as microfinance, the maritime industry, and consulting.

Global Careers (www.globalcareers.com). Job listings searchable by career type, but relatively few positions.

PlanetRecruit (www.planetrecruit.com/channel/int). Based in Great Britain, this site emphasizes British postings and lists international jobs in various categories.

The Riley Guide (www.rileyguide.com/internat.html). Lists numerous international career websites and country-specific job banks.

Goinglobal (www.goinglobal.com). "Grassroots intelligence" on international careers at this site founded by Mary Anne Thompson, author of *The Global Resume and CV Guide*. The bulk of the site's resources on finding a job and living in twenty-three countries are contained in documents you can download for a fee.

The United States Office of Personnel Management (www.opm.gov). Provides links to job postings throughout the U.S. government.

Written Resources

There are many books and brochures providing insight into international careers. Often it is best to begin with general books that outline different career fields—like this one. There are also books on specific careers in government, banking, nonprofit organizations, and really any career that you might imagine. These guides provide an introduction to the career field and often discuss the skills and qualifications necessary for a particular occupation.

Next, you might want to explore literature that is produced by the specific organizations or companies that are of greatest interest to you. The Internet has made this process much easier—simply locate the website of your organization of interest and click! Multilateral organizations, federal agencies, and nonprofit organizations all have excellent websites or informational literature available for the asking. Banks and businesses have annual reports and recruiting brochures, also readily available, most of the time online, along with electronic job and internship listings and information. All of this material can provide helpful information on organizational functions, jobs and internships, and career development.

Directories of businesses, banks, nonprofit organizations, and consultants (see the Recommended Reading on page 340 of this book) are available in your city or college library. These provide names, addresses, and sometimes contact information for specific employers. They may be especially helpful in identifying organizations in cities, states, and countries other than your own.

Finally, it is very helpful to look at specific job listings, which can be found on the Internet and in newspapers, trade publications, and career offices. Job (or internship) listings often provide very specific information about what an actual job entails, which job titles might be appropriate for your level of education and experience, and the qualifications that are in demand by employers in a particular career area. There are many such books listed in the Recommended Reading of this text, organized under each career field.

Career Services Offices

If you are in school, you should consult your career office during each stage of your career decision. As discussed above, a knowledgeable career counselor can be enormously helpful in expanding your job horizons. He or she will not make a career decision for you but can act as a sounding board for your questions and concerns, as well as provide guidance during your search.

Career offices also offer online listings and links, career libraries, panels, and conferences that offer information about different career opportunities and the important chance to network with professionals in the field. Note, however, that job searching is still a personalized process, and individual contacts are important. This brings us to the next source of career research.

Informational Interviewing

I will never forget the powerful presentation of one senior professional at a career panel I attended. He opened his remarks by saying that when he speaks to a group of approximately fifty students, generally thirty will approach him at the end of a panel for questions; only five might ask for a business card; and if he has a good day, only two will call to follow up for an informational interview. Those are the only two he might—he informed the surprised group—consider hiring.

Obviously, the informational interview is a key component in the international job search. The best way to get up-to-date information on a specific type of job is to speak with individuals who are actually performing the kind of work you are thinking about.

Whom should you approach for an informational interview?

Do you have friends or relatives working in organizations with international interests? If so, make an appointment to speak with them. Get names of alumni in specific international occupations from your school and ask them about their work. Find out how they prepared for their careers, how they obtained their jobs, what their career development has been. In particular, get information about what they do on a daily basis. A detailed description of their functions may provoke boredom, curiosity, or enthusiasm in you; whatever the reaction, this information provides one more indication of your suitability for that field of work.

How do you arrange an informational interview?

There are essentially two ways to request an informational interview, either over the telephone or in written form. Both methods are acceptable, so pick the one that makes you most comfortable. If you choose to telephone someone directly, make sure that you have planned what you want to say (i.e., how to introduce yourself, your reason for calling, how you obtained their name) so that you sound professional and respectful of their time. Try to arrange a face-to-face meeting, but if that is not possible, see if you can schedule a telephone appointment.

Writing—generally through e-mail these days—has the advantage of letting the person you are contacting know in advance the purpose of your call, but you must be sure to take the initiative and follow up promptly. Do not expect the person to call you—you are the one with the request! It is advisable not to attach a copy of your resume to the e-mail because that may imply a job search rather than an information search; rather, describe your background and goals in a brief paragraph, along with the subjects you hope the person can address in your meeting.

Finally, don't forget to send a thank-you note (e-mail thank-you notes are very appropriate, though they should be somewhat more formal than the average e-mail correspondence) and keep in contact with the people you meet. It is a common courtesy (but one that is often overlooked, much to the dismay of professionals) to keep individuals with whom you meet apprised of your progress, particularly if they referred you to a particular person or organization.

Informational Interview Dos and Don'ts

Do: Be on time
Dress professionally
Bring a notepad and pen
Prepare and review a list of questions in advance
Be prepared to briefly summarize your career goals
Bring a resume (do not offer it but have it in case it is requested)

Don't: Ask for a job
Waste time with questions you could have read in organizational brochures or on websites
Appear unfocused or unsure of why you are there
Expect them to take the lead—this is YOUR appointment!
Feel you are imposing on their time—most professionals enjoy what they do and helping individuals explore options in their particular field. Enjoy the chance to meet new, interesting people!

THINGS TO CONSIDER WHEN DOING YOUR RESEARCH

The Outlook for Each Occupation

Suppose you are favorably disposed toward a particular international occupation. There are several questions you'll need to ask. What sort of future does it have? Is it in a growing industry or a shrinking one? What will it look like in five to ten years? For example, if you are interested in a career in human rights, where is the international community focusing its attention and efforts? In the 1980s, human rights activists were busiest in Central America; today, as governments in Central and Latin America stabilize, the field is increasingly responding to abuses in Africa and Asia.

Career Mobility

Currently, you can expect to change jobs—and actually, careers—several times over the course of your lifetime, and you will want to be fairly certain that your career of choice allows for future mobility. Sometimes you will want to stay in the same general field but switch sectors. If you start in an international banking career, for example, and later wish to transition into government, the skills and experience you have learned will strengthen your credentials for work with the Treasury Department, the Export-Import Bank, and other government agencies dealing with matters of international finance.

If, to take a very different example, you should decide to switch from banking to an unrelated career in theater, you'll have less immediate mobility. One
student I worked with recently decided to leave a career in international affairs
to attend medical school and, obviously, had to take a big step back in order to
begin to move forward in her newly chosen profession. The choice of quite a
different career may mean returning to school or otherwise gaining credentials
to make you attractive to an employer in that field.

Fortunately, movement between careers these days has become the norm,
making employers increasingly tolerant of individuals who decide to make a
major change in vocation. If you can explain the reasoning behind your decision, and it sounds rational and well thought out, most employers have no
problem with a change.

Salaries and Tax Exemption

The salary of a job is obviously something that you will take into consideration.
Salaries in the field of international affairs vary greatly by sector and by the
amount of experience you are able to bring to the table.

In the United States, salaries for recent bachelor's degree graduates range
widely, from the high teens to low twenties for nonprofit or entry-level media
jobs, to the high thirties and forties for jobs in banking or consulting. Government jobs, often thought to offer low salaries, can be higher than other sectors
and provide excellent benefits. Federal jobs can sometimes pay lower than
state or local government jobs in a large state but will often offer more exposure to international issues. If you have a master's degree, you can expect to
earn more ($45,000–$60,000 in banking and business; a GS–9 in federal government brings in around $30,000; and nonprofit and media organizations
range from $20,000 to $40,000-plus, depending on the organization, sector, and
your prior experience). Joint degree students can often command more, because of their combined expertise and skill base.

Working overseas can be lucrative. Although the base pay may be the same as
in the States, fringe benefits attached to overseas jobs may double or even triple
your stated salary. You may be granted a cost-of-living allowance if you are stationed in a country where the cost of living exceeds that in the United States. If
you are posted to a country where there is war or significant civil unrest, there
may be a differential in salary to compensate for the danger. Free housing may be

provided, as well as return trips to the States to visit family. You may also be re-imbursed for the expense involved in sending your children back to school in the United States or to private school in the country in which you are living. One good website for overseas salary calculations is (www.homefair.com/homefair/cmr/cmr.html).

Two excellent articles available at Monster.com summarize the pros and cons of taxes for expatriates: http://international.monster.com/workabroad/articles/tax/ and http://international.monster.com/workabroad/articles/taxwise.

HOW CAN YOU GAIN EXPERIENCE?

Internships

I always advise the typical graduate student to do a minimum of two or three internships over the course of their study. Naturally, the ideal number depends on an individual's particular background. For instance, if someone has two years of banking experience and is returning to get a master's degree in order to advance more quickly in her company, she will need fewer internships than the student who wants to make a career change into banking with no prior banking experience. And in general, students interested in fields like nonprofit organizations or media that do not have regular recruiting cycles may need more internships to build a broader network. But returning alumni, no matter what their profession, almost always tell students that their internships were a critical factor, if not the determining factor, in obtaining their first job out of school.

Look for internships in your field of interest. Internships may be paid or unpaid, but they almost always involve an educational, or learning, component. They are an excellent way to get a foot in the door, and they provide valuable skills and training that are critical in today's competitive marketplace. An internship gives you many helpful contacts and can provide you with a mentor if you're lucky, as well as a new network for later job hunting. Interns are often assigned a substantive project of value to the organization. Reimbursement is not always received, but academic credit may be given if you are a student. Time spent on the job may vary from one or two days a week during the academic semester to five days a week during the summer. Internships illuminate the pressures, peculiarities, and pleasures of different careers and are a good way to try a particular career field without committing to it for a longer period of time.

Internships in Various Sectors

Government. Government agencies have long been traditional internship employers, although some agencies have lost funding for paid internships due to recent government downsizing. Nonetheless, programs still exist, and information is available on the homepages of each agency. In the United States, USAJOBS (www.usajobs.opm.gov/index.htm) functions as a hub for federal jobs and employment, including summer positions. Jobs and internships geared toward students are located at www.studentjobs.gov/index.htm. Summer jobs are also available, and they are listed in *Summer Job Opportunities Announcement No. 414*, an annual brochure available starting the last week of December from the Federal Job Information Centers, located in major cities (see www.nyonline.com/dc/gov/manual/fjic.htm for a list by state) and college career offices. Get it as soon as it is issued because deadlines for submitting applications are sometimes as early as January.

International and Nonprofit Organizations. Most international organizations have formal internship programs to which you can apply. One note of advice: Many require several months' lead time to process an application, so be sure to check deadlines carefully; these are available on agency websites. You might also propose your own internship by writing or e-mailing directly to a division of interest, either domestically or overseas.

Nonprofit organizations are great internship employers. Some programs are structured, though many are very informal. Because there is always plenty of work to go around, interns at nonprofits are often given a great deal of responsibility in a short period of time. Another plus is that interns may sometimes be hired into permanent positions when they arise because nonprofits generally have less formal recruiting procedures and positions are often filled through networking with contacts in the field.

Media Employer. Internships are almost mandatory in the field of media and communications, and in media organizations paid opportunities, in particular, are rare. Newspapers often have structured programs with early fall application deadlines, whereas broadcast and production internships are somewhat less deadline-driven. Obviously, exceptions occur, so give yourself enough time to explore your options. Be persistent and creative in approaching companies. Many media employers that don't have a structured program may be open to taking interns on an ad hoc basis. If you aren't successful with the main domestic internship programs, consider applying directly to foreign offices or bureaus.

Private Sector.   Some years ago, many large businesses and banks with international interests had regular summer programs that employed graduate students working toward these careers. Now, however, the size of these programs has been whittled down to the selection of a very few highly qualified and talented students. You must often be enrolled in school to be considered, and deadlines are early—late fall and early winter in most instances.

Note: If you are specializing in international business or banking within your M.A. in international affairs, you will find yourself competing with M.B.A. students for the few internships or summer associate positions available. The M.B.A. students may have an edge in the private sector because in general they will have more proficient technical skills demonstrated through actual business work experience and thus need less training to become productive in a short-term assignment. On the other hand, you may have the edge in international assignments because of your language skills and your knowledge and experience in a specific region.

Overseas Internships.   The experience of work abroad can be one of the strongest items on your resume; it is also one of the most difficult to attain. Very few organizations—whether they are businesses, banks, nonprofit organizations, government, or multilateral organizations—will pay your transportation abroad for a job lasting only two or three months. They may, however, be open to negotiating accommodations and a small stipend to cover your basic costs, especially if you bring relevant experience to their organization. In addition, there is the problem of work permits (see Chapter 3). If you can get overseas on your own, however, your chances improve considerably. Contact the foreign branches of American or international organizations directly for possible internships; these include U.S. government agencies, UN agency offices, businesses, banks, wire services, and nongovernmental organizations (NGOs) in whatever country you happen to be. To that end, the Council on International Educational Exchange (633 Third Avenue, New York, NY 10017, [888] COUNCIL) coordinates work and study abroad programs in many countries. Information, downloads, and order forms for materials are available at its international website (www.councilexchanges.org or in the United States at www.us.councilexchanges.org).

Monster.com has some excellent articles on overseas internships (see http://international.monster.com/workabroad; click on "For Students").

A few words on summer jobs. A summer job, as opposed to an internship, is always paid but is not necessarily substantive or educational in nature (you could end up spending thirty hours a week photocopying or filing). But summer jobs can help you to earn money for living expenses and gain exposure to an organization that you might not otherwise be able to access—temping at an international bank, for example. A summer job can also be used to subsidize a more rewarding unpaid internship.

Making the Most of Your Internship

Before You Begin
Establish the parameters of the internship with your employer, outlining your responsibilities as well as your specific responsibilities. Obviously, you will need to be flexible as work situations change, but this measure will help assure that you have a meaningful, educational project. Don't be afraid to ask for input in the process of developing this informal roadmap. Read about the organization and the field so that you are aware of current industry trends and any challenges that the organization may be facing.

On the Job
Take time to meet your coworkers and display a visibly positive team attitude.

Show initiative and creativity. Ask for advice or counsel if you need it. Be on time and display professional behavior at all times.

With Your Boss
Ask for feedback after two to four weeks so that you know what you are doing well and what might need more attention.

Periodically, give your boss a memo or an e-mail describing the work you have accomplished. It should be brief and concise. This will tell your supervisor what he or she needs to know in case you are not in the office when a question arises; more important, it provides a basis for constructive feedback.

Internship Resources: Selected Internship Websites

InternshipPrograms.com (www.internships.wetfeet.com/home.asp). Run by career guidance company WetFeet, this internship site lets you post your resume, search a database of internships, and research companies and careers.

InternWeb (www.internweb.com). Extensive resources on internships, including a database of positions, advice articles, and a newsletter.

CareerPlanit (www.careerplanit.com/world/internship.cfm). Offers a searchable database of internships. Select "Worldwide" for the broadest list of opportunities.

JobWeb (www.jobweb.com/experiential/jintern.htm). Links, articles, and databases on summer work, internships, and fieldwork.

Backdoorjobs (www.backdoorjobs.com). This site features adventure-oriented summer jobs and internships. The emphasis is on outdoor sports, camping, environmental expeditions, and cross-cultural experiences. International internships are featured at www.backdoorjobs.com/worldwide.html.

INTERNships INTERNational (www.rtpnet.org/intintl). Website for a company that coordinates internship postings in ten international cities (Bangkok, Budapest, Capetown, Dresden, Dublin, Glasgow, London, Melbourne, Paris, Santiago).

CampusCareerCenter (www.campuscareercenter.com/students/intern.asp). Current college students can register here to read articles and search databases on internships.

Council Exchanges (www.councilexchanges.org). As described above, this organization provides opportunities to work, teach, study, or volunteer abroad.

Directories of Internships—A Sampling

The Internship Bible, by Mark Oldman and Samer Hamadeh, Princeton Review, 2002.

Peterson's Internships, Peterson's Guides, 2001 (published annually).

Peterson's Summer Jobs for Students, Peterson's Guides, 2001 (published annually).

The Back Door Guide to Short-Term Job Adventures: Internships, Extraordinary Experiences, Seasonal Jobs, Volunteering, Work Abroad, by Michael Landes, Ten Speed Press, 2001.

The Best 106 Internships, by Mark Oldman and Samer Hamadeh, Princeton Review, 2000.

Internship Success: Real-World, Step-by-Step Advice on Getting the Most out of Internships, by Marianne Ehrlich Green, McGraw Hill-NTC, 1998.

Alternatives to the Peace Corps: A Directory of Third World and U.S. Volunteer Opportunities (9th ed.), by Joan Powell and Joanna Powell, Food First Books, 2001.

Vacation Work's International Directory of Voluntary Work (7th ed.), by Louise Whetter and Victoria Pybus, Vacation-Work, 2000.

How to Live Your Dream of Volunteering Overseas, by Joseph Collins, Stefano Dezerega, Zahara Heckscher, and Anna Lappe, Penguin USA, 2002.

The Successful Internship: Transformation and Empowerment, by H. Frederick Sweitzer and Mary A. King, Wadsworth, 1998.

The Access Guide to International Affairs Internships, edited by Bruce Seymore II and Matthew T. Higham, Access: Washington, 1996 (out of print).

Preparing to Lead: College Women's Guide to Internships and Other Public Policy Learning Opportunities in Washington, PLEN (Public Leadership Education Network), 1992.

If you are interested in a particular organization, don't hesitate to approach an appropriate official of that organization, whether or not it has a formal internship program. Internships can sometimes be worked out if you take the initiative and propose a project of benefit to the company as well as to yourself.

Academic Work

You can also expose yourself to an occupation through academic work. If, for example, you have been looking into a journalism career but are still unsure about whether you will enjoy it, take a course or two in writing and reporting. It won't be long before you get an idea of your competence in the field as well as an indication of how comfortable you might feel as a practicing journalist.

If you decide that taking a course for credit is too much of an investment in time and money because of your career uncertainties, the next best thing is to audit a course. Listen to the lectures and class discussions. Auditing won't be as helpful as doing all the class work, but it will take a minimum of time while gaining some background in the subject matter.

Site Visits

Another way to investigate a potential career is to visit a job site. If, for example, you think you might be interested in a banking career, visit a bank just to get a sense for what goes on. Get the "mood" of the place. Is this the right atmosphere for making your own special impact on the professional world, whether your aims are for money, prestige, self-expression, security, service, or a combination of all of these and more?

Unfortunately, this type of impression and information gathering cannot always be practiced. Some federal government agencies—e.g., the Department of State or the Office of the Secretary of Defense—are naturally very difficult to access. In this instance, you will have to find someone to invite you in as a guest.

WHAT ARE THE RIGHT QUALIFICATIONS?

How Important Is Knowledge of Language and Culture?

Language Fluency

Even though English is probably the most widely spoken language of global business, fluency in a language is becoming more and more important, but how critical it is depends on the sector in which you are searching. For the Foreign Service of the Department of State, language ability is respected but is not required among your qualifications—initially. If you have no foreign language capability, you will be placed immediately in a rigorous language training program. Even if you are fluent in one or more languages, you may be assigned to a different country or region and be sent for retraining.

For the United Nations, knowledge of at least two official UN languages (English, French, Spanish, Chinese, and Arabic) is required, but equally important is a firm grounding in economics, economic development, and area studies and significant prior work experience. This is generally the case for international development and human rights work as well. One student I recently worked with had excellent experience but was turned down by a large development organization because he failed his French fluency exam.

For businesses with large international markets, knowledge of languages is highly desirable, but more important is relevant work experience and a background in technical business subjects such as accounting, finance, and marketing.

Cultural Awareness and Understanding

Understanding and developing strong working relationships with professionals from other countries depend not only on a knowledge of language but also on a knowledge of culture—the customs and traditions of a people that make them distinctive. Without this understanding of culture, you may find yourself confusing and, even worse, antagonizing others when you are simply trying to develop a rapport.

For example, conducting a business lunch in Mexico is very different from a business lunch in London or Singapore. The same is true for business meetings. Knowing about the importance of nonverbal communication like eye contact and handshaking and understanding cultural business norms is key. In Latin America, for example, relationships are very important. Spending some time to get to know your colleagues will definitely give you more credibility than simply charging into a room and stating your agenda, as is typically done in the United States. In Asia, silence is used as an effective communication tool, while in the United States, individuals tend to be uncomfortable with silence.

How do you learn about the country and culture in which you are working? Many companies and government agencies provide cross-cultural training sessions for their employees, where country experts and previous expatriates participate and share experiences and knowledge about living and working in that field. If your organization does not offer such a service, you might want to request it as part of your negotiation package before accepting an offer. Much has also been written on this subject: *Kiss, Bow, or Shake Hands: How to Do Business in Sixty Countries* (Terri Morrison, Wayne A. Conaway, and George A. Borden, Adams Media Corporation, 1995) is a popular book in the field. Websites such as www.monster.com, www.oag.com, and www.economist.com have useful sections on cultural differences and how to deal with them.

You should also take time to read extensively about the history and politics of the country you intend to visit or live in. Take a course at a local college that will help you understand multicultural differences of the region you are going to visit. Whatever your reason for going to a foreign country—to sell a product, to understand people and culture, to research, or simply for pleasure—you will be more successful in achieving your goal if you are sensitive to the meaning of the customs you will be encountering in your daily life abroad.

It certainly helps, too, to locate a cultural mentor who has worked or is currently working in your country of interest. Ask him or her about the differences he or she sees and has experienced, and how situations have been effectively handled. A cultural mentor can help you troubleshoot challenges as they arise. Hopefully, in turn, you can eventually become a cultural mentor for someone else embarking on an international assignment.

Do You Need a B.A.? M.A.? Ph.D.?

Two commonly asked questions are "How far will a B.A. get me?" and "Do I need a Ph.D.?"

A B.A. is a good—and necessary—starting point for most jobs. In some careers, such as the Foreign Service of the Department of State, if you can pass the written Foreign Service exam with your accumulated knowledge, you have the same chance of eventual entry as the Ph.D. In other government jobs, a B.A. will qualify you for some entry-level jobs. A B.A. is usually necessary for analyst positions in business and banking. An entry-level position in nonprofit organizations can be obtained with a B.A, and if you apply with a Ph.D. you may find that you are perceived as being overqualified.

As for the second question—"Do I need a Ph.D.?"—the answer again must be hedged. In essence, the value of the doctorate depends on the kind of job you are seeking. If you are after a teaching job at any level over junior or community college, the Ph.D. is necessary. If you wish to go into policy analysis and research (e.g., in international relations, regional studies, or international economics), the Ph.D. will be exceedingly helpful. If you are after a career in international banking, business, or journalism, the Ph.D. may be irrelevant or considered a liability—unless you have a persuasive answer to the question "Why did you pursue a doctorate instead of courses in accounting, finance, marketing, or journalism?" Skepticism toward pure academics is liable to be encountered by a Ph.D. trying to break into these fields.

A further warning: Don't begin a Ph.D. just because the extra years in academia will postpone the fears and frustrations of job hunting. The economic climate some years from now may be better—or worse. So why postpone the inevitable unless the extra degree will help you toward your international job objective? In other words, know your motivation for getting a Ph.D. Know how you will use it and what it will do for you.

In general, an M.A. is an optimum degree for most international jobs. In Chapter 2, we will explore different options for master's programs that will prepare you for international work.

CONCLUSION

Even after informing yourself thoroughly about a career, you may still hesitate to make a decision. You are fairly sure but not absolutely clear. You may also be concerned that any decision will commit you to a specific career for the rest of your life.

It is important to recognize that there will almost always be a degree of uncertainty in any career choice you make. It is the rare individual who will be absolutely certain that the path he or she is taking is the absolute right one. It is only when you are actually at work that you will really know the atmosphere, the people, the details of the job, and all those other intangible points that sometimes make the difference between liking and not liking one's work.

When you have reached the stage of 80 or 90 percent certainty, perhaps it is time to relax. No choice is irrevocable or totally binding.

2

Careers and Academics: The Link

THIS CHAPTER WILL focus on the vital connection between your academic work and the attainment of your career goals.

In planning your curriculum, you ideally should work backward from your career objective. Your starting point should be "What do I want to do *after* I have my graduate or undergraduate degree?" Try to answer this question before you finish—and preferably before you *start*—your international studies.

After you have spent some time considering the issues discussed in Chapter 1—What skills do you want to use? What lifestyle issues are important? Do you prefer economics to finance? What are your language skills?—the other necessary decisions fall into place: first, the most appropriate degree to pursue; second, a major or specialization within your academic program; and third, the selection of courses within this concentration. By knowing where you want your academic work to lead, you will be able to choose the courses best suited to helping you reach your goal.

In some cases, the choice of a specialization is an obvious one. If you want a career in international banking, you will pursue either an M.A. or an M.B.A. and take courses in international finance and banking; and if you want your future to be in international development, you will specialize in something like economic development, international health, or microfinance, depending on which subfield you wish to enter.

However, if you wish to enter the Foreign Service or become a foreign correspondent, your choice of specialization is less obvious. You may approach your goal a number of ways, depending on your area of interest: foreign policy, environment, or international economics.

The above progression—starting with a career choice and working backward to specialization and courses—represents the ideal. Furthermore, it avoids the expense and misfortune of deciding during your last semester before graduation that you want to pursue international marketing only to discover that you have not taken any of the required courses for jobs in that field.

STRAIGHT TALK ABOUT GRADUATE SCHOOLS AND CAREER OPPORTUNITIES

As we discussed in Chapter 1, a master's degree is required for most professional jobs in international affairs. However, relevant work experience is just as important, if not more so, in the current job market. Employers want to know that you have successfully performed in a particular position and had on-the-job training, not just that you are *prepared* to do a certain job.

In fact, it is strongly suggested that you get practical training in the form of internships, and preferably full-time work experience, *before* you apply to graduate school. For some programs, it is an absolute prerequisite to admission. (Two years is usually the minimum amount recommended.) Working "in the real world" not only allows you to acquire job skills and make contacts with professionals in your field of interest; it also enables you to decide whether a particular career is really for you. After a couple of years, if you do decide to attend graduate school, you will have the advantage of bringing your experiences to the classroom.

A Decision to Attend Graduate School

When I graduated from college, I took a position as a program assistant with a large conservation and development organization in Washington, D.C. The work was a perfect match for my career interests, but my position did not give me enough responsibility for direct decision-making. I spoke with many senior program officers and vice presidents in the organization who advised me on how to become qualified for these types of positions. Invariably the answers were the same: Get a graduate degree in an appropriate sector and get field experience.

Within a year, I had joined the U.S. Peace Corps and was doing health and community development work in a small village in Cote d'Ivoire. After three years of working in West Africa, I returned to the United States and began applying to graduate schools of international affairs that had particularly strong programs in economic and political development.

My prior professional experience and fieldwork were invaluable to me in helping me focus during graduate school. Knowing why I had returned to school and what I intended to get out of the experience facilitated the process of choosing classes and developing a functional concentration. My goal was to test the practicality of my fieldwork against current academic theories to see if what I had encountered could be explained or better understood through analytical and comparative studies.

Is there a downside to graduate school? Yes and no. There are certainly opportunity costs. Graduate school takes an enormous amount of time and energy if you want to do well, and the constant pressures of reading and research can be a little overwhelming. Free time is a scarce commodity. So is money. The upside to all of this is that after completing the degree, you are immediately qualified to compete for better jobs at higher salaries. Graduate school can speed your entry into more autonomous, decisionmaking positions in almost any field.

Some Popular Graduate School Options

Obviously, there are many ways to achieve your professional goals. Below are just a few of the many types of graduate schools that can prepare you for a career in international affairs.

Schools of International Affairs

The Association of Professional Schools of International Affairs (APSIA; www.apsia.org) is an international membership association of 28 graduate schools of international affairs and 15 affiliated institutions based in the United States and abroad. These schools are "dedicated to advancing global understanding and cooperation by preparing men and women to assume positions of leadership in world affairs."

All of the schools, affiliated with major universities, offer two-year M.A. programs and offer coursework in economics, history, political science, language, management, and policy analysis, combined with specific concentrations in regional and functional areas.

The member schools and their websites provide helpful information about programs and curricula, including applications and financial aid deadlines and procedures, career and alumni services, and often actual applications:

The American University
School of International Service
www.american.edu/academic.depts/sis/

Columbia University
School of International and Public Affairs
www.sipa.columbia.edu/index.html

Duke University
Terry Sanford Institute of Public Policy
www.pubpol.duke.edu/

The George Washington University
The Elliott School of International Affairs
www.gwu.edu/~elliott/

Georgetown University
Edmund A. Walsh School of Foreign Service
www.georgetown.edu/sfs

Harvard University
John F. Kennedy School of Government
www.ksg.harvard.edu/

The Johns Hopkins University
The Paul H. Nitze School of Advanced International Studies
www.jhu.edu/~sais

Princeton University
Woodrow Wilson School of Public and International Affairs
www.wws.princeton.edu/

Syracuse University
Maxwell School of Citizenship & Public Affairs
www.maxwell.syr.edu/ir/irmain.htm

Tufts University
The Fletcher School of Law and Diplomacy
www.fletcher.tufts.edu/

University of California at San Diego
Graduate School of International Relations and Pacific Studies
www-irps.ucsd.edu/

University of Denver
Graduate School of International Studies
www.du.edu/gsis

University of Maryland
School of Public Affairs
www.puaf.umd.edu/

University of Michigan
Gerald R. Ford School of Public Policy
www.spp.umich.edu

University of Minnesota
Hubert H. Humphrey Institute of Public Affairs
www.hhh.umn.edu/

University of Pittsburgh
Graduate School of Public and International Affairs
www.gspia.pitt.edu/

University of Southern California
School of International Relations
www.usc.edu/dept/LAS/ir/

University of Washington
Henry M. Jackson School of International Studies
jsis.artsci.washington.edu/

Yale University
Yale Center for International and Area Studies
www.cis.yale.edu/ycias/

Carleton University (Canada)
Norman Paterson School of International Affairs
www.carleton.ca/npsia/

L'Institut d'Etudes Politiques de Paris (France)
Fondation Nationale des Sciences Politiques
www.sciences-po.fr/accueil.htm

Ritsumeikan University (Japan)
Graduate School of International Relations
www.ritsumei.ac.jp/kic/ir/index-e.html

St. Petersburg State University (Russia)
School of International Relations
www.dip.pu.ru/english/oldfmo/home_en.htm

Stockholm School of Economics (Sweden)
www.hhs.se/

University of St. Gallen (Switzerland)
Swiss Institute for International Economic and Applied Economic Research
www.unisg.ch/org/siaw/web.nsf/wwwPubhomepage/webHomepageEng

HEI (Switzerland) (Institut Universitaire de Hautes Études Internationales, Genève)
Graduate Institute of International Studies
heiwww.unige.ch/

Non-APSIA Schools of International Affairs/Relations

The London School of Economics and Political Science (www.lse.ac.uk) offers master's and Ph.D. degrees in international relations, as well as other, more specialized master's degrees in subjects related to international employment. It has a reputation for being more theoretical in nature. Its international student body and excellent reputation make it another option to consider.

Other Schools with International Affairs Programs:

DePaul University, International Studies Program (condor.depaul.edu/~intstuds)

Florida International University, Graduate Program in International Studies (www.fiu.edu/orgs/intlrel)

Fordham University, Graduate Program in International Political Economy and Development (www.fordham.edu/iped)

George Mason University, International Commerce and Policy Program (www.gmu.edu/departments/t-icp)

Howard University, Ralph J. Bunche International Affairs Center (www.howard.edu/rjb)

International University of Japan, Graduate School of International Relations (www.iuj.ac.jp)

Monterey Institute of International Studies, Graduate School of International Policy Studies (www.miis.edu)

Rutgers State University of New Jersey, Center for Global Change and Governance (http://andromeda.rutgers.edu/~cgcg)

Seton Hall University, School of Diplomacy and International Relations (http://diplomacy.shu.edu)

Universidad Externado de Colombia, Externado (www.uexternado.edu.co)

University of Chicago, Committee on International Relations (http://cir.uchicago.edu/index.html)

University of Miami, School of International Studies (www.miami.edu/international-studies)

University of Toronto, Munk Center for International Studies (www.library. utoronto.ca/ir)

Schools of Business Administration

Several M.B.A. programs have gained strong reputations in the international business community—Columbia, Wharton/The Lauder Institute at the University of Pennsylvania, Harvard, and Stanford are probably the best known. In order to be a competitive candidate for admission into a strong M.B.A. program, according to Tom Fernandez, former assistant dean for career services at Columbia's Graduate School of Business, you will need strong quantitative and computer skills, approximately four years of prior relevant work experience, with at least two in the same job, demonstrated leadership and academic achievement, and, for international work, language fluency and cultural adaptability.

The Association to Advance Collegiate Schools of Business (AACSB) is the foremost accrediting agency for B.A., M.B.A., and Ph.D. programs in business administration and accounting. The association is headquartered in St. Louis (view www.aacsb.edu/ to access information about graduate schools, in business and to research international schools of business). There is also a section of helpful links, publications, workshops, and seminars. Publications including *U.S. News and World Report*, *Financial Times*, and *BusinessWeek* produce annual rankings of the top business schools. *U.S. News* also ranks public affairs schools. According to *U.S. News* in 2002, the top five schools with international business specialties are, in order of rank:

1. Thunderbird American Graduate School of International Management
2. University of South Carolina (Moore)
3. University of Pennsylvania (Wharton)
4. New York University (Stern)
5. Columbia University Graduate School of Business

Thunderbird boasts an international student body from 80-plus countries, representing more than half its class. Additionally, its curricula go beyond traditional international business training to include language study, international casework, and political economy. The USC Master of International Business Studies (MIBS) program includes a guaranteed five-month overseas internship with a multinational company. Columbia offers the advantage of a joint business and international affairs degree at the same university. The top schools according to the *Financial Times* in 2002 are:

1. University of Pennsylvania (Wharton)
2. Harvard Business School
3. Columbia University Graduate School of Business
4. Stanford University Graduate School of Business
5. University of Chicago Graduate School of Business
6. Insead (Paris)
7. MIT (Sloan)
8. New York University (Stern)
9. London Business School
10. Northwestern University (Kellogg)

If you are considering a graduate school in international business, it might be wise to attend a school with a Center for International Business Education and Research (CIBER). CIBER is located in twenty-eight universities across the United States and administered by the U.S. Department of Education. Its purpose is to serve as a regional and national resource for business students and academics. CIBER aims to increase global competitiveness of U.S. companies by training students to succeed in today's international business environment. Students mainly benefit from the programs that CIBER sponsors on campuses, from the faculty they recruit, and from the corporate relationships that they build. A website for more information on CIBER is www.mgmt.purdue.edu/centers/ciber. Another option is GlobalEdge at globaledge.msu.edu/ibrd/ibrd.asp. A list of the government-supported CIBERs can be found at www.ed.gov/offices/OPE/HEP/iegps/cibegrantees.html.

Schools of Law

The American Bar Association (ABA) publishes an annual book of ABA-approved law schools, which includes information on enrollment, financial aid, tuition, faculty, LSAT scores, libraries, employment prospects, and websites. It is $19.95 and available in most bookstores or through the ABA Service Center.

U.S. News and World Report also rates law schools in its annual review of U.S. graduate schools. In Chapter 12 of this book, there is additional information about U.S. law schools with strong reputations in international law.

You may contact the American Bar Association for more specialized referrals at 750 North Lake Shore Drive, Chicago, IL 60611, (312) 988–5000, www.abanet.org. Also check out the Association of American Law Schools (AALS) at www.aals.org.

Schools of Public Health

A master's degree in public health is excellent preparation for a career in international health, which may mean working in the areas of population, epidemiology, AIDS, health education, or refugee assistance. By contacting the Association of Schools of Public Health, you can receive a list of the 28 accredited schools of public health in the United States and Puerto Rico. These schools educate more than 15,000 students a year from the United States and abroad. Professionals work in government, nonprofit, and private-sector organizations. The schools that have strong international reputations include: Harvard University, Columbia University, Johns Hopkins University, University of Michigan, University of California at Berkeley, University of California at Los Angeles, Emory University, University of North Carolina at Chapel Hill, and Tulane University.

For more information, contact the Association of Schools of Public Health, 1660 L Street NW, Suite 204, Washington, DC 20036, (202) 296–1099, www.asph.org.

Schools of Journalism

Those interested in pursuing a career in international journalism or communications may consider studying for a master's degree in journalism. Within the degree program, students generally focus their studies on specific areas, such as electronic journalism, newspaper and magazine journalism, photojournalism, public relations, advertising, and, increasingly, telecommunications and new media. Many graduate programs offer coursework on international issues, such as health, social policy, politics, and the environment.

Graduate programs with strong reputations include: the Medill School of Journalism at Northwestern University (offering a joint degree with the

Fletcher School of Law and Diplomacy), Columbia University (which has a joint degree with the School of International and Public Affairs), the University of Florida, the Annenberg School for Communication at the University of Southern California, the University of North Carolina at Chapel Hill, the University of Missouri at Columbia, the Newhouse School of Public Communication at Syracuse University, and the University of California at Berkeley. JournalismJobs maintains a list of journalism programs at www.journalismjobs.com/general_links.cfm.

Other Academic Alternatives

There are obviously other degree options you may be interested in exploring: architecture, environmental science, public policy and administration, and social work. Don't limit yourself to what is described above—there are many paths to your final destination!

PURSUING A JOINT DEGREE

Increasingly, people are enrolling in joint degree programs. Having both an M.B.A. and an M.A. may make you more attractive to many employers, but remember it is no substitute for professional experience. Still, the trend to pursue studies in related fields to deepen expertise is increasing as employers look to hire those with specializations in a certain field. In addition to an M.B.A., many international affairs programs offer joint degrees with law, journalism, public health, and urban planning.

Studying for joint degrees isn't for everyone. It generally costs more and takes longer because you have to fulfill requirements demanded by both schools. It's a good idea to be extremely focused and to speak with career and academic professionals to determine whether both degrees are necessary in order to achieve your career goals. For instance, if your goal is to do senior policy work for Amnesty International, it is probably a good idea to pursue joint degrees with a law school and school of international affairs. If your goal is to work in business reporting, you will probably gain more if you focus on media, economics, and financial coursework offered at a school for international affairs, rather than pursuing both an M.A. and an M.B.A.

Tips When Investigating Graduate Schools

According to MarJean Knokey, director of admissions at the Fletcher School for Law and Diplomacy, here are five important things to consider when exploring the possibility of graduate school:

1: Determine your strengths, interests and needs—will this program/school meet your needs and do its goals meet yours? For example, if you are interested in telecommunications, does the school have a concentration in that field? Do you want significant faculty interaction? If so, what are the schools with a smaller faculty-student ratio?

2: Consider the size, location, and culture of the program. The culture of a school can shape your experiences: Is it conservative or liberal? How diverse is its student body? Does it encourage flexibility in planning your curriculum, or is there a rigid set of requirements? Does it have a bias in favor or private-sector or nonprofit work?

3: What are the employment and internship opportunities that are offered? Does the office of career services seem accessible and helpful?

4: What is your competitiveness as a candidate? Look into profiles of the average student—how do you compare academically and professionally? Is this a realistic option for you?

5: What is your commitment to the field? Graduate school is expensive and a large commitment of time. Do you really want to make the leap?

3

Conducting an Overseas Job Search

JOB SEARCHING IS a difficult task, whether in the United States or abroad. Getting a job overseas is plagued with challenges similar to those at home, plus a few challenges unique to international employment. Of these, the most important consideration is that the majority of countries—including the United States—insist that their nationals receive priority in the local job market. This means that a foreigner usually must have a work permit, which is not at all easy to obtain. Often one must find a job before a permit is issued. The employer in turn is given the difficult task of showing that the job opening cannot be filled satisfactorily by a native of that country. Long forms of justification must often be completed by the employer, who will clearly not relish the bother unless the foreigner to be employed has qualifications vastly superior to the local competition.

How, then, can you maximize your chances for getting a job overseas? This chapter will provide some ways to try and break down the barriers to international employment, offering tips on how to begin the search, as well as how to use internships and teaching as ways to establish yourself overseas, and explain the tremendous advantages that students have for securing short-term stints abroad.

START THE HUNT AT HOME

The best way to ensure success is to start the job hunt *before* you leave the United States. If you are able to find a job abroad while you are still here, it sometimes simplifies the problem of legalizing your work status. With a job promise under your belt, you may receive a work permit or at least diminish the procedural hassles in getting yourself legalized.

Immediately, however, you run up against a different set of difficulties. Before you are offered a job, you usually must have an interview. If you're in the United

States, how do you arrange this interview with an employer who may be 12,000 miles away? Sometimes interviews may be arranged with foreign employers who are visiting the United States on business, but this does not happen frequently. "Interviews" can also be conducted using e-mail. Usually the only way to get a conventional interview is to pack your bags and travel overseas. This also has the added advantage of allowing you to network personally with other organizations and contacts, rather than depending solely on phone, fax, and e-mail. In most cases, you are at a distinct advantage if you are in-country.

Hook into an American Organization with Operations Abroad

One student, whom I will call Rachel, spoke fluent Chinese and wanted to get a job in China. She targeted a small U.S. company that had extensive trade operations with China, and she was eventually was hired as a trade associate. After one year, the company sent her to Beijing to establish a small office. She was their first permanent employee from the United States in China.

As you can see from Rachel's experience, another way to minimize permit problems is to get a job with a U.S. organization with overseas operations. After working there awhile, you might be able to ask for a transfer overseas.

Also, before you leave the United States, explore job possibilities with the headquarters of American banks and businesses that have a branch in the country you would eventually like to be. You might not be paid to be sent overseas, but if you decide to go on your own initiative, you may at least be able to carry with you an introduction from headquarters to the branch manager in the country where you will be going. The difficulty with this is that the trend is to hire nationals for overseas foreign offices. An American-educated Russian, for example, has several advantages over a Russian-speaking American doing business in Russia. He or she knows the culture as a native, is absolutely fluent in the language, may be paid in local currency (which is less expensive for the company), and is not likely to leave for a more familiar culture. Nonetheless, it is probably easier to transfer to an overseas position after some time within a U.S. multinational company than to convince a foreign employer to hire you, particularly in a country with a well-educated applicant pool.

Explore Work with a Foreign Company in the States

Another option is to secure work with a foreign company with operations in the United States such as a British bank or a Chilean importer, for example; after proving yourself stateside, your supervisor may be able to arrange a stint at their headquarters. If not, perhaps while on the job you have met professionals from headquarters or other overseas offices with whom you can network.

Consider Being a Stringer

Those interested in writing can arrange to submit articles from abroad to the wire services—Associated Press, United Press International, Agence France-Presse, Reuters—to large metropolitan or small-town dailies and to magazines. There is no guarantee that your articles will be accepted, but if they are, you will be paid (hopefully). Another advantage of being a stringer is that you may avoid being burdened by work permit problems. Stringing offers ample freedom, but for a beginning writer it can take a long time to develop enough contacts and material to make a decent living at it. Trying to a write about a foreign country you have just arrived in is difficult; expect to take some time to get to know the ins and outs of the culture and society. Many stringers take other work while developing their expertise. If you plan to work as a freelancer, exercise some care in choosing your country or region. Large, dominant countries offer plenty of interesting news but have the disadvantage of being heavily covered already by established bureaus and correspondents. Smaller, more peripheral places will give you more opportunities to do original stories, but the challenge in this case is to get editors back home to take any interest in your subject. The good news for your career is that foreign-desk editors tend to respect anyone with the guts to pick up and freelance in a distant land. A useful primer on international writing is *The World on a String: How to Become a Freelance Foreign Correspondent* by Alan Goodman and John Pollack (Henry Holt, 1997).

Don't Forget about Alumni!

Before going abroad, get names and addresses of alumni from your school who are living or working in the countries where you expect to be. The alumni network is a potent force in leading you directly or indirectly to a job.

CONSIDER TEACHING ENGLISH

English has rapidly become an international lingua franca, especially in business. In countries that have close economic ties with Western countries, particularly the United States and Britain, many jobs require knowledge of English. Increasingly, English also is being used as a common means of communication between people with different mother tongues. This is especially true in Asia and Europe. While demand for English teachers has leveled off in some regions, such as Eastern Europe, many developing countries offer growing opportunities. Among wealthier nations, Japan remains a popular choice for English teachers, as it combines exotic appeal with relatively high wages. Japanese journals in America often carry ads for this type of work; a qualified applicant can write to these Japanese institutes and might be offered a job without an interview. Once a position is obtained, a work visa is readily forthcoming from the Japanese Embassy in Washington or the Japanese Consulate General in New York. This is an exceptional situation, admittedly, but you will probably be searching out many exceptional circumstances in order to land a job overseas. If you are interested in teaching English in a Japanese or Chinese school or college, rather than in a language institute, the procedure is somewhat different. Consult Chapter 11.

AN INTERNSHIP MAY BE YOUR BEST BET

One of the best ways to get yourself overseas is to try to set up an internship in the country in which you'd like to live. While you will almost definitely have to pay your own travel expenses and may have to accept a job without pay, you will get a foot in the door. An internship will allow you to learn about the work environment, and if you prove yourself to be valuable, an employer may be able to justify hiring you as a consultant or as a full-time employee. If the prospects for such a position look bleak, be grateful for the experience and the chance to network within the city you are in, and be sure to honor your commitment to your internship employer. Years down the road, they might just remember you.

Do Some Background Research

Consult the classified ads of major newspapers, such as the *Times* (London), *Le Figaro* (Paris), *Die Welt* (Hamburg), and *Messagero* (Milan). Obviously, the web is a phenomenal resource and has made the gathering of information from overseas much easier. The more organizational research you have done, the more prepared you will be to talk to an employer or an alum once you get overseas. A word of caution, though—nothing replaces *being there*.

Thailand: One Student's Experience

Thailand is an exciting place to be. On the one hand, it is a developed country, lacking few amenities; on the other hand, it has all the mystery and exotic qualities of a still-developing country. Thailand perhaps can best be summed up by picturing a man praying at a Buddhist temple by the side of the road—except the man is wearing an expensive suit and talking on a cell phone at the same time!

As Thailand continues to develop, more and more businesses and organizations are opening offices there. Thus, there are many opportunities, but there is also a lot of competition. The best way to get a job in Thailand is to network, network, network. Especially in the nonprofit area, contacts are extremely important. A great way to make those contacts is to first get an internship. I spent last summer working for UNICEF in Bangkok. Not only was this a great experience professionally, but it also helped me to meet a lot of different people. However, be warned that most internships in Thailand will be unpaid.

When I returned to the United States, I spent the next six months e-mailing and faxing all my contacts, and my contacts' contacts. I got in touch with several alumni living in Thailand for advice. This developed into quite a circle of people, as everyone seems to know everyone in Thailand's NGO/UN community. However, despite having interned in Bangkok, I encountered many obstacles to finding a job. One of the biggest obstacles is the distance. Understandably, many organizations do not want to hire you sight unseen. Furthermore, you must convince the organization that it should hire you instead of a Thai, or a foreigner who already lives in Thailand. As Thailand develops more and more, there is less of a need for the expatriate consultant, and Thais are especially sensitive about this. It is therefore extremely important to be respectful in Thailand, especially to your boss and elders. Furthermore, UN agencies are cutting back and are even thinking of leaving Thailand in a few years. Thus, UN jobs are harder and harder to come by. This is unfortunate, because UN jobs in general pay quite a bit more than NGO jobs, which brings me to my last big obstacle: money. The salary paid to work for an international or domestic NGO in Thailand will probably be enough to live on, but not a lot more. In conversations with potential employers, I made sure that they knew that I was willing to work for a short-term contact.

Finally, after about six months of e-mailing and faxing, I landed a six-month contract with an international NGO.

I quickly learned that even the hiring process is quite different from what Americans are used to. There is little talk of money, and almost no negotiating is done. Unlike working for an American firm, where there would be a lot of back-and-forth conversation about remuneration and the type of work one would be doing, little of this is done in Thailand. This creates a lot of uncertainty for the foreigner. But these cultural differences also make Thailand a great place to work. It is difficult to get a job there, but if you're willing to be flexible, and perhaps take a low-paying job at first, it will pay off.

Germany: Another Student's Story

As I began planning to work abroad in Berlin, Germany, after college graduation, I asked colleagues and friends whether they had connections there and was surprised at how quickly my list of contacts grew. I sent letters to schedule short meetings and turned up several leads to pursue. I also contacted the German Embassy in Washington, D.C., for current information on work and residency permits. To work in Germany legally, Americans must have both a residency permit *(Aufenthaltserlaubnis)* and a work permit *(Arbeitserlaubnis)*.

The first step to getting a residency permit is to register at the local police station in Berlin. After this, I went to the Residence Authority responsible for my district and filled out a form, provided two passport photos, a letter from my hometown police station saying I had never committed a felony, proof of support (a bank statement) and health insurance, an acceptance letter to a language school, and my passport. A college diploma and letter of sponsorship from a German friend are also helpful. I then paid approximately DM 80 and received my residency permit. Generally, Americans are given a one-year permit, which can be renewed.

A work permit is more difficult; if you are offered a job, an employer will assist you with the paperwork, which must prove to the Labor Authority that a foreigner has a special skill that justified hiring them instead of a German. Often the Labor Authority will post the job in the paper for up to five months to see whether a German candidate can be found. Generally, it is easier to get a work permit if you already have a residency permit; remember, though, that your work permit is valid only at the company that sponsored you. If you change jobs, you need to get a new permit. As an official student at a German university, you can work without a permit for three months per year.

Another option available for Americans, which I took advantage of, is to register as self-employed. This works well if you intend to do things such as freelance translation, writing, research, or leading tours for foreigners who don't speak German. The first step in this process is to write a proposal of what you would like to do—a simple one-page letter will suffice. Submit this letter to the Residence Authority, which passes it to the Labor Authority. After doing this, I received a call to confirm my plans and ask questions about how I planned to do my work. Finally, I received a letter requesting that I bring in my passport, I paid another DM 80, and the permission to work was written into my passport.

The final step was to request a tax number from the Finance Authority. Then, I was legally able to work, but only at the specific tasks indicated in my permit. I learned that I was also responsible for my own health insurance and taxes, so I carefully kept all work-related receipts.

As you can see, there are always jobs to be found if you have initiative and no preconceived ideas of the level or type of work you are willing to accept. It especially helps to target a country with a lot of opportunities, as opposed to a country in an economic crisis or one with a large qualified candidate pool and high unemployment. Using your student status is helpful, whether to secure an internship or get a short-term work permit. And background research and networking are both vital to a successful search.

Catapult's JobWeb (www.jobweb.org/catapult), which links to numerous job listing sites by region, has a large overseas list, including sites from Ireland to China, and everywhere in between. Check it out!

Monster.com (www.monster.com) also has a Global Gateway that links to jobs worldwide. The Work Abroad page has articles on a variety of job choices, relocation information, cultural issues, and regional tips and information.

Most of the websites listed in Chapter 1 also have international job listings: Escape Artist (www.escapeartist.com), Overseas Jobs (www.overseasjobs.com), and Job Pilot (www.jobpilot.com).

IF YOU ARE A STUDENT

The prospects for students are brighter than for individuals not in school, especially in Great Britain, Ireland, France, Germany, Costa Rica, New Zealand, Canada, Jamaica, South Africa, and sometimes Australia (depending on the school you are attending). In these countries, the Council on International Education Exchange (CIEE) in New York can be of help. For a fee of $300–$475 (depending on the country), you can get a short-term work authorization as well as information on housing and general literature on living and working abroad plus access to potential employers prior to departure. Once you are in-country, CIEE provides an orientation session, and participants are then able to access their complete job bank. The length of the authorization varies from one country to another—up to three months in France, longer in other countries. No guarantee of a job goes with the authorization, but with one in hand you obviously have a better chance of connecting with a job. Brochures can be downloaded as PDF files from their website or ordered through the mail.

In China and Thailand, CIEE offers five-month and ten-month teaching contracts for fees of $1,300 to $1,495; in these cases the organization does arrange paid employment, accommodation, and other services. You do not have to be a student for these contracts.

Council on International Educational Exchange
>205 East 42nd Street
>New York, NY 10017
>(888) 268–6245
>www.ciee.org

CIEE also has extensive resources for both minority and disabled students; be sure to access their website for more information.

Since the difficulties and procedures for getting permits to work abroad vary among nations, get detailed information on the problems you will face before you leave the United States from the particular embassies (in Washington) or consulates (usually in New York) of the countries where you want to work. The State Department (www.state.gov) maintains online fact sheets about countries, which can be a useful start. Some travel guidebooks, such as *Lonely Planet* and the *Time Out* city guides, provide information on work regulations. If you are a student, be sure to mention that fact, since you will probably find fewer obstacles in your path toward summer or part-time employment.

Two More Possibilities for Students

International Association of Economic and Management Students (AIESEC)

>135 West 50th Street, 20th Floor
>New York, NY 10020
>(212) 757–3774
>www.aiesec.org

This association offers a worldwide program of work traineeships. Students are placed in positions in industry abroad year-round, with placements anywhere from six weeks to a year and a half. AIESEC currently focuses on work placements, youth development exchange projects (community development projects), corporate social responsibility, entrepreneurship, and regional/bilateral exchanges. Students receive a stipend to cover living and incidental expenses. Several thousand students are placed annually in traineeships in 87 participating countries in Europe, Africa, Latin America, Australia, and Asia. In order to qualify for an internship, students must work through a local chapter, agreeing to attend an orientation and also pay a registration fee of $500. Interested students should first visit AIESEC's homepage at www.aiesec.org to locate a chapter near them in order to participate.

Association for International Practical Training (IAESTE/US)

10400 Little Patuxent Parkway, Suite 250
Columbia, MD 21044–3510
(410) 997–2200; fax: (410) 992–3924
www.aipt.org

This organization operates four training programs: the IAESTE program for college and university students majoring in technical fields; the Student Exchanges Program for college and university students studying nontechnical subjects; a Career Development Exchanges Program for young professionals and recent graduates in most fields; and a Professional Visitor Program for professionals wishing to come to the United States for short-term experiential education in their fields. Students of engineering, architecture, mathematics, and the sciences can obtain on-the-job training with employers in countries all over the world. Traineeships usually last from two to three months during the summer. Some longer-term placements are possible by special arrangement. Trainees receive a maintenance allowance and pay their own costs of travel.

AIPT trainees must be at least 18 years old and less than 35 years old. All trainees are paid a competitive wage by the host employer; programs last from three weeks to 18 months (except the Professional Visitor Program). All AIPT programs carry application and processing fees. For more information, interested candidates should contact the association in Maryland or access their website.

4

Landing the Job

AFTER YOU HAVE identified an international career area that interests you, planned your curriculum to reflect this interest, and done some occupational research to learn more about the area, you should then begin to tailor your resume and begin exploring possible job and internship options.

RESEARCH AND NETWORKING

The first stage of the job search involves uncovering the many kinds of international opportunities available. These opportunities are so diverse and numerous that Part Two of this book is devoted entirely to helping you find ways to research career fields, access organizations in which jobs or internships may be available, and gain insights into some of the necessary qualifications.

As you will recall from Chapter 1, the first step is to research the field that interests you and the organizations that are doing the work that you might like to do. Through informational interviewing (see Chapter 1), you begin the invaluable process of networking with professionals who will not only offer you advice but also keep you informed about internship or job possibilities. Studies have shown that approximately 80 percent of all jobs are obtained through networking, so it is important to focus on people, not paper.

Still, an effective resume is critical, and a strong cover letter that presents your credentials will usually make a big impact on a potential employer.

Having done the research, you are finally ready to plan your search, either for an internship or a permanent position. Until now you have been preparing yourself—through self-assessment, school, and research—for an international career. Now, it is time to use the training and knowledge you have gained to impress employers with your qualifications so that you get the job you want.

No matter what field you have in mind—banking, law, government, non-profit, or media—any strategy you use to reach your goal will require three things: (1) a cover letter, (2) a resume, and (3) an interview. You will almost never get a job without an interview, and you will ordinarily not get an interview without first submitting a letter and resume. The trick, then, is to make your letter interesting enough to make someone want to read your resume, which in turn should be impressive enough to lead to an interview.

Many books (some of them listed in the Bibliography) have been written on letters, resumes, and interviewing techniques. There are also many excellent websites to help you, and several will be recommended throughout this chapter. Here are a few pointers to get you started.

When Should You Start Looking for Work?

The lead time for international jobs is often longer than for other types of work. In government jobs, the time between initial application and a job offer may be as long as 12 months because the security check itself may take up to six months. Jobs with multilateral organizations may also take 6–12 months because of the many levels of approval needed.

For jobs with government and international organizations such as the United Nations, then, begin the application process 6–12 months before you want to start working. With other types of international work, count on a lead time of three to five months.

RESUMES

A resume is essentially a profile of your professional and educational background. It should be easy to read, have a clearly identifiable focus, and relay your accomplishments and responsibilities. The kind of resume used depends in turn on the number of your career objectives and how closely defined they are.

There is no perfect resume. This means that you should research a variety of formats, then make your own decisions (perhaps in consultation with a career counselor) on the style that presents your credentials in the strongest, most favorable light.

Ideally, your resume should be no longer than one page, particularly for jobs in the private sector. For academic or research positions, and for many non-profit fields, two or more pages are acceptable. Definitely include your education (undergraduate and graduate) and experience (work, internships, etc.).

The final section(s) may comprise a variety of subjects, depending on what you want to convey. Common topics include: computer skills, languages, publications, extracurricular activities, and presentations/conferences.

If you are applying directly from school, you should start with your educational experience; if you are currently in the workforce, begin with professional experience. Be sure that at the top of your resume you have a physical address, phone number, and e-mail address where you can be reached.

On the following pages you will find some examples of different resumes. Review each and notice certain key issues it raises about the motivation and background of the applicant.

In all of these resumes you will find certain characteristics that often make a positive impact on employers.

- *They emphasize achievements and accomplishments.* Not "Subscription manager of the *Journal,*" but "As subscription manager of the *Journal,* increased circulation by 60 percent." Not "Conducted career workshop," but "Organized career workshop that assisted students in effective job searching."
- *They utilize phrases rather than narrative paragraphs.*
- *They show a focus on a particular field.*
- *They list education and experience in reverse chronological order.*
- *They include part-time employment and internships.* Part-time jobs and internships have several features in common with professional jobs: discipline, punctuality, ability to work with people. All are considered relevant in the job hunt, especially if they relate to your field of interest. There is no need to specify whether the work is paid or unpaid.
- *They do not give references.* No names or addresses should be listed. Rather, a separate sheet of paper with the names and addresses of your references should be typed and ready for distribution at the request of a potential employer.

If I Have Two Concentrations, Should Both Be Emphasized on My Resume?

This depends on the job for which you are applying. In some cases, your chances increase because of the two specializations offered. In other cases, only one background is relevant. If, for example, you have a dual background in

Resume 1: Focus on International Communications

Education

Columbia University, School of International and Public Affairs, New York

Master of International Affairs (M.I.A.), Harriman Institute Certificate, expected May 2004

Honors: Pepsico Fellowship, Harriman Institute, 2002–2003; Philip E. Mosely Fellowship, Columbia University, 2001–2002

Washington University, St. Louis, Missouri

B.A. *Magna Cum Laude* in History, minors in Economics and Russian, May 1992

Honors thesis: "The Foreign Relations of Hungary, 1939–1944: An American Perspective"

Experience

The Economist, Business Reporting Intern, London, June–Aug. 2002

- Proposed, researched, and wrote articles for the Business and Finance sections. Topics included: the reform of Russia's power industry, the sale of a major Hungarian bank, the future of Russian oil, the demise of a German conglomerate.

Freelance Writer, Budapest, Hungary, Jan. 2000–Aug. 2001

- Published in *Euromoney, Wall Street Journal Special Sections, The Banker, Tornado, Business Central Europe.*
- Conducted extensive interviews in English, Hungarian, and Russian for articles on economics, politics, and the IT sector.

Budapest College of Foreign Trade, Visiting Lecturer, English Department, Jan. 2000–Aug. 2001

- Taught courses on American and British newspaper vocabulary. Lectured on American, British, Hungarian culture.

Reuters, Correspondent, Budapest, July 1998–Dec. 1999

- Produced reports on the currency market, equity and debt markets, company analyses, political news.
- Covered corporate and governmental news conferences, edited colleagues' work, monitored radio and television stations.

Budapest Business Journal, Reporter, Budapest, June 1997–June 1998

- Wrote 3–4 articles per week on the telecom and IT sectors, foreign trade. Created features on business and social themes.
- Traveled to eastern Hungary to research and write in-depth report on small border town becoming an important trade center.

The Moscow Times, Reporter and Researcher, Moscow, Dec. 1995–June 1996

- Generated 40 articles under deadline pressure about privatization, the oil industry, the constitutional court, the stock market.
- Researched and authored in-depth article about a corrupt industrial tycoon who was challenging Yeltsin for the presidency.

***Moscow News,* Chief Style Editor, Moscow, Feb. 1994–Dec. 1995**
- Supervised team of three; responsible for editing 150 pages of news each week.

Freelance Writer and Photographer, Washington and Moscow, Nov. 1992–Dec. 1995
- Journalism and op-ed pieces appeared in the *Dallas Morning News, Detroit News, St. Louis Post Dispatch*, and others.

***Demokratizatsiya,* Issue Editor, (Vol. II, No. 1), Washington, March 1993–Feb. 1994**
- Created and oversaw 170-page special issue focusing on U.S. policy toward the former Soviet Union.
- Supervised staff of ten through all phases of publication process: article solicitation, editing, and production.

***The National Interest,* Assistant Editor, Washington, Aug. 1992–Jan. 1994**
- Reviewed and critiqued unsolicited manuscripts; edited articles and formatted pages in Quark publishing software.

Skills
- Fluent in Russian and Hungarian; intermediate French.
- Familiarity with Lexus/Nexus and various web-based search engines. Proficiency with Microsoft Word, Excel.

Resume 2: Focus on International Development

Education

M.A., International Development and Social Change
Clark University, expected May 2004
Thesis: "Power and Vulnerability in Toubkal National Park, Morocco: Perspectives"
B.A., English/Sociology
University of Connecticut, 1994

Awards

FULBRIGHT SCHOLAR, Toubkal National Park, Morocco
J.William Fulbright Research Scholarship, January 2002–October 2002
Completed a 9-month study of the environmental and social impacts associated with ecotourism in Toubkal National Park, Morocco. Methodology included surveys conducted with local and international tourists in 5 languages, participatory focus groups with park-affected communities, interviews with Moroccan ministry officials, assessment of tour company policies, evaluation meetings with local and international NGOs.

RESEARCH ASSISTANT, Marketing and Research Department
Clark University, Spring 2001
Adapted senior faculty publications for the university's Interactive Learning and Research website.

TEACHING ASSISTANT, Sociology Department
Clark University, Fall 2000
Graded papers, tracked class attendance, facilitated small group projects, maintained office hours, assisted professor with 100 students in introductory sociology class.

NATIONAL SCHOLAR ATHLETE
University of Maryland, Spring 1991
University of Connecticut, 1991, 1994

Professional Experience

CONSULTANT, Writing Center
Clark University, November 2002–current
Assist graduate and undergraduate students with all aspects of writing, including style, grammar, organization, editing. Currently supporting dissertation for doctoral candidate.

ASSISTANT TO THE DIRECTOR, International Development and Social Change Department
Clark University, January 2001–December 2001
Assisted director in grant and proposal writing; organized and facilitated retreat for 50 graduate students, 10 faculty members; coordinated prospective student visits; coordinated on-campus conferences; corresponded with faculty and students; maintained director's calendar; shared management of departmental office for 80 graduate students.

TECHNICAL COORDINATOR, Morocco
Peace Corps, June 1998–September 1998
Developed curriculum, educational materials for a 13-week technical training program, utilized participatory methods in Environmental Education and Rural Community Development; instructed 18 Peace Corps trainees in preparation for their field assignments; published comprehensive technical resource manual including training design and objectives.

COMMUNITY/ENVIRONMENTAL EDUCATOR, Morocco
Peace Corps, June 1996–September 1998
Assessed Rural Community Development potential of 23 villages between 50–500 residents each within 20-kilometer valley located inside Toubkal National Park; conducted Participatory Rural Appraisal meetings with communities; taught environmental education to primary school students; recruited, trained, and supervised teachers at the National Environmental Education Teachers training program.

ENVIRONMENTAL EDUCATOR, Wiscasset, Maine
Chewonki Foundation, May 1994–February 1996
Prepared environmental and natural history lessons; helped maintain working organic farm; led groups of 10–12 students through 5-day residential encampments; guided extended sea kayaking, canoe, and backpacking trips.

Skills

LANGUAGES

Moroccan Arabic (fluent)

Standard Arabic (proficient)

Tashelheet (local dialect, fluent)

French (written, proficient)

English (native speaker)

GEOGRAPHIC INFORMATION SYSTEMS

Idrisi

ArcView

CONFLICT NEGOTIATION

PARTICIPATORY RURAL APPRAISAL

RECOGNITION

Fulbright research featured in *The Chronicle of Higher Education* (Winter 2002, forthcoming issue), quarterly *Fulbright Morocco Newsletter* (Summer 2002); response letter published in *Newsweek International* (September 2, 2002); selected presenter at U.S. Peace Corps In-Service Training, Close of Service Conferences; requested translator at *Kasbah du Toubkal*, Morocco, conference (September, 2002).

Resume 3: Focus on International Environmental Work

Education

Johns Hopkins University   Washington and Bologna

School of Advanced International Studies (SAIS)

Master of Arts in International Relations with Distinction   2002

Bologna Center Diploma in International Affairs   2001

- Concentrations: International Development; Energy and Environment
- Awards: SAIS Academic Excellence Committee Fellowship; Bologna Center Fellowship
- Relevant Courses: East European Economies in Transition; International Trade; Monetary Theory; Finance in Development; Energy, Environment in Eastern Europe and Former USSR; International Environmental Law

University of Colorado at Denver   Denver and Moscow

Bachelor of Arts in International Affairs, *summa cum laude*   2000

- Concentrations: Political Science, Communication, History
- International College, UC Denver in Moscow 1996–1998
- Awards: Outstanding Graduating Senior; Chancellor's Scholars and Leaders Fellowship
- Honors thesis: "International Development: UNICEF and Arsenic Groundwater Contamination in Bangladesh"

Georgetown University   Prague, Czech Republic
American Institute on Political and Economic Systems
- Analyzed merits of democracy and open markets in former   Summer 1997
  communist countries

Moscow State Institute for International Relations (MGIMO)   Moscow, Russia
- Fellowship from Polish government for 1-year course in International   1995–1996
  Relations

Experience

SAIS Foreign Policy Institute, The Protection Project   Washington, D.C.
Legal Research Intern   January 2002–Present
- Assisted in drafting legal section of Human Rights Report on trafficking in persons

School of Environmental Sciences, Jadavpur University   Kolkata, India
Intern   Summer 2001
- Assessed involvement of Indian and Bangladeshi governments in arsenic crisis
- Evaluated feasibility of arsenic removal and remediation plants in West Bengal and
  Bangladesh
- Educated villagers on basic hygiene, importance of alternative water sources to prevent ar-
  senicosis

Center for Constitutional Studies and Democratic Development,
** Youth Organizing Institute**   Vukovar, Croatia
Program Assistant   June 2001
- Led orientation of 28 Balkan youth leaders and 15 international faculty members
- Acted as assistant to Danube river conflict simulation and seminar on the environment
- Liaised with Vukovar Peace Institute to arrange logistical, technical, and administrative
  support

Fourth Arsenic World Conference   San Diego, USA
Organizational Assistant   June 2000
- Assisted in managing conference with 200 delegates on arsenic groundwater contamina-
  tion in Asia
- Organized networking of Colorado health experts and environmental engineers prior to con-
  ference

University of Colorado at Denver, Chancellor's Scholars and Leaders   Denver, USA
Program Coordinator   1998–2000
- Nominated "Speaker of the Year" to Colorado Leadership Luncheon 2000
- Coordinated 50 student volunteers and office staff at university's leadership program
- Implemented successful campus-wide PR campaign increasing engagement in commu-
  nity service
- Assisted in organizing conference to develop comprehensive public transportation in lieu of
  urban sprawl

Additional Information

Languages: Fluent English, Polish, Russian, Hindi; Working Italian; Conversational Spanish; Survival German.

Citizenship: Poland and United Kingdom

Latin American studies and economics, both count heavily if you apply to the U.S. Agency for International Development or the InterAmerican Development Bank. In still other cases, it may be that your economics will be the more attractive specialization and your Latin American studies of subsidiary or no importance. In other words, know the type of job for which you are applying, so that the appropriate part of your background can be emphasized on your resume and in your interview.

Note: If you were not born in the United States, you probably do not have to prove your credentials as an expert in the part of the world you come from. Therefore, unless you have overriding reasons for taking an academic major in the area of your birth, it would be helpful to have some specialization related to the functional area in which you'd like to work, such as in business, economics, or journalism.

Check out these three excellent websites for articles and tips on writing resumes:

- Monster.com (http://resume.monster.com)
- The Career Journal (*Wall Street Journal* Career Site; www.careerjournal. com/jobhunting/resumes/index.html)
- Hot Jobs (www.hotjobs.com/htdocs/tools/index.html); go to "Resumes"

JOB SEARCH CORRESPONDENCE

Constructing Cover Letters

A cover letter serves both as an introduction to your resume and as a sample of your writing ability. It has three main components: an *introductory paragraph*, in which you introduce yourself and state your purpose for writing (include a referral name if possible); the *body of the letter*, in which you mention certain skills that you have developed and relate them to the job/internship for which you are applying; and a *closing paragraph*, thanking the employer for his or her consideration and making polite plans for follow-up.

For excellent cover letter advice, check out these three sites:

- Hot Jobs (www.hotjobs.com/htdocs/tools/index.html); go to "Job Searching"
- Monster.Com (http://resume.monster.com/coverletter)
- The Riley Guide (www.rileyguide.com/letters.html)

Below you will find some sample letters. They are not meant to be followed closely; in fact, you would be doing yourself a disservice if you did so, since cover letters are a very personal thing. They are included to expose you to the general style of cover-letter writing and to allow you to start thinking about how to construct the kind of letter that you think will present your credentials in the strongest and most favorable light. Above all, letters should reflect your personality and style, while respecting the protocol and formality of the process.

To Whom Should Letters and Resumes Be Sent?

One student, whom I will call Linda, approached me one day quite dejected about her job search; she had sent out more than fifty letters but received only rejection letters, if any response at all. Upon probing, I learned that all of her letters had been sent to the human resources department of various organizations; she hadn't even bothered to get the name of someone to send them to! Of course, it takes time to research the organization in order to determine the name and title of the person who will actually supervise the screening and interviewing process. It takes work to determine exactly where to apply, but the effort to network into the organization has a much greater payoff, and this will much more often result in a real lead.

We discussed other techniques, including informational interviewing, using alumni to figure out who is responsible for hiring in a particular organization, and how to retarget some of those same organizations by writing letters to a department head. Approximately two weeks later, Linda was thrilled to have secured several interviews—well worth the time it took to research and send her cover letters to the right people.

If you have no contact in an organization, you may automatically assume that you should apply to the human resources division. This depends on the organizational structure—and whether you are applying for an advertised position that specifically instructs you to do so. Often, however, human resources offices are deluged with resumes, and they get filed in a place where they are never reviewed again.

There are certain characteristics of successful letters:

- Keep the letter brief—no longer than one page.
- Always address the letter to an individual, never to "Sir or Madam."
- Emphasize achievements and accomplishments rather than responsibilities.
- Be concise; remember that this will be used as a writing sample.
- Refer to your resume (which should be attached).
- Request consideration for an interview.
- Make it easy for the employer by pointing out parts of your background that are pertinent to the job for which you are applying.
- Address things from the employer's point of view (i.e., not "I want to do so and so," but "My skills in . . . will help you. . . .")

Here are three examples of letters used in the application process. They can be sent either via e-mail or hard copy (fax is generally preferred); if sent as e-mail, include the letters in your correspondence as an attachment. *Note:* Always scan your attachments for viruses prior to attaching and e-mailing them to a prospective employer.

Letter in response to a job announcement at school or in the classified ads
Letter asking if opportunities exist / For an informational interview
Follow-up/Thank-you letter (after the interview)

Proofreading Is Key

Each year, I receive calls from frustrated alumni who help hire recent graduates. But when they advertise jobs, they often receive resumes and cover letters from students that contain typos. Most employers who find errors in your spelling and grammar will stop reading and automatically throw your materials in the wastebasket. Alums are no different: Your application is seen as a reflection on them, and they probably wouldn't pass along an embarrassing resume to the individual who is hiring. *Note:* Proofread your letters and resumes before sending them out.

1. Letter in Response to a Job Announcement at School or in the Classified Ads

33 West 72nd Street
New York, NY 10024

April 13, 2003

Mr. Scott Sawyer
Manager, Emerging Markets Research
Citibank
230 Park Avenue
New York, NY 10017

Dear Mr. Sawyer:

I am writing to apply for the research position that I saw advertised at Georgetown University's Office of Career Services. I am interested in a career in emerging markets focused on Latin America and believe that I have the qualifications to contribute to your operations in that area.

As the attached resume indicates, I have recently graduated from the School of Foreign Service at Georgetown, where I focused on International Banking and Finance. My coursework includes accounting, money and financial markets, business finance, international banking, and economies in the developing world. I have also completed three courses in graduate level economics. The quantitative skills that I have developed through these classes will allow me to effectively analyze financial data and create models through which country or company risk may be assessed.

My previous work experience at Merrill Lynch as a summer intern provided me with experience in credit analysis and exposed me to a fast-paced work environment where it was important to work closely as part of a team to produce high-quality research on a timely basis. I have strong research and writing skills, developed through my prior work experience as an economic analyst for the Department of the Treasury. Additionally, I have traveled extensively through Latin America, speak Spanish fluently, and am beginning coursework in Portuguese. I believe that my language skills, as well as the analytic abilities detailed above, would allow me to effectively contribute to your work in Latin American emerging markets research.

Thank you for your consideration. At your convenience, I would enjoy meeting with you to review my background in relation to the position.

Sincerely,

Jeanette Gomez

2. Letter Asking If Opportunities Exist/For an Informational Interview

April 1, 2003

Ms. Cecilia Brown
Vice President, Human Resources
Public Health International
Washington, D.C. 20006

Dear Ms. Brown:

I am writing at the recommendation of your former colleague, George Smith, who has been very helpful as I have been researching careers in international public health. He suggested that you might be willing to meet with me briefly to provide some advice as I begin my job search in this field.

I am particularly interested in the work of Public Health International because of the work you do in the area of child survival. After two years in the Peace Corps, working on maternal-infant health issues and health education in Bolivia, I returned to the United States to pursue a Master's in public health at Johns Hopkins University. I graduated recently and am pursuing positions in the field as a program officer—either in Latin America or Africa. I am enclosing a resume for your review.

I would very much appreciate the opportunity to speak with you about possible openings with PHI. Please allow me to call you within the next two weeks in the hope that we can meet at your convenience. Thank you.

Sincerely,

Kelly Cooke

If You Have One or More Job Objectives

How does your strategy change if, for example, you have one job objective or three objectives? If you know you are going into international journalism and that's all that concerns you, your job strategy is relatively simple. Not only is your target well defined and easily identifiable, but the search itself

3. Follow-Up/Thank-You Letter (After the Interview)

927 Charles Street
Seattle, WA 98143

August 17, 2003

Mr. George A. Sims
Regional Coordinator, International Trade Division
Department of Economic Development
Seattle, WA 98144

Dear Mr. Sims:

Thank you for the opportunity to meet with you yesterday and discuss a policy analyst opening with Seattle's International Trade Division of the Department of Economic Development.

I appreciated the opportunity to learn more about the needs of your department, particularly with regard to your increasing activity in Southeast Asia. I was impressed by the growing importance of an in-depth knowledge of the ASEAN countries and believe that my language skills in Malai and Thai will allow me to assist with promoting exports to the region. Additionally, my work experience in San Francisco's Department of International Trade has provided me with knowledge of the working of a city agency, and it has given me a deeper sense of the importance of writing and analytic skills when researching markets and advising potential businesses. The job opportunity we discussed sounds extremely rewarding and I hope you will give my application further consideration. I look forward to the possibility of working with you.

Sincerely,

Lawrence Golden

will be facilitated. You will ordinarily have one resume that is clearly focused toward that goal. You can draft one general cover letter, which you will be able to tailor specifically to the different jobs and organizations to which you are applying.

Suppose, however, you have had a specialization in international media and there are three kinds of jobs you would like to explore: public affairs with a nonprofit organization, print journalism, and broadcast production. With three such varying objectives, you would probably do well to draft three versions of your resume, each with a slightly different focus to emphasize those parts of your education and experience that are pertinent to the job for which you are applying. Accordingly, your three resumes should be accompanied by different types of cover letters, each geared to the specific objective mentioned in the accompanying resume.

According to Eric Schlesinger, senior human resources officer at the World Bank, "Your resume and cover letter create your first impression when you are corresponding with potential employers. All that they will know of you is what you tell them. Therefore, remember to focus quickly on the positives in your background that are directly related to the job in which you are interested."

INTERVIEWING TECHNIQUES

We now come to the last stage of the job hunt and one of the most important. You have invested a lot of time and energy all along the way: the self-knowledge you have poured into the job hunt; your decision of a career objective and the appropriate choice of courses to support this objective; the extensive research you have undertaken to identify your targets; the hours you've sweated over your letters and resumes.

All this effort has paid off. You have impressed an employer who has the job you are after and you have been invited for an interview. This is the moment that counts. The whole career planning process you have diligently developed over the years has brought you within striking distance of the job you want.

Interviewing is as much an art as a science. Much of the result will depend on the chemistry between personalities, and there's not much you can do about that. Furthermore, intangible factors like mood and the employer's frame of mind may be outside your control.

However, there is much you can do to prepare effectively for an interview. First, read what you can about the organization and try to speak with people who are familiar with its work and its reputation. Then, carefully review your resume and try to pick out experiences in your past that are relevant and transferable to the job or internship at hand.

One of the most important things you can do to increase your effectiveness as a candidate is to *practice* answers to possible interview questions. Make a list—or review a list in a book about interviewing—and jot down some notes to each answer. Then practice articulating the answers out loud—to a mirror, to a friend, to a career counselor, or on a cassette tape. While you obviously don't want to sound "rehearsed" and unnatural, you do want to sound like you have anticipated some of the employer's questions and have thoughtfully considered what is relevant in your background to express. This is almost impossible to do without practice, particularly in an interview, which can make you a bit anxious, to say the least!

On the Actual Day of the Interview

Be sure that you get a restful night of sleep; then look over your notes again and review the organizational materials. Of course, your clothing should be professional. Always err on the side of formality, even if the organization seems a bit more casual. So, a suit is usually in order, preferably in a conservative color like navy, gray, or brown, though a tie or a scarf can add some color.

Know the directions to where you are going and leave plenty of time to get there. It is a good idea to arrive approximately ten minutes early—in case you need to use the restroom, get a drink of water, or just examine your environs and the atmosphere of the office.

Twelve Interviewing Tips

1: *Know the organization.* Read all available literature on it. Consult annual reports, brochures, and websites. This knowledge will increase your confidence during the interview and show the employer your motivation for the position.

2: *Prepare questions you wish to ask the interviewer.* These should be based on your research of the organization's functions, plans, and problems. Don't ask obvious questions that you could have answered yourself by reading their literature.

3: *Know the points about yourself that you wish to make.* The insertion of this material into the discussion is a skill that comes with practice. Don't wait until the last moment, when you are at the door saying good-bye, then suddenly blurt out, "By the way, I forgot to mention that I'm president of the student association. Oh yes, I'm also. . . ."

4: *Evaluate your strengths and weaknesses before the interview.* You will be asked about them and expected to give specific examples to back up your assertions. Sometimes a weakness can be presented as a strength, e.g., being highly demanding of other people.

5: *Expect the unexpected.* Some interviewers may insist on doing all the talking; others may lean back and ask, "What are all the things I should know about you?" leaving you an open field for the next 25 minutes. Fortunately, most interviews involve some level of conversation, with questions and answers on both sides.

6: *Be familiar with the parts of an interview.* Most are divided into roughly five parts:
  A. Introduction, meant to establish a rapport and put you at ease ("How are you?" "What a lovely view from your window.")
  B. Discussion of your qualifications, background, and career goals ("Why do you want a career in _____?" "Where do you see yourself in ten years?")
  C. Discussion of requirements of the job opening
  D. Attempt to relate your qualifications to the job
  E. Summary/Close. ("You can expect to hear from me in two weeks.")

The order of the above may vary. Sometimes a discussion about job requirements will precede the discussion of your qualifications. Sometimes an employer may not specifically probe the relationship between your qualifications and the job requirements, but even if it isn't voiced, the employer will certainly be attempting to do this mentally, so the more you can help with direct links, the better.

7: *Remember the employer's point of view and base your case on how you can be useful to the employer.* An employer is less interested in what they can do for you than what you can do for them.

8: *Be prepared to explain your motivation.* "Why do you want to work in international economics?" or "Why are you applying to our particular firm?" are common types of questions. If you are honestly enthusiastic about the job, don't hesitate to express your enthusiasm.

9: *Don't raise questions about salary, vacations, or benefits during your first interview.* If asked about salary, indicate a range and that it is negotiable—know the salary range of the type of job and set your figure accordingly.

10: *Always tell the truth.* As someone once said, "You will have less to remember."

11: *Stress accomplishments and achievements, rather than duties and responsibilities, in any past employment.* ("As circulation manager of the school magazine, I increased subscriptions by 50 percent.") You are not being immodest. You are making it easier for the employer to come to the conclusion that, of his six interviewees, you are the most capable.

12: *Keep the initiative, if possible, for future contacts* ("Shall I call you in two weeks to see how my candidacy is coming along?"). Don't sit by the phone waiting for employers to call, unless they have specifically stated they will contact you within a definite time frame. Be pleasantly surprised if they do contact you at the appointed time. If they don't, give them a few days' leeway, then phone to determine the status of your candidacy and express continuing enthusiasm for the job.

Above all, be yourself. Let the interview reflect your personality. If in a banking interview you find yourself giving an interpretation of what you think a banker should be, you might want to consider whether banking is really the career you're after.

Some organizations—particularly businesses and banks—have special forms on which an interviewer evaluates each candidate. Here are two examples.

Bank A rates candidates on the following factors:

Introductory material
Oral communications skill
Self-confidence
Appearance
Social effectiveness

Education
Ability to reason logically
Level of overall academic accomplishment

Ability to apply academic background

Apparent maturity of judgment

Work experience

Apparent motivation to succeed

Significance of summer work to career goal

Prior leadership roles

Ability to work with others

Self-direction

Overall management potential

Maturity of career objectives

Commitment to banking

Bank B rates candidates on the following factors:

Interpersonal/social skills

Ease in working with clients and associates

Effectiveness of communication skills

Ability to develop and maintain client confidence

Judgment/analytical skills

Ability to reason logically

Planning and organizational skills

Affinity for numbers

Motivation/internal drive

Realistic career objectives

Achievement orientation

Commitment to banking

Every factor in each bank's assessment is given a numerical rating. The ratings are added and candidates with a high total are invited back for further interviews. Candidates below a certain numerical level do not receive an invitation to return.

You may well wonder how some of the above factors, such as "achievement orientation" or "overall management potential," are evaluated. Often, employers look for previous experiences to exemplify these two areas, like academic success for the first, and experience in leadership activities, organizational skills, and strong interpersonal skills for the latter.

Most important, you should note that academic standing is one factor among many in Bank A's assessment; in Bank B's, grades are not directly evaluated at all, although they are taken into consideration under "judgment/analytical skills" and "motivation/internal drive."

Many organizations look for the "rounded individual," preferably one who has a number of extracurricular interests, social presence, and at least average intelligence.

Academic standing and grades are more important if the job under discussion is in research, requiring intellectual capacities. Other jobs may put a premium on social effectiveness or leadership abilities.

After the Interview

Sit down as soon as possible and assess the interview in a notebook or a journal. Note the names of the people with whom you spoke, important things to remember about the organization, points you feel you expressed well, and things you wish you had done better. Write down any questions you may have to ask at a follow-up interview or conversation. Be sure to write a thank-you note to whomever you interviewed with, preferably within forty-eight hours.

The first interviews may well be grueling, but as you gain experience, the encounter with employers should become more familiar and thus more comfortable. You will be trying to impress upon the interviewer that you are the right person for the job; the interviewer will be trying to assess your qualifications and personality in relation to the job available.

Good luck!

For practice interviewing, tips, articles, and tough questions, check out these websites:

The Riley Guide for networking, interviewing, and negotiation (www. rileyguide.com/netintv.html)

Monster.com (http://interview.monster.com)

Wall Street Journal Careers (www.careerjournal.com/jobhunting/interviewing/index.html)

PART TWO

The International Job Market

5

The Federal Government

EXECUTIVE BRANCH JOBS

The federal government is in the midst of significant changes in the post–September 11 era. After the Reinventing Government era of Bill Clinton and Al Gore, President George W. Bush has faced the challenge of revamping and reorganizing our international security apparatus, including the creation of the new Office (then Department) of Homeland Security. Consequently, there is definitely an increase in the number of jobs in intelligence, law enforcement, and special operations (see information under CIA, FBI, and Department of Justice later in this chapter for more information on these areas).

Additionally, according to a spokesperson in the Office of Communications at the U.S. Office of Personnel Management (OPM), the Bush administration is asking each agency to carefully examine its mission. This initiative was in effect prior to 9/11 but has become even more urgent since the attacks, as budget numbers are more critical and funds are being diverted to deal with new security needs and the economic impact of the tragedy. Thus, hiring is definitely happening, steadily, but with a strong strategic perspective—jobs that were emptied are not simply being filled. Rather, responsibilities are being examined to see if the vacant position is critical to the mission of the agency, or if a different sort of job/profile is needed.

There has been a lot of talk recently about a "human capital crisis" in the federal government. This phrase refers to the number of anticipated retirees and the need for the government to have a well-developed pipeline of future leaders. However, OPM Director Kay Coles James prefers to think of this challenge as a "human capital opportunity" to replenish the federal workforce with new ideas and twenty-first-century skills. OPM recently completed an in-depth study to look at the actual numbers of individuals who are eligible to retire in the next five years and determined that only 19 percent of those eligible to retire actually plan to leave the workforce. Thus, the numbers trumpeting an exodus of 30–50 percent may be significantly overrated.

That said, opportunities in federal hiring are strong. The number of jobs involving international issues is increasing as the global economy becomes more interdependent. Some of these positions are available to those of you with a bachelor's degree, while some require a master's degree. And most federal jobs do not require a specific degree, so if you don't have a college education, there are still opportunities for you, particularly in administration and information technology.

It is difficult to generalize about international jobs within the federal government. The opportunities are vast—from being an intelligence analyst for the CIA to implementing a USAID-funded women's health project in Guatemala to assisting companies who are drawing upon the experience of the Commerce Department to export their goods. While the largest concentration of federal jobs is in the Washington, D.C., area, thousands also exist around the country and around the world.

There are many agencies in the executive branch that have a strong global focus—certainly, the Department of State, the U.S. Information Agency, the Agency for International Development, the Peace Corps, the Department of Commerce, the Overseas Private Investment Corporation, and the Export-Import Bank come immediately to mind. There are also myriad jobs in the intelligence community, in the midst of a major reorganization, but traditionally the National Security Agency, the Central Intelligence Agency, the Defense Intelligence Agency, the Office of the Secretary of Defense, the Justice Department, and the Federal Bureau of Investigation (FBI). However, practically all agencies have an international division and are worth exploring. Most students in international affairs who are looking for a federal government job think only of the aforementioned internationally oriented U.S. agencies, but don't forget to think "outside of the box." Consider a broader spectrum of agencies that also have positions of potential interest; for example, the Department of Labor, Department of Agriculture, Department of the Treasury, and Department of Energy all have international divisions and employ individuals with international backgrounds.

As you may imagine, salaries are not as high as in the private sector (see Table 5.1 for the federal government salary schedule later in this chapter). Still, government salaries allow you to live quite comfortably and rise with experience, and benefits are excellent.

Applying for Federal Employment

The Office of Personnel Management has developed USAJOBS to assist individuals interested in exploring federal employment. It is composed of three user-friendly components for conducting your personal job search. USAJOBS provides access to federal jobs—as well as some state and local government jobs—and updates the information on a daily basis. In many instances, job seekers can apply for positions online. Obviously, since it is available through the Internet, you can access the information day and night, seven days a week.

The Outstanding Scholar Program

If you are a current or recent college graduate, you might be eligible for the Outstanding Scholar Program. This is a special hiring authority for grades GS–5 through GS–7 that allows agencies to hire you directly, in a much simpler way than a typical posting. Positions in the following occupational fields are not covered by the Outstanding Scholar Program: accounting and auditing; engineering; physical sciences; biological sciences; and mathematics.

In order to be eligible, applicants must be college graduates (from any major)and have maintained a grade point average (GPA) of 3.5 or higher on a 4.0 scale or have graduated in the upper 10 percent of their graduating class or major university subdivision, such as the school of business. Students who are interested in the Outstanding Scholar Program may apply in the fall of their senior year—up to nine months before completing all the

---

Midlevel Jobs

Midlevel positions, such as economist, research analyst, or financial analyst, are generally for those with graduate degrees. For midlevel grades GS–9 through GS–12, individuals should apply directly to the agency that they are interested in or for which they feel the most qualified. You may find that your international background and experience may or may not be relevant. Don't necessarily let that deter you from applying. If you should be offered a job in the domestic operations of a government agency, you may wish to consider it. Once inside, you may be given priority for possible job openings in the agency's international division. At first, though, even an international job in one of these domestic-oriented agencies probably will involve primarily work in Washington with only occasional trips overseas.

The official website for jobs and employment information may be accessed at www.usajobs.opm.gov

Step 1: Log on to the Web or Call the Telephone Employment Information System

USAJOBS, the federal government's employment information system, is easily accessible. Through the Internet, job seekers can access current job vacancies worldwide, employment information fact sheets, and applications and forms. In some instances, you can apply for jobs online. The USAJOBS website also has an online resume builder feature that allows individuals to create electronic resumes specifically designed for applying for federal Jobs.

If you do not have computer access, you can use the USAJOBS automated telephone system. This interactive voice response system can be reached at (478) 757–3000 or TDD (478) 744–2299. By telephone, job seekers can access worldwide current job vacancies, employment information fact sheets, and applications and forms and, in some instances, apply for jobs by phone.

Step 2: Obtaining the Vacancy Announcement

OPM advises that once you find a job of interest, you should next obtain a copy of the vacancy announcement—again, through the Internet or telephone system. The vacancy announcement is an important source of information, as it comprehensively lists the details you need in order to apply, including specific job responsibilities, job location, educational background required, closing/deadline dates for applications, and salary.

Step 3: Follow the Application Instructions

You may apply for most jobs with a resume, and the Office of Personnel Management's resume builder allows you to create a resume that fits most standard federal jobs. For jobs that are filled through automated procedures, federal agencies may require that you submit a resume and/or other specialized forms. Jobs with unique requirements may also occasionally require special forms.

OPM stresses that whichever application method you choose, be sure to carefully follow the application so that you aren't disqualified on this basis.

requirements of the program, including GPA or class standing. However, be prepared to produce appropriate documentation (e.g., a copy of a college transcript) at the time of appointment. In order to apply, check the USAJOBS website; Outstanding Scholar opportunities are often posted there. You can also contact an agency directly to inquire about how it uses the Outstanding Scholar Program.

Special Tips

You don't have to wait to be summoned for a job interview once your written materials (e.g., resume and cover letter and/or the special form for federal employment) are submitted, but you can increase your chances immeasurably by taking certain actions:

1. Do Your Agency Research

While your papers are being processed, consult the websites for each agency, which contain a great deal of information, including the mission of each agency, current projects, regional offices, internships, and hiring information. Also, try to locate a copy of the *U.S. Federal Yellow Book,* which provides information on the chain of command in these offices.

Agency websites will also enable you to identify additional sections within each agency of particular interest. The *Federal Yellow Book* gives the names of individuals in charge of those sections. University career offices can be helpful as well in providing you with contacts in some government agencies.

2. Plan a Trip to Washington, D.C., or the City in Which You Are Seeking Federal Employment

Since most government agencies do not recruit on campus, you will have to first lay the groundwork for face-to-face meetings in Washington. Obviously, if you are a midcareer professional, you will need to invest in a trip to Washington, D.C., to do some networking. Initial communication with an agency might consist of a brief cover letter and a resume. E-mail or fax your correspondence to the director of the international division or office to which you are applying, or, ideally, to an alumnus/alumna or other contact that you have been given. You can sometimes send e-mails to more than one office within the same agency.

Try to make contact with individuals two to four weeks before a planned visit to Washington. Mention the approximate date of your trip and indicate that you will phone or send a follow-up e-mail to the recipient of the letter for a possible appointment.

Phone or e-mail for an appointment at the time indicated. E-mail has greatly facilitated the process of setting up such informational meetings, and often you will find that you receive a positive response to your meeting request.

If you impress a potential employer, he or she may ask you to submit your application for formal consideration when vacancies arise.

It's smart to check the various addresses of the offices you will be visiting on a map of downtown Washington before making appointments. Knowledge of agency locations and careful planning can double the number of people you can see in a day.

A final note on this subject: Avoid scheduling your trip to Washington during major holiday periods in order to increase the likelihood of meeting with top management.

3. Use Contacts Whenever Possible

According to Judy Kugel, who was director of career services at the prestigious John F. Kennedy School of Government at Harvard University from 1980 to 1997,

> From my 17 years of helping Kennedy School graduate students looking for federal government jobs, I do not know of a single student who found employment by submitting documents to OPM. Our graduates who are working in every federal agency, found their positions through their networking initiatives. Without exception.

After reading all of the information about OPM, applications for federal employment, and governmental hiring mechanisms, this quote must make you wonder why the bureaucratic procedures outlined above were included. And you are probably wondering if I agree with Judy Kugel? I do. As noted in the earlier chapters in this book, informational interviewing and networking are a key component of the international affairs job search, and federal government is a case in point. However, it is not uncommon to be later asked to go back and apply through official channels. Thus, familiarizing yourself with OPM and federal hiring procedures can only help your job search. *But who you know and who knows you will ultimately almost always get you the job.*

Presidential Management Intern Program

The Presidential Management Intern Program (PMIP) is a government-wide effort to attract outstanding graduate students into the federal service who have the potential to become top-level career executives. Established by executive order in 1977, it provides access to internationally oriented civil service positions, which are otherwise very difficult to obtain.

Each year, between 250 and 400 exceptionally talented individuals receive Presidential Management Internships (PMIs), through which they may apply for a two-year appointment in the government agency of their choice. They may be assigned to staff units in administrative and managerial services or to operating program or policy offices. Individuals enter at a GS–9 (currently, approximately $35,000) and are promoted to GS–11 or GS–12 by the end of two years. At the end of their internship, depending on the quality of their performance, they may be granted Civil Service status without further competition. To give you a sense of the competitive nature of the process, in 2001, 623 finalists were chosen from 1,800 applicants.

A unique component of the PMIP is its career development orientation. Each group of incoming interns receives orientations, attends training programs, and may participate in a rotational program that allows each individual to rotate to another division within his or her agency or to another agency altogether. For example, an intern in the Environmental Protection Agency (EPA) might be able to do a rotation to the Department of State or the Office of Management and Budget. This allows for new experiences, learning, and, of course, a larger professional network.

You are allowed to apply for a PMI *only* during the fall of your last year of graduate school. Written applications, which include a resume, must be received by October 31 of the year in which you are completing your graduate (M.A. or doctoral) work. If your written application is accepted, you participate in a rigorous oral assessment, which takes place in January or February. Finalists are notified, generally, in late March or early April; the next step is to interview for specific job openings within the government.

Application materials are available at graduate schools in the early fall of each year. If not available on your campus, applications can be obtained by checking the PMI website at www.pmi.opm.gov.

Types of Jobs

There are many federal government agencies, some large, some small. In this section you will find a list of most major federal agencies, a summary of the activities

A DAY IN THE LIFE

Day in the Life of a Former PMI

The year I applied there were hiring freezes at State, Treasury, and Commerce, and very few jobs for internationally oriented people. It became apparent after about a month of informational interviews that I was not going to have any luck getting the kind of Japan- or Asia-related position I was looking for. So, about midsummer, I decided that I would use the leverage of the PMI to go for agencies whose work seemed most interesting. I targeted the EPA . . . since I had virtually no environmental experience, I offered to do an internship—unpaid—for EPA's international office while I looked around for other prospects there. By luck, the international office created a slot that fall that required a knowledge of trade, and they threw in some Japan-related responsibilities for me as well. Incidentally, while I was interning, contacts I had made in other agencies came through for me, and I turned down jobs at Treasury and [International Trade Administration] during the autumn.

I had something of an unusual PMI experience in that I did not rotate like many PMIs, mostly because I was given a very substantive portfolio; I was put in charge of the UN program portfolio, and I was able to take on responsibilities that most people wouldn't get until several years into their government career, at the very least. Soon after that NAFTA got hot, and I felt that my position was allowing me to take on increasing responsibilities in a high-profile and somewhat technical field.

Without question, the greatest advantage of the PMI experience is that it is often the only dependable entree into government, particularly for international work. Equally beneficial, once you are in, is the relative freedom you have to tailor your experiences to your career goals. While the supervisory attitude varies quite a bit across agencies, supervisors recognize that you have a particular status as a PMI and that some deference should be paid to your long-term aspirations. This is not typically the case with a GS–9.

One warning I did not heed, or really give any thought to at all, but that I would now give anyone planning a career in civil service, is that, in many agencies, advancement comes to a halt for a good period of time at about my level for most people—that is, around a GS–14 or 15. At that level, it's not all that easy to change positions, and—unlike the private sector—policy positions do not translate all that well into similar businesses. The result is that, while my day-to-day responsibilities are probably as interesting as most comparable private sector jobs (if not more so), competent people in policy jobs often feel a bit stuck. The way forward is not as clear as in the private sector, where you can expect advancement—either within your organization or through job-hopping. ⌊L⌋

of the organization, information about the types of jobs and internships available, procedures for applying, and recommended academic and work backgrounds.

International Development Cooperation Agency (IDCA)/ Agency for International Development (USAID)

Ronald Reagan Building
1300 Pennsylvania Avenue

Washington, DC 20523–1000
(202) 712–0000
fax: (202) 216–3524
www.info.usaid.gov
Mailing Address for Recruitment Unit:
M/HR/POD/SP, 2.08, RRB
Washington, DC 20523–2808
fax: (202) 216–3418

USAID operates U.S. economic and humanitarian assistance programs in four regions: sub-Saharan Africa, Asia (Near East), Europe and Eurasia, and Latin America and the Caribbean.

The agency uses loans and grants in its development assistance program. It focuses on critical problem areas in developing countries, such as rural and private enterprise, development, nutrition, family planning and health (particularly infant and child mortality), illiteracy, education and human resources, the environment, natural resources, science and technology, and democracy and governance. Specific programs under the purview of USAID include Foreign Disaster Assistance, Food for Peace, and Economic Support.

USAID is currently focusing on supporting democracy, promoting economic growth, agriculture and trade, delivering humanitarian assistance, improving public health, and the environment.

At the time of writing, USAID had openings for the New Entry Professional Program (Foreign Service), Midlevel Hires (Foreign Service), and Civil Service positions. USAID's International Development Intern (IDI) program has been discontinued and replaced by the **New Entry Professional (NEP) Program**, which the agency uses to recruit for the Foreign Service. The selection process is extremely competitive. Applicants are evaluated based on academic credentials, related development experience, and other qualifications. Training begins in Washington and can take up to 18 months.

New entrants are appointed as career candidates at the Foreign Service level 4 or 5 (roughly equivalent to GS–11 or GS–12 in the U.S. Federal Competitive Civil Service). Successful applicants are paid according to their position's level, are typically posted abroad, and are given a clear career path to top executive positions. USAID does not require applicants to take the foreign service exam. Non-U.S. citizens may consider applying directly to overseas missions since direct hires from headquarters must be Americans. The only other entry-level hire into USAID is through the PMI Program.

USAID positions are quite varied and, therefore, require different kinds of training. The following list provides some idea of the background required for particular positions within AID:

- **Program officers** are generalists who advise the mission director on policy, planning, and evaluation of AID programs. International affairs, economics, political science, or regional expertise in developing countries are appropriate background studies, and significant work experience is desired.
- **Agricultural/rural development/natural resources officer economists** advise senior USAID and host government officials on agriculture and rural development; participate in project design and development; and manage and evaluate programs. A background in an agricultural specialty, an environmental specialty, anthropology, rural development/sociology, or natural resources and at least three years of specialized experience is essential for these positions.
- **Contract/commodity management officers** help coordinate and award USAID-financed commodity programs. The position requires a bachelor's degree in business, finance, public administration, law, or banking with an emphasis on commerce or trade and at least three years of related work experience.
- **Democracy officers** assist host-country leaders in furthering democratic initiatives in their country. Requires either a J.D. (law) degree or graduate degree in international affairs, public administration, or related social science and at least three years' experience in a related field.
- **Program economists** study economic conditions in countries applying for U.S. assistance. A graduate degree in economics and at least three years of pertinent professional experience are basic requirements.
- **Education/human resources development officers** analyze, advise, and assist with the development of host-country educational systems and human resources. Duties include participation in policy formation and program and project design. A graduate degree in education, psychology, sociology, anthropology, or communications and at least three years of specialized experience is required.

- **Environment/natural resources officers** advise senior USAID and host government officials to identify and develop programs to remedy environmental problems; promote sustainable development; and provide technical analysis and input for contract negotiations and grant agreements. Requires a graduate degree in environmental, biological, or related physical science or in an applied ecological science and at least three years of related professional experience. Courses in international economics and development are desirable.
- **Food for Peace officers** assist in the planning and implementation of USAID food and emergency projects and programs. Requires a graduate degree with a concentration in economics, business or finance, public administration, agricultural or social sciences, and at least three years of relevant experience.
- **Financial management officers** maintain USAID's accounting system and provide financial and statistical data. Requires a bachelor's degree and course work with a CPA or M.B.A. and at least three years of related work experience.
- **Health/population/nutrition officers** assist in managing family planning, nutrition, HIV/AIDS, and other health projects. Requires a graduate degree in a related field including public health, health sciences, business, or economics and at least three years of related experience.
- **Housing/urban development officers**, through the Office of the Environment and Urban Programs, assist in designing and monitoring USAID's shelter and urban environmental programs for low-income families in developing countries. Requires a graduate degree preferably in urban planning, public administration, economics, or finance and at least three years of related work experience.
- **USAID private enterprise officers** advise and assist host-country leaders from both the public and private sectors in furthering the emergence of a market economy in their country. Requires a graduate degree or related coursework in international affairs, finance, economics, or law and at least three years of related work experience.

Hiring.   There is no written examination for AID's Foreign Service positions, including the NEP program. To start the selection process, applicants should look for specific vacancy announcements on USAID's website and contact Barbara Ellington-Banks, via e-mail or at (202) 712–0665. If you have experience in a specific country or region, include your preference in your cover letter that accompanies your resume. Overseas USAID offices determine their own needs for short-term employees. In addition, foreign language proficiency is required for work in the field. Language training, if needed, is provided in Washington before departing on a foreign assignment.

Candidates are first screened to ensure that they meet the qualifications for one of the occupational specialties. The second screening will evaluate the applicant's knowledge of economic development issues and test his or her writing ability. All applicants for each specialty are rank-ordered. Those ranked highest come to Washington for interviews.

As with the Foreign Service exam of the Department of State, there is a long wait between application and eventual appointment. Similar to the Foreign Service, once through the NEP Program and appointed to a permanent position within USAID, you will spend a major part of your career overseas.

Central Intelligence Agency (CIA)

Recruitment Center
P.O. Box 4090, Dept: Internet
Reston, VA 20195
(703) 482–1100
www.cia.gov

The CIA is perhaps the most significant government agency providing intelligence information in the formulation of foreign policy. Although the clandestine operations appeal to the movie-going public because of their melodramatic content, the bulk of CIA work has to do with intelligence gathering and analysis. The gathering is done primarily in the field; the analysis, at headquarters in Langley, Virginia.

Each year the size and emphasis of the CIA recruitment program vary. There was a surge in applications, and some increase in demand, following the terrorist attacks on September 11, 2001. Further changes in recruiting may occur as the agency's role shifts to emphasize counterterrorism and as cooperation with other agencies is increased. In general, the CIA is interested in candidates with extensive life experiences, e.g., overseas experience, or a bachelor's or graduate degree in international affairs or another useful field, fluency in foreign languages, and an ability to translate original material, rather than conversational ability.

Another basic skill the CIA values is international economics, to be used in the collection, research, and measurement of data relating to the economic performance of foreign countries. Additional disciplines used by the CIA are abstract mathematics, business administration, computer science, engineering, international politics, physics, and chemistry.

The CIA prefers that applicants apply online. Otherwise, resumes can be mailed to the above address, stating the position being applied for on the envelope. It can take between two months and a year for your application to be processed. Each applicant undergoes a thorough background check, character assessment, medical exam, psychological exam, and polygraph test, in addition to the usual government screening. You must be a U.S. citizen to work for the CIA. The Clandestine Service Training Program has been established for those interested in the clandestine side of CIA operations. The two-year program is intense and highly competitive. It consists of formal study and on-the-job training. If you don't hear back from them within 90 days of application, assume that either there were no available positions or that you were not selected.

Those interested should send a cover letter, transcript, and resume to:
CST Division
P.O. Box 4605, Dept: Internet
Reston, VA 20195

The CIA also offers three highly competitive programs for students. Those accepted are paid and receive benefits. The Undergraduate Student (Co-op) Trainee Program places students at the agency's headquarters. The CIA's Internship Program is similar but seeks candidates with specific background studies useful to the agency. Students work in Washington for either a combination semester and summer internship or two 90-day summer internships. Those accepted work with and receive may of the same benefits as permanent employees. Students who have completed their undergraduate studies can apply to the Graduate Studies Program, which is open to students of international affairs, languages, economics, physical sciences, and engineering. Those selected should be starting their first or second year of graduate studies after the internship and, as with all the internships, must relocate to Washington.

To apply for any of these programs, send a resume, cover letter, and academic record to the main recruitment address, citing which program you are applying to.

Defense Intelligence Agency (DIA)

The Pentagon
Washington, DC 20340–0001
(703) 697–1757; (202) 231–8228 for recruitment
www.dia.mil

Another intelligence agency is the DIA, which is the intelligence arm of the Department of Defense. The DIA's mission has changed dramatically since the end of the Cold War and the Gulf War. Key areas of emphasis now include assessing battle damage, monitoring weapons proliferation, and supporting peacekeeping operations. DIA officers provide information to U.S. weapons planners and policymakers in the Department of Defense and Joint Chiefs of Staff. Less glamorous aspects of its work include analysis of military capabilities of various countries, transportation intelligence, photo interpretations, and economic analysis of foreign military production and expenditures.

Most DIA jobs are at the Defense Intelligence Analysis Center on Bolling Air Force Base in Washington. A small number of employees work at the Armed Forces Medical Intelligence Center in Maryland and at the Missile and Space Intelligence Center in Alabama. Attachés are assigned to embassies around the world, and DIA liaison officers are assigned to each unified military command.

DIA is staffed by civilian and military personal. Screening processes for applicants are similar to those at the CIA. Applicants must be U.S. citizens. The agency prefers candidates with training in engineering, international relations, economics, math, the sciences (including toxicology, environmental science, military science, and political science), history, information technology, statistics, or regional studies. Foreign language skills are highly valued. Salaries range from about $31,000 to $86,000, plus comprehensive benefits. Applications can be submitted via the agency's website.

For students, the DIA runs an Academic Semester Internship Program for undergraduates and graduates at universities in the Washington, D.C., and

Security Clearances

According to Rachel Kopperman Foster, USD (Comptroller) in the Office of the Secretary of Defense: "There are two basic types of clearances that a person coming into the government would get: Secret and Top-secret. There are levels of clearances above this—but none of these would apply to a person coming on board—and besides, they're classified.

"A secret clearance is just a basic background check to make sure that a person has no outstanding warrants or hasn't been arrested or convicted of a crime. It is a fairly quick process—but can still take a few months if the organization doing the check is backed up."

Kopperman Foster goes on to explain that top-secret clearance generally takes anywhere from three to four months to a year and a half. You should be prepared to provide every address and job you've had for the past ten or more years, along with the names and contact information for several friends, close family members, and acquaintances. (It helps if you first track down reliable people in these potentially faraway places who know you and can vouch for you, and provide this to the investigator to make the job easier.) The length of the clearance may be impacted by several factors:

- First, in order to get clearance, your arrest history and credit history are checked.
- Your friends and neighbors (over the course of your life) should expect a phone call or personal visit, during which they will be asked questions about your character.
- If you have spent much time overseas, especially in countries that are not considered allies, the check is definitely lengthened. Notes Kopperman, "I have personally known several people who have spent summer vacations in Russia, China, etc. who have waited close to a year and a half to get their clearance—so be prepared to earn a living some other way while you wait."

Given the above, it is critical that all of the information you provide is accurate. It is much better for you to take a little bit of extra time to locate old friends and neighbors and provide a correct address and phone number than to merely list the last known. This is true even if you haven't been overseas. The investigator will not clear a person for top-secret until he or she has conducted enough personal interviews to feel confident that the person is not a security risk.

Maryland area. It also has an Undergraduate Training Assistance Program that employs high school seniors, providing them with tuition assistance, summer employment, and a guaranteed job in their field of study after graduation. Additionally, the DIA's Intelligence Community Fellowship Program allows entry-level professionals to enroll in the Master of Science of Strategic Intelligence program at the Joint Military Intelligence College.

Export-Import Bank of the U.S. (Eximbank)

811 Vermont Avenue, NW
Washington, DC 20571
(202) 565–3946
www.exim.gov

For more than 60 years, the Eximbank has helped finance and facilitate more than $300 billion in the sale of American goods and services. Although about 85 percent of U.S. manufactured exports are sold without the Eximbank's support, many exports cannot be financed by the private sector alone. Eximbank, accordingly, plays a limited but critical role in the U.S. exporting effort. Specifically, it assumes commercial and political risks that private financial institutions cannot undertake and assists U.S. exporters in meeting the competition of officially supported foreign export credit. Eximbank offers programs in working capital guarantees, export credit insurance, guarantees, and direct loans.

The personnel of Eximbank have degrees in economics, finance, banking, business, and accounting. These skills—and preferably a minimum of two or three years in banking—are highly recommended. Contact the agency for specific information about its internship program, which has traditionally been paid, but because of budget constraints, this cannot be guaranteed. It is open to both undergraduates and graduate students.

Foreign Service of the Department of State

Recruitment Division
Department of State
P.O. Box 9317
Arlington, VA 22219
(202) 647–6575
http://careers.state.gov

Foreign Service jobs exist in the Department of State in Washington, D.C., other U.S. locations, and in U.S. embassies and consulates abroad. Some 4,200 Foreign Service officers (FSOs) serve the department in more than 265 embassies and consulates in 160-plus countries. Today, the Foreign Service is incredibly diverse. Candidates must be at least 20 and no more than 59.

Foreign Service officer duties are divided into five career tracks called Cones.

- *Political officers* follow political events within the host county and report significant developments to the State Department. They convey U.S. government views on political issues to foreign governments and may accompany higher-level officials of the embassy as note-takers when they meet with host government officials. Finally, political officers assist visiting U.S. officials and represent the United State at selected official functions, ceremonies, and meetings.

  In Washington, political officers analyze reports from overseas, prepare guidance for embassies, and brief senior State Department officials. They also work closely with other U.S. government agencies and with foreign embassies in Washington.
- *Economic officers* are responsible for providing their post and Washington with information and analysis on significant economic developments in the host country and for advancing U.S. economic and commercial policies, interests, and goals, including assistance to U.S. business representatives. Economic officers may support or conduct bilateral negotiations on economic and commercial issues; participate in the development of Country Commercial Programs; and provide support for specific U.S. trade promotion programs.

  In Washington, economic-commercial officers analyze reports from the field and work with other offices within the State Department and with other agencies such as Treasury, the U.S. Trade Representative, the White House, Commerce, the Environmental Protection Agency, the Federal Aviation Agency, the Fund, the local and/or U.S. Chamber of Commerce, other trade entities, and Congress.
- *Administrative officers* abroad manage the support operations of U.S. embassies and consulates. They are responsible for budget and fiscal planning, maintenance of vehicles and other property, procurement of supplies, negotiating leases for housing, general financial functions, travel arrangements for officers and their dependents, and human resources.

They also play a leadership role in the local American community to foster goodwill and cooperation on matters of mutual interest.

- *Consular officers* serving overseas protect the interests of American citizens traveling or residing abroad. They help Americans who have been in serious accidents abroad or have other emergencies; visit U.S. citizens in prison to try to ensure that Americans in foreign jails are fairly treated; issue birth certificates to Americans born abroad; register absentee voters; and take testimony for U.S. courts. They also process applications for nonimmigrant and immigrant visas and monitor migration issues of interest to the U.S. government.
- *Public diplomacy officers* administer cultural and information programs to explain the complexities of American culture and the current U.S. foreign policy agenda to foreign audiences. Within this cone, cultural affairs officers oversee programs that might employ visiting U.S. academic and cultural leaders to speak on key multilateral or bilateral issues. They also manage a variety of exchange programs like the Fulbright and Humphrey Fellows, which bring individuals from other countries to the United States to study. Information officers, sometimes known as press attachés, serve as embassy spokespersons handling all media inquiries about official U.S. government policy. They might write speeches, arrange press conferences, try to place public affairs pieces with the local media (print, TV, and radio), and develop relationships with local media professionals.

Coursework.   Although there is no specific curriculum you should take, almost any course at a school of international affairs will be useful. Certainly you should know basic economic theory and its application to current economic issues; U.S. foreign policy, history, and geography; and cultural affairs, as well as current policy issues such as narcotics control, the environment, and human rights. The State Department recommends, overall, a good general education with a background in English, management, history and government, literature, business, public administration, social sciences, trade, and, of course, the broad international affairs curriculum.

Application for the Foreign Service Officer Program.   In the application booklet for the Foreign Service exam there are sample questions that you can self-score to see your areas of strength and weakness. Address gaps in knowledge by taking the appropriate courses or by reading on your own. If, for example, you are weak on cultural matters, you should read the art, book, and theater sections of any of the weekly news magazines or the Sunday *New York Times.* At a minimum, you should be able to identify major American names and their contributions in each cultural field. If you are weak in economics or U.S. history, read a basic text in these subjects. If you know little of the functions of U.S. embassies and can't describe what a consular officer does, glance through some of the reference books listed in the official study guide you may order from information in the Foreign Service Examination application booklet.

How to Apply for the Exam.   An application booklet describing the exam format and listing sample exam questions is available throughout the year and may be ordered via the website noted above. You may also register for the exam and order study materials through the website. The booklet can also often be picked up in college and university career offices.

The exam varies slightly from year to year, but it takes the form of a multiple-choice test with questions covering English expression, international relations, economics, U.S. history, and geography, as well as American art, literature, and culture. It also covers the historical antecedents of international affairs, foreign political systems, micro- and macroeconomics, trade issues, the U.S. Constitution and political process, and the U.S. educational system. All facets of U.S. foreign policy, customs, and culture are stressed, since FSOs need a solid background in American studies to be effective U.S. representatives abroad.

Each year approximately 10,000 applicants take the Foreign Service written exam. However, 2002 saw a massive increase in the number of exam takers and set a record at about 25,000! Secretary of State Colin Powell's popularity, along with post–9/11 activities, may be the reason for this increase, though the State Department has been working very hard to conduct greater outreach and hire more officers than usual through an aggressive recruitment campaign.

If you pass the written examination you are invited to an oral assessment, which is offered in Washington and several other sites around the country. In general, approximately 2,000 pass each year and become eligible to take the oral assessment. Eventually, around 150 may be given probationary appointments for a period of five years. Afterward, these appointments may be tenured into permanent positions. Obviously, these numbers will increase as the State Department works to increase the number of officers in its ranks.

For the first time ever, in 2002 the Foreign Service written exam was offered twice in one year as part of the State Department's new aggressive recruitment effort. The department plans to hire 5,000 new employees over the next three years (2002–2005). This will increase its staffing levels by more than 1,400, notes Niels Marquardt, director of the agency's new Diplomatic Readiness Task Force.

Oral Assessment and Other Tests.   Candidates who pass the written examination are invited for a daylong oral assessment that includes a variety of things:

1. An oral presentation in which the candidate presents a demarche (oral presentation) to the examiner.
2. The candidate resolves three hypothetical problem-solving exercises based on administrative, consular, and public affairs scenarios.
3. A group negotiation exercise that the candidate participates in along with several other finalists.
4. An actual panel interview with three Foreign Service officers.

If you are successful in the oral assessment, you will then be investigated to determine eligibility for a security clearance. A medical exam is required, as is a 1,000-word autobiography and transcripts from each institution of higher learning that you attended.

A final review panel weighs each candidate's qualifications against those of other candidates. The names of those who pass the entire examination and selection process will be placed in rank-order on a list of eligible candidates. Candidates wanting informational/cultural affairs work should request to be placed on a United States Information Agency list. There is also a commercial register for the Department of Commerce. All others will become career candidates with the Department of State.

If your passing grade is low, your name will be placed toward the bottom of the list, and unfortunately you may never be called. If you have not been given an offer within a year and a half, your chances grow progressively slimmer as new applicants with higher scores are placed above your name on the register.

Timing.   The length of time between applying to the Foreign Service and getting a job offer requires patience. The security check takes from four to six months, sometimes longer if you have lived abroad. Then comes your medical exam.

The length of the entire process, starting with the written exam through receiving an initial assignment, can be close to one year, sometimes more. Thus, if a job with the Foreign Service is your primary career objective, it is a good idea to keep yourself open to other options, particularly short-term consultancies, while you embark on the process.

Foreign Service Specialists.   The Department of State offers additional career opportunities in specialized functions, including technical support and administrative services in information management, medical, and facilities maintenance. For example, job titles include: information management technical specialist, office management specialist, regional English language officer, regional medical officer/psychiatrist, and diplomatic security special agent.

These appointments do not require taking the written exam, but candidates must meet specific education or work experience requirements and pass an oral assessment. Information is available through the Department of State website at www.careers.state.gov.

Languages.   Knowledge of a foreign language is not essential to be hired into the Foreign Service. If you do not have a second language, however, you will not be granted tenure until language competency is acquired. Officers and specialists attend foreign language classes at the Foreign Service Institute, which offers training in more than forty languages, depending on a post assignment.

There is a strange twist to the language question. If you have language competence in Arabic, for example, you may assume you will spend all or most of

A
DAY
IN THE
LIFE

Thoughts on the U.S. Foreign Service Exam

I took the oral exam in March 1993 at the old Foreign Service Training Center, along with eleven other examinees. After writing one or two essays on fairly broad and bland topics, the demarche began. I was to play the role of an administrative officer at the U.S. Embassy of "Ruritania" who was responsible for coordinating the impending visit of the U.S. secretary of state. Using the handful of cables (State Department telegraphs), memos, and note paper the examiner gave me, I was asked to (a) prepare a demarche (a presentation made to foreign government officials to convey a U.S. position) outlining the arrangements the embassy wanted to see implemented; (b) deliver the demarche to two Ruritanian foreign ministry officials; and (c) write a reporting cable on the outcome of the demarche. My objective was not necessarily to deliver on everything the Department of State was requesting—and I don't think the examiners/Ruritanians would have let me—but rather to work with the Ruritanians to come up with a mutually acceptable agreement.

My last exercise before lunch was to answer (orally) three hypotheticals, such as: "You're a consular officer. You receive a call late at night from a hotel owner who is irate because a drunk American has broken a window at the hotel. The American doesn't have the money to pay for the repairs, and the hotel owner is threatening to have him thrown in jail. What do you do?"

None of the hypotheticals, nor the demarche for that matter, ask you to envision yourself as an ambassador, or to pretend that you are in the middle of the SALT II talks, or to report on major geopolitical events. Instead the examiners may ask you to play-act the more bread-and-butter work of Foreign Service officers.

After lunch, the examiners seated six of us examinees around a large round table for the group exercise. Six examiners sat in an outer ring behind us. We were told that we were each representing a different section of an embassy (e.g., the U.S. Information Service, Commerce, the Economic Counselor, etc.) and that we were there to decide how to distribute a set amount of funds among different development projects the embassy wanted to sponsor in our host country. Each of us was assigned one project to study and present to the group; afterward we would have to decide which ones we would implement. We didn't have to insist that our projects be funded if we felt that someone else had a more promising project. As it turned out, I was the only person willing to forego her project. I think that some of the candidates felt they had to dominate the discussion in order to impress the examiners, but that did not necessarily facilitate consensus. I kept a tally of the budget, and as time ran out I tried to remind the group that we had to come to a decision soon. We finally did.

your career in the Middle East. Not so. The department will try to use your language skills, but it will not guarantee that all your assignments will be in a specific country or area. In fact, you may specifically be assigned to a non-Arabic-speaking area to expand your knowledge of the world and a variety of foreign policy problems.

First Assignment.   Your first assignment is usually at an American embassy overseas, and you are not given a choice in the location. You may rotate positions there, spending time in each of the career tracks. At the end of your two-year tour of duty you will have learned a great deal about the operations and functions of all parts of an embassy. In general, you should expect about two-thirds of your career to be spent overseas, the rest usually in Washington, D.C.

Internships

The State Department administers several student employment programs that enable students to get experience in a foreign affairs environment through on-the-job experience. Some of the positions are at headquarters in Washington, D.C., and others afford the opportunity to work abroad in an embassy overseas. Positions are both paid and unpaid, and many are available during spring, summer, or fall. Specific and clear application information is available by clicking on "Student Programs" and then "Student Internships" at the Department of State website (http://careers.state.gov). Beyond internships, there is a cooperative education program, fellowship programs for students of color, a summer clerical employment program, and a Thomas Pickering Foreign Affairs/Graduate Foreign Affairs Fellowship Program.

Public Diplomacy and Public Affairs, Department of State (formerly the United States Information Agency)

Office of Recruitment, Examination and Employment
United States Department of State
HR/REE, SA–1
2401 E Street, NW, 5H
Washington, DC 20522
(202) 261–8888; fax: (202) 261–8841
www.state.gov

The U.S. Department of State's undersecretary for public diplomacy and public affairs now directs the public relations, cultural, and educational exchange programs formerly run by the United States Information Agency (USIA), which was absorbed by the department in 1999.

Cultural presentations for overseas audiences, logistical support for libraries, English-teaching programs abroad, and programs for visitors from overseas all come within the purview of Public Diplomacy and Public Affairs. The best known of these exchanges is the Fulbright or academic exchange program, which enables more than 800 Americans to study or conduct research in more than 120 countries annually. Applicants applying for Fulbright Full and Travel Grants must be U.S. citizens and hold a B.A. or equivalent. Each year the program also brings approximately 5,000 foreign leaders in all fields to the United States and administers a program for the exchange of young people from 15 to 30 years of age.

Foreign press centers and the WORLDNET interactive TV programs are now part of the department's Bureau of Public Affairs, which works to help Americans understand the importance of foreign affairs. Public affairs specialists disseminate information about the work of the department through newspapers, radio, television, speeches, briefings, and the department's website.

If you are interested in this type of work, recruiting is now done centrally by the State Department, either via Foreign Service or Civil Service, depending on the position. USIA's regional offices have been merged with State Department offices in the same areas. Depending on the job, the posting may be abroad as a Foreign Service officer or specialist, or in the United States.

Journalism and cultural studies in particular are desired. Regional expertise, languages, foreign policy, international relations, and administration are also helpful.

Requirements.   In most cases the timing and procedure are the same as for the Foreign Service. You will be required to take the Foreign Service officer exam. Get the FSO exam booklet in August or September so that you can submit your application before the October deadline (see address listed above).

As with the Foreign Service, the length of time between applying and getting an offer is long, so you might choose to explore other career opportunities and keep your options open.

Inter-American Foundation (IAF)

901 North Stuart Street
10th Floor
Arlington, VA 22203
(703) 306–4301
www.iaf.gov

The IAF is an independent government corporation that supports social and economic development in Latin America and the Caribbean. It makes grants primarily to private indigenous organizations that carry out self-help projects benefiting the poor. It has also arranged with the Inter-American Development Bank to channel some of its resources to foundation projects, such as workers' self-managed enterprises, credit and production cooperatives, self-help housing, agricultural extension services, legal aid clinics, a bank run by and for workers, peasant associations, and informal education. Because of recent reductions in financial assistance by major donor countries, the foundation has focused on increasing the economic stability of grassroots development by forming alliances among NGOs, private enterprises, and the public sector.

The variety of activities of the IAF defines the different backgrounds needed by this agency: economics, economic development, Latin American studies, finance, agriculture, labor, cooperatives, banking, housing, law, industrial management, statistics, labor relations, and a fluency in Spanish and Portuguese.

International Broadcasting Bureau

330 Independence Avenue, SW
Washington, DC 20237
24-hour job line: (202) 619–0909
e-mail: bjludwic@ibb.gov, lybrown@ibb.gov
www.ibb.gov

The International Broadcasting Bureau (IBB), including the Voice of America, was formerly part of the now-defunct U.S. Information Agency. It now operates independently, with policy guidance from the Secretary of State. The bureau produces and broadcasts radio programs in English and 53 foreign languages for overseas audiences and is meant to provide news and information to all parts of the globes, including those that don't have access to free media. It comprises the Voice of America (VOA), WORLDNET Television and Film Service, Radio and TV Marti, and an engineering directorate. It also operates Radio Free Europe/Radio Liberty (RFE/RL) and Radio Free Asia (RFA) under congressional oversight.

The VOA (www.voa.gov) broadcasts almost 700 hours of programming to an estimated 90 million people each week. Writers and editors produce mostly news-related programs in VOA's Washington, D.C., newsroom, from its 23 news bureaus worldwide and from its network of stringers and part-time reporters.

The Office of Cuba Broadcasting Radio broadcasts to Cuba on the VOA's Cuban Service, or Radio and TV Marti, began in 1985 and 1990. Named for Cuban patriot Jose Marti, this program provides "news, commentary, and other information about events in Cuba and elsewhere to promote the cause of freedom in Cuba."

Radio Free Europe/Radio Liberty and Radio Free Asia offer daily news, analysis, and current affairs programming in their respective regions.

IBB uses the latest satellite technology through its **Office of Engineering and Technical Operations** to beam important programs live to foreign audiences through local TV stations. It also acquires and produces videotape programs and films for distribution through its overseas posts.

Management handles administrative, personnel, and comptroller services.

IBB Programs uses press and publications to project an accurate image of the United States and its foreign policy abroad. Foreign media reaction to U.S. policies is reviewed, speakers are recruited, and exhibits are displayed overseas. Programs publishes 14 magazines in 20 languages and distributes pamphlets in more than 100 countries.

Relevant qualifications for work at the IBB range from standard journalism skills for print and electronic media to computer, engineering, and management abilities. Knowledge of international affairs and regional expertise are obvious assets. For foreign correspondent positions with VOA, international reporting experience, knowledge of the local language and culture, and the ability to work in a mixture of media (print, radio, and television) are important qualifications. Apply for specific positions directly via the bureau's website or through the contacts listed above.

The IBB also offers unpaid quarterly internships in Washington for current undergraduate and graduate students. Applications are accepted on a rolling basis but should be submitted at least six weeks in advance to allow time for processing. Interns should have some background (academic or work experience) in broadcasting, journalism, and international affairs. Successful candidates receive on-the-job training, developing skills in voicing, directing, producing, and writing as they rotate among the most important divisions of the

News and English Broadcast Complex. There are opportunities in radio, television, overseas bureaus, public affairs, civil rights, management, and other administrative areas beyond journalism. For internship information visit the IBB website or write to:

Janice Albritton-Pollock
International Broadcasting Bureau
330 Independence Avenue, SW
Room 1543
Washington, DC 20237
(202) 619–3117; fax: (202) 205–8427
e-mail: lybrown@ibb.gov

National Security Agency (NSA)/Central Security Service

College Recruitment Program
National Security Agency
9800 Savage Road
Fort Meade, MD 20755–6000
Attn: Office of Employment (M 322)
(301) 688–6524 or (800) 669–0703
www.nsa.gov

The National Security Agency/Central Security Service is charged with two national security missions:

1: The foreign signals intelligence (SIGINT) mission allows for an effective, unified organization and control of all foreign signals collection and processing activities of the United States. NSA is authorized to produce SIGINT in accordance with objectives, requirements, and priorities established by the Director of Central Intelligence with the advice of the National Foreign Intelligence Board.
2: The information system (INFOSEC) mission provides leadership, products, technical advice, and services to protect classified and unclassified national security systems against exploitation through interception, unauthorized access, etc. The mission also supports the director of the NSA in fulfilling his responsibilities as executive agent for interagency operations security (OPSEC) training.

NSA puts a premium on people with advanced degrees in electronic/electrical and computer engineering and in mathematics. NSA is also interested in people with proficiency in certain foreign languages, particularly Slavic, Asian, and Middle Eastern languages. An ability to translate from original sources, rather than conversational ability, is required. Most NSA jobs are in the United States, although occasional travel abroad may be required.

Requirements

In order to be considered for employment with the NSA, you must be a U.S. citizen. All NSA employees hold a minimum top-secret clearance. A thorough background investigation is conducted in order to ensure suitability. A polygraph exam and psychological assessment battery are also administered to all potential employees. Applicants usually must take an aptitude test, called a professional qualification test, which measures the aptitudes and abilities the NSA needs. This test is usually given annually in November.

The first step in applying for an NSA job is to submit a resume along with academic transcripts. If you meet the criteria, you will be contacted to set up a site visit, at which time you will be interviewed and polygraphed.

Office of the United States Trade Representative (USTR)

600 17th Street, NW, Winder Building
Washington, DC 20508
(202) 395–3000 or (202) 395–7360
www.ustr.gov

The U.S. Trade Representative is responsible for developing and coordinating U.S. international trade, commodity, and direct investment policies as well as the direction of all trade negotiations. Negotiators, analysts, and support staff all work in the office on policymaking and negotiations. Staffs are maintained in Washington and Geneva. Most USTR employees began their career with the Department of Commerce and then transferred to the USTR; it is not a place for entry-level candidates. A high degree of skill in economics, with an emphasis on trade and negotiations, is required of applicants for the rare job opening that develops in this office. A law degree or Ph.D. in economics is preferred.

The USTR also operates an unpaid internship program open to undergraduate and graduate students (U.S. citizens only). Assignments include research, analyses, statistics, briefings, report writing, organizational duties, letter writing, and more. Typically, 20–30 interns are selected each year from about 300 applicants.

Overseas Private Investment Corporation (OPIC)

Human Resources Management

1100 New York Avenue, NW

Washington, DC 20527

(202) 336–8400; job vacancy hotline: (202) 336–8683; internship information: (202) 336–8683

www.opic.gov

OPIC is an independent agency that assists American companies investing in more than 140 developing nations and emerging market economies. It does this by providing U.S. investors with political risk insurance and financial assistance to support their investments in these countries. OPIC finances investment projects through direct loans and guarantees and provides the investor with various services such as counseling and country investment kits. The investors may be large or small, corporate or individual.

OPIC has seven departments: Insurance, Finance, Investment Funds, Investment Development, Legal Affairs, Management Services, and Financial Management and Statutory Review. All projects supported by OPIC must assist in the economic or social development of the country and also be consistent with the economic and foreign policy interests of the United States. OPIC insurance is of particular importance in protecting investments against: (1) the ability to convert into U.S. dollars any local currency received by investors as profit; (2) the loss of investments from nationalization or confiscation of facilities; and (3) war, revolution, or insurrection.

Since many OPIC functions revolve around insurance and finance, a background in either or both is essential. Economics, economic development, banking, and statistics are also helpful. OPIC offers internships for the fall, spring (unpaid), and summer (often paid) semesters. Interns must be enrolled at least part-time in a relevant degree program. OPIC generally seeks graduate students (M.B.A., international affairs, or economics programs, etc.), law students, and some junior- or senior-level undergraduate students. OPIC employees must be U.S. citizens and are required to obtain security clearances.

Peace Corps

The Paul D. Coverdell Peace Corps Headquarters
1111 20th Street, NW
Washington, DC 20526
(800) 424–8580
www.peacecorps.gov

The Peace Corps is an independent agency with a specialized task of training people from developing nations. Since the organization was established in 1961, more than 165,000 volunteers have served in more than 135 countries throughout Africa, Asia, the Pacific, Central and South America, the Caribbean, Central and Eastern Europe, and Eurasia. Though Peace Corps volunteers continue to work in the more traditional fields of agriculture, education, forestry, health, engineering, and skilled trades, they are also working in new areas such as business, the environment, urban planning, youth development, and teaching English for commerce and technology expertise.

The Peace Corps requires three to five years of work experience and/or a college degree. Generalists (with a B.A.), graduate students, and professionals in business, economics, agriculture, education, engineering, fisheries, the health professions, and other areas are encouraged to apply for field positions.

A living allowance in the local currency is given to cover housing, food, and essential expenses. When service is completed, volunteers receive a $200 readjustment allowance for every month served. Volunteers may also qualify for cancellation or deferment of certain government-backed educational loans.

Occasional full-time, paid positions may also be available in Washington headquarters, where policy is set, personnel are processed, and work in the field is supervised. Those with administrative or finance backgrounds are needed. Country director positions abroad may also open up.

To apply, you must first complete a lengthy application form. If selected, you enter an 8–14 week training program followed by a two-year assignment in a developing country.

Special Note: Returning Peace Corps volunteers who are looking for another international job should read the *Bulletin of Career, Educational, and Re-entry Information and Opportunities for Returned Peace Corps Volunteers*, a bimonthly publication of the Peace Corps that includes current openings in the private and public sectors of the United States and openings abroad. This publication is available through the Washington, D.C., Peace Corps office.

The Peace Corps Master's International Program.   The Peace Corps has a partnership with more than 20 schools offering master's-level studies in fields such as forestry/national resource management, public health/nutrition, teaching English to speakers of other languages (TESOL), business, and urban planning. Volunteers receive three months of language, as well as technical and cross-cultural training. Upon completion of Peace Corps service, volunteers return to the United States to complete any final degree requirements. Benefits include a $5,400 readjustment allowance earned upon completion of 27 months of service, career counseling, and academic credit for Peace Corps service. For more information call (800) 424–8580 or (202) 606–9322, option 2, extension 2226, or request an information packet at www.peacecorps.gov/gradschool/masters/index.cfm.

U.S. International Trade Commission
Director of Personnel
500 E Street, SW
Washington, DC 20436
(202) 205–2000
e-mail Joyce Douglas: jdouglas@usitc.gov
www.usitc.gov

USITC is an independent, quasijudicial agency that provides objective trade expertise on the impact of imported products on U.S. industries. The commission has a trade monitoring system that investigates whether increased imports of articles produced in other countries are causing market disruptions in the United States. It also directs actions against unfair trading practices.

The commission states that it is primarily interested in applicants with the following backgrounds: international economics, international trade, marketing, and international law. There are almost no entry-level positions available.

Domestic Agencies with International Operations

The following agencies have international divisions or departments but also work on a domestic policy level. In all cases, the focus here is to highlight international opportunities, both in terms of jobs and internships. Sometimes, it is a good idea to take a job in the domestic operations of your agency of choice, then gain experience and apply for jobs in the international area.

Department of Agriculture (USDA)

Director, Personnel Division
Foreign Agriculture Service
14th Street and Independence Avenue, SW
Washington, DC 20250
(202) 720–2791
www.usda.gov

The **Foreign Agriculture Service (FAS)** of the Department of Agriculture is the export promotion agency for U.S. agriculture. FAS collects information about global supply and demand and analyzes trade trends and emerging market competition. It improves access in the global marketplace for U.S. farm products through representations to foreign governments and through participation in trade negotiations. The FAS also appraises overseas marketing opportunities and offers technical assistance programs to those in U.S. agricultural trade.

Of particular interest to students of international affairs is the global operation of FAS. It maintains an overseas network of 75 posts in more than 130 countries. Those working abroad report and analyze world agricultural production, trade, and policies affecting U.S. agriculture. USDA has a variety of opportunities for interns, volunteers, students, and experienced professionals. These are described in detail on its website.

Department of Commerce

Office of Human Resources Management
1401 Constitution Avenue, NW
Room 5001
Washington, DC 20230
(202) 482–4807
www.doc.gov

This department, with a wide variety of programs, offers unusual opportunities for those with an international background and business interests.

The International Trade Administration (ITA) is the lead unit in the department and aims to promote world trade and strengthen the international trade and investment position of the United States. It staffs 134 overseas offices in 78 countries. Within ITA, there are several offices that may be of interest to you.

- *The Office of Market Access and Compliance* provides U.S. businesses and policymakers with in-depth country analysis. It also works to expand access to overseas markets, remove international commercial barriers, and promote U.S. exports. It is broken down into four geographic areas: Europe, the Western Hemisphere, Asia and the Pacific, and Africa and the Near East. Each of these offices has responsibility for trade and investment issues with countries in its area. ITA also has a specific program for big emerging markets, which includes the following countries or regions: Mexico, Argentina, Brazil, the Chinese Economic Area, the ASEAN countries, South Korea, Poland, Turkey, and South Africa.
- *The Office of Trade Development* advises domestic business on international trade matters and emerging high technology.
- *The Office of Import Administration* is responsible for safeguarding the American economy from unfairly priced imports.
- *Foreign Commercial Service (FCS)* of ITA. The FCS is a part of the Foreign Service system and helps U.S. exports enter new markets abroad while protecting U.S. business interests abroad.

Besides the offices within ITA, other sections in the Department of Commerce hold interesting job opportunities. For example, the **Bureau of Export Administration** issues export licenses and develops export control polices, and the **Bureau of Industry and Security** works closely with other governments to limit the export of goods and technology that have the potential to create weapons of mass destruction.

Also under the Department of Commerce is the **Office of the Deputy Assistant for Tourism.** It fosters tourism and trade development and represents the United States in tourism-related meetings with foreign government officials. It also gives technological assistance for international tourism development.

The **Economics and Statistics Administration (ESA)** produces and analyzes economic and demographic data.

The **Office of International Affairs** at the **National Telecommunications and Information Administration** provides information and analysis on global communications and technologies.

The **National Oceanic and Atmospheric Administration (NOAA) Office of Global Programs** assesses changes in the Earth's environment. NOAA leads a multinational effort to establish research centers that examine the global climate system.

Experience in international economics, trade, commerce, marketing, area studies, languages, and business administration is desired. A combination of two or three will be particularly helpful. A technologic and scientific background is suggested for the other departments. Various opportunities are described at www.commerce.gov/jobs.html, while Commerce Opportunities On-Line allows you to search and apply for jobs directly at www.jobs.doc.gov.

Department of Defense (DOD)

Office of Assistant Secretary of Defense
International Security Affairs (ISA)
1400 Defense Pentagon
Washington, DC 20301–1155
(202) 697–5737
www.dod.gov; for jobs: www.defenselink.mil/other_info/careers.html

The Department of Defense is America's main security and defense agency. Within DOD, you should pay particular attention to the **International Security Affairs Division.** ISA develops defense positions in political-military and foreign economic affairs, including arms control and disarmament. Among its functions are negotiating and monitoring agreements with foreign governments concerning military facilities and the status of armed forces. Policy guidance is provided to military personnel stationed in U.S. embassies and to U.S. representatives at international organizations and conferences.

Academic studies of optimum use are national security, military technology, international economics, U.S. foreign policy, Russian studies, Chinese studies, and East Central European studies and languages. The Presidential Management Internship (PMI) is an excellent way, and often the only way, to enter DOD as a civilian.

Department of Energy (DOE)

Assistant Secretary, International Affairs
1000 Independence Avenue, SW
Washington, DC 20585
(202) 586–4670
www.energy.gov

DOE promotes efficient energy use and researches alternative energy sources. Its **Office of Policy and International Affairs** (www.pi.energy.gov) develops and implements U.S. international energy policies and deals with energy emergencies. It provides the energy perspective on all international negotiations between the United States and other nations. The office also develops policy options on energy relationships between producer and consumer nations, analyzing the options' impact on these relationships and on U.S. energy objectives. The DOE makes policy recommendations regarding the international oil industry and assesses world price and supply trends. Of particular importance is the office's role in evaluating the future adequacy of world energy resources. Important qualifications include a background in engineering, economics, and energy matters.

Department of Health and Human Services (HHS)

Administration for Children and Families Office of Refugee Resettlement
370 L'Enfant Promenade
Washington, DC 20447
www.acf.dhhs.gov/programs/orr
(202) 401–9246
or (202) 619–0257

The **Office of Refugee Resettlement** works to aid refugees abroad and help those admitted to the United States to resettle and adapt to new lives. It develops, recommends, and issues program policies and procedures. It also evaluates and supports the states and other agencies in refugee-related issues. Courses in health, medicine, human rights, international law, and regional studies may be useful. Hiring is generally done centrally by the Department of Health and Human Services.

Department of Justice (DOJ)

U.S. Department of Justice
950 Pennsylvania Avenue, NW
Washington, DC 20530–0001
(202) 353–1555
www.usdoj.gov

Immigration and Naturalization Service (INS)
425 I Street, NW
Washington, DC 20536
For employment: 800 K Street, NW
Washington, DC 20536
ATTN: Employment Services
(202) 514–4301
www.ins.usdoj.gov/graphics/index.htm

Drug Enforcement Administration (DEA)
Office of Personnel
2401 Jefferson Davis Highway
Alexandria, VA 22301
(202) 307–1000; for special agents: (800) DEA–4288
www.dea.gov

Federal Bureau of Investigation (FBI)
J. Edgar Hoover Building
935 Pennsylvania Avenue, NW
Washington, DC 20535–001
(202) 324–3000
www.fbi.gov

The Justice Department's **Office of International Affairs** (OIA) (www.usdoj.gov/criminal/oia.html) supports the U.S. attorney general, senior officials, the DOJ's Criminal Division, the State Department, Interpol, and other agencies in the formulation and execution of transnational criminal justice enforcement policies, including international extradition proceedings, prisoner transfers, money laundering, cyber crime, and mutual legal assistance. The OIA has field offices in Rome, Mexico City, and San Salvador.

The **Immigration and Naturalization Service (INS)** administers the immigration laws relating to the admission or deportation of aliens and naturalization of citizens. The **Board of Immigration Appeals** is the highest tribunal in immigration matters.

Also of interest to those with international backgrounds is the **Drug Enforcement Administration (DEA)**, which conducts domestic and international investigations of major drug traffickers and exchanges information with certain foreign countries.

The **Federal Bureau of Investigation (FBI)** has extended its criminal investigations overseas. Foreign liaison officers work at more than 40 posts around the world with American or local authorities on criminal matters within FBI jurisdiction.

In these immigration and drug and law enforcement functions, economists, investigators, lawyers, statisticians, and those with a strong background in international affairs or area and language studies are needed. Special agents for the DEA or the FBI are hired directly; applicants should hold a bachelor's degree and have three years' work experience or the equivalent. DEA and FBI special agents must complete a special agent interview process, which includes a rigorous background check and a psychological suitability test. For more information about job vacancies or internship possibilities consult the agency's website.

Department of Labor

Bureau of International Labor Affairs (ILA)
Room C–4325
Frances Perkins Building
200 Constitution Avenue, NW
Washington, DC 20210
(202) 693–4770
www.dol.gov/ilab

The **Bureau of International Labor Affairs** carries out the international responsibilities of the Department of Labor. Under the direction of the undersecretary for international affairs, the bureau helps to formulate international economic trade and immigration policies affecting American workers. ILA also represents the United States in trade negotiations and in such international bodies as the World Trade Organization (WTO), the International Labor Organization (ILO), and the Organization for Economic Cooperation and Development (OECD). The bureau also provides direction to the U.S. labor attachés at embassies abroad and studies child labor practices around the world. The bureau is organized into the following offices: the Office of International Economic Affairs, the Office of International Organizations, the Office of Foreign Relations, the National Administrative Office, and the International Child Labor Program.

Department of Transportation (DOT)

Assistant Secretary for Aviation and International Affairs
Department of Transportation
400 7th Street, SW
Washington, DC 20590
(202) 366–5580 or (202) 366–4000
www.dot.gov

Maritime Administration
Department of Transportation
400 7th Street, SW
Washington, DC 20590
(800) 996–2723
www.marad.dot.gov

Federal Aviation Administration
Department of System Safety
800 Independence Avenue, SW
Washington, DC 20591
(202) 366–4000
www.nasdac.faa.gov or www.faa.gov

The Department of Transportation aims to enlist the cooperation of federal, state, and local governments, carriers, labor, and other interested parties in achieving a more effective transportation network throughout the United States.

Under the DOT is the **Maritime Administration,** which administers programs to aid in the development and promotion of the U.S. merchant marine. There is also the **Federal Aviation Administration**, which promotes civil administration abroad by exchanging aeronautical information with foreign aviation authorities, negotiating international agreements to facilitate the import and export of aircraft. Its Office of System Safety includes the Global Analysis and Information Network, which works to develop a worldwide partnership with members of the aviation community.

Environmental Protection Agency (EPA)

Human Resources Headquarters
1200 Pennsylvania Avenue, NW
Washington, DC 20460
(202) 564–8111
www.epa.gov

The purpose of the Environmental Protection Agency is to protect public health and safeguard and improve the environment. The EPA aims to check and/or eliminate pollution of all types, from excess garbage to noise to radiation. Many of those activities encompass international research and cooperation. For instance, the EPA has developed several binational and multiagency programs to protect and improve the environment along the U.S.-Mexico border area. The office is also involved in providing guidance to U.S. representatives at international conferences dealing with environmental matters.

The EPA employs about 18,000 people across the United States. In-depth academic studies and experiences (either internships or full-time work) in economics, environment, energy, population, and related courses are of major importance in getting the midlevel rating of interest to this organization. For job vacancies go to www.epa.gov/ezhire. For internship opportunities consult www.epa.gov/epapages/epahome/intern.htm or the various EPA offices, which may be accessed from EPA websites.

Executive Office of the President

Office of Management and Budget (OMB)
725 17th Street, NW

Washington, DC 20503

(202) 395–3080

www.whitehouse.gov/omb

The major function of the **Office of Management and Budget** is to make government service more efficient and economical. OMB has two national security programs of potential interest: the **National Security Division,** reachable at (202) 395–3884, and the **International Affairs Division,** at (202) 395–4770. These divisions concentrate on the international aspects of the following OMB functions: assisting the president in evaluating budgets for the foreign-oriented agencies (Department of State, USIA, NSA, CIA, and the Department of Defense) and keeping the president informed of the work proposed, initiated, and completed by these agencies.

A midlevel rating with a significant background in international economics, business administration, and international affairs is helpful in getting a job at OMB. Applicants should forward copies of their resume and transcripts to OMB's Office of Human Resources, which has the reputation of being one of the best and most responsive throughout the federal government.

Federal Reserve System

International Finance Division

Board of Governors of the Federal Reserve System

20th Street and Constitution Avenue, NW

Washington, DC 20551

(202) 452–3880 or (800) 448–4894

www.federalreserve.gov

Twelve Federal Reserve Banks located throughout the country and the Board of Governors in Washington, D.C., constitute America's federal banking system. The board's primary function is to formulate monetary policy. To assist the board, there is a staff of more than 1,000 employees assigned to various divisions, among which is the **International Finance Division.** This division analyzes international policies and operations of the Federal Reserve, major financial and economic developments abroad that affect the U.S. economy, and problems related to the international monetary system. Staff members of the division serve on U.S. delegations to international financial conferences and maintain liaisons with central banks of foreign countries.

As you might guess, the most pertinent curriculum to prepare for jobs in the International Finance Division includes international economics, international finance, money and banking, accounting, and statistics. A Ph.D. in one of these fields is often preferred, but talented individuals with an M.A. and relevant experience are given fair consideration and frequently hired.

The board also offers paid and unpaid summer internships for students planning careers in economics, finance, and computer science, particularly in the divisions of Banking Supervision and Regulation, Information Technology, and Research and Statistics. Details of job vacancies and internships can be found at www.federalreserve.gov/careers/default.cfm.

National Aeronautics and Space Administration (NASA)

NASA Office of External Relations, International Relations Division
600 Independence Avenue, SW
Washington, DC 20546
(202) 358–2345 or (202) 358–0000
www.nasa.gov or www.nasajobs.nasa.gov

NASA conducts research for the solution of problems of flight within and outside the Earth's atmosphere. It also arranges for the most effective use of U.S. scientific resources with other nations engaged in space activities. The international division is divided into three divisions: the Space Flight Division, the International Relations Division, and the Mission to Planet Earth.

A science, engineering, and aeronautical background is clearly indicated for technical jobs; at the same time, there are some jobs in administration for which a background in accounting, human resources, or public administration is helpful. Job openings and internship opportunities are posted online.

National Science Foundation (NSF)

Division of International Programs
4201 Wilson Boulevard
Arlington, Virginia 22230
(703) 306–1234 or (703) 292–5111
www.nsf.gov

The National Science Foundation supports many programs for scientific research. Its **Division of International Programs** encourages American participation in international science programs and activities. The division also fosters the exchange of information between scientists in the United States and those in foreign countries. Other international programs include the exchange of American and foreign scientists and engineers, as well as travel to international conferences. The NSF also lists other federal and science and technology agencies that have international programs on its website (www.nsf.gov/ home/external/fedint.html). A scientific background in addition to public policy, economics, or regional expertise is helpful, and it is wise to consider an internship with the NSF before applying for a full-time job.

Federal Pay Schedule

The table on the opposite page shows salaries for certain federal job levels as of January 2003. Salaries may well be higher by the time you read this. For a complete set of pay scales by location, go to the U.S. Office of Personnel Management (www.opm.gov/oca/payrates).

LEGISLATIVE BRANCH JOBS

The search for government jobs does not end with the obvious executive agencies. The legislative branch offers a variety of positions with international content. Unlike the executive branch, the legislative branch does not rely heavily on the Office of Personnel Management or Civil Service ratings. Leave your resume in the placement offices of the House and Senate, but spend more time in cultivating contacts with staff assistants and their friends in congressional offices. This network is usually the *key* to available jobs in the legislative branch.

Senate and House

House Foreign Affairs Committee
House Office Building
New Jersey and Independence Avenue, SE
Washington, DC 20515

Senate Foreign Relations Committee
Senate Office Building

Table 5.1: Salary Table 2003-GS

(2003 General Schedule Incorporating a 3.10% General Increase, Effective January 2003)

Annual Rates by Grade and Step

GRADE	STEP 1	STEP 2	STEP 3	STEP 4	STEP 5	STEP 6	STEP 7	STEP 8	STEP 9	STEP 10	WITHIN-GRADE AMOUNTS
GS-1	$ 15,214	$ 15,722	$ 16,228	$ 16,731	$ 17,238	$ 17,536	$ 18,034	$ 18,538	$ 18,559	$ 19,031	VARIES
2	17,106	17,512	18,079	18,559	18,767	19,319	19,871	20,423	20,975	21,527	VARIES
3	18,664	19,286	19,908	20,530	21,152	21,774	22,396	23,018	23,640	24,262	622
4	20,952	21,650	22,348	23,046	23,744	24,442	25,140	25,838	26,536	27,234	698
5	23,442	24,223	25,004	25,785	26,566	27,347	28,128	28,909	29,690	30,471	781
6	26,130	27,001	27,872	28,743	29,614	30,485	31,356	32,227	33,098	33,969	871
7	29,037	30,005	30,973	31,941	32,909	33,877	34,845	35,813	36,781	37,749	968
8	32,158	33,230	34,302	35,374	36,446	37,518	38,590	39,662	40,734	41,806	1,072
9	35,519	36,703	37,887	39,071	40,255	41,439	42,623	43,807	44,991	46,175	1,184
10	39,115	40,419	41,723	43,027	44,331	45,635	46,939	48,243	49,547	50,851	1,304
11	42,976	44,409	45,842	47,275	48,708	50,141	51,574	53,007	54,440	55,873	1,433
12	51,508	53,225	54,942	56,659	58,376	60,093	61,810	63,527	65,244	66,961	1,717
13	61,251	63,293	65,335	67,377	69,419	71,461	73,503	75,545	77,587	79,629	2,042
14	72,381	74,794	77,207	79,620	82,033	84,446	86,859	89,272	91,685	94,098	2,413
15	85,140	87,978	90,816	93,654	96,492	99,330	102,168	105,006	107,844	110,682	2,838

SOURCE: **http://opm.gov/oca/payrates**

First Street and Constitution Avenue, NE
Washington, DC 20510

According to a legislative assistant on the hill, there are three major types of jobs on Capitol Hill through which you can work on various aspects of foreign policy.

Committee staff positions generally allow you to put to use particular area or functional expertise. Generally requiring a significant amount of prior relevant work experience, the bulk of these assignments are on the Senate Committee on Foreign Relations (foreign.senate.gov) and the House Committee on International Relations (www.house.gov/international_relations). However, one Capitol Hill staffer recommends that you also include in your search other committees that have an international purview. For example, the Senate and House Appropriations Committees have two subcommittees that allocate funds for international operations and foreign assistance; in addition, the Senate Armed Services Committee and the House National Security Committee also have peripheral involvement in international affairs.

Committee assignments are very difficult to secure, as they almost always are given to those with prior Hill experience. Thus, it is often a good idea to seek a position in an office of a staff member who is active on one of the committees in which you are interested. It may be easier to obtain a position in a more junior legislator's office; the best time to job search on the Hill, obviously, is immediately after an election cycle.

Two types of entry-level positions in a senatorial or congressional office are described below.

There are **legislative assistant** positions in every senator's and representative's personal office. Responsibilities include researching and preparing background and legislation, although, because staffs are usually "stretched thin," according to a Hill professional, "you will not have the luxury of focusing on one area for these assignments. . . . However, they can be quite rewarding and entail interesting work with the chance to advance policy ideas through legislation, especially if the member has a particular foreign policy interest and/or if he or she is a member of one of the committees involved in foreign affairs."

Legislative correspondent positions involve drafting responses to the thousands of pieces of constituent mail received by each legislator. Legislative correspondents often find that they're doing the real grunt work of the office, but in fact writing the replies offers a good opportunity to research and familiarize yourself with the myriad of issues of interest to the public. And because there is relatively high turnover in these positions, they are a good way to get your foot in the congressional door. Obviously, good writing and diplomacy skills are essential.

Internships

Internships are almost always unpaid on Capitol Hill, but they are an excellent way to begin to network and make contacts that are vital to the job search unless you are very well connected in your home state. They are also an excellent way to gain experience, which is often required for a Hill position. The concept of internships on Capitol Hill is quite common, and almost every office has, or has had, students or individuals who wish to work on the Hill volunteer in some capacity or another.

Congressional Budget Office (CBO)

Ford House Office Building, 4th Floor
Second and D Streets, SW
Washington, DC 20515–6925
(202) 226–2628
www.cbo.gov

The Congressional Budget Office was established in 1974 to provide Congress with an overview of the federal budget and to enable it to make decisions on spending and taxing levels. The office is the mechanism through which Congress weighs priorities for the allocation of national resources. It prepares budget studies relating to U.S. defense and international economic programs. The CBO also examines the impact on the economy and the federal budget of foreign programs, such as commodity agreements, aid, tariff and subsidy programs, and international monetary agreements. The CBO hires people with M.P.A. and M.B.A. backgrounds and, occasionally, those with a master's degree in international affairs.

General Accounting Office (GAO)

National Security and International Affairs Division

441 G Street, NW
Washington, DC 20548
(202) 512–4320
www.gao.gov

The General Accounting Office is in the legislative branch of government and reports directly to Congress. It analyzes the efficiency and effectiveness of the operations of federal government agencies in the executive branch. Its recommendations ostensibly lead to improved management practices in these agencies. Even though the GAO is in the legislative branch, it uses Civil Service ratings for entry positions. Job openings are listed on its website.

The **National Security and International Affairs Division (NSIAD)** focuses on national security issues and foreign policy problems. Reviews are conducted at several federal agencies, including the Department of Defense, the Department of State, and the Department of Commerce. Typical of these reports are *Foreign Assistance and Combating HIV/AIDS in Developing Countries*; *Foreign Investment Issues Raised by Taiwan*; *Proposed Investment in McDonnell Douglas*; and *Foreign Technology: Federal Process for Collective Dissemination.*

Library of Congress

Congressional Research Service
101 Independence Avenue, SE
Washington, DC 20540
(202) 707–5000
www.lcweb.loc.gov

The title of the Library of Congress is deceptive and does not hint at the scope of its functions. True, the library has an extensive collection of books on every subject and in a multitude of languages and it administers the copyright laws. It also engages in a variety of research tasks of an international nature.

The **Congressional Research Service (CRS)** works exclusively and directly as the research arm of members of Congress and their staffs. Employees provide in-depth policy analysis, legal research, and fact-finding research in addition to presenting seminars and briefing members and staff. The CRS responds to more than 500,000 congressional requests annually. Its jobs website is located at www.loc.gov/crsinfo/crsjobs2.html.

In addition, the CRS has a well-known, respected internship program in the **Central Research Section of the Foreign Affairs and National Defense Division**. Interns work on projects on U.S. foreign policy organizations, major weapons acquisition decisions, arms control and nonproliferation, international organizations, and global crises. The internship is unpaid, though students may earn college or graduate school credit. Visit www.loc.gov/crsinfo/volunteer for details.

HELPFUL RESOURCES

The following publications will give you additional information on each government agency, its functions, organization, and top personnel:

Washington Information Directory
Congressional Quarterly, Inc.
1414 22nd Street, NW
Washington, DC 20037
www.cqpress.com
Published annually.

Federal Yellow Book directory and *Congressional Yellow Book* directory
Washington Monitor, Inc.
1301 Pennsylvania Avenue, NW
Washington, DC 20045

The former lists the top-level employees of the federal agencies; the latter lists members of Congress as well as their committees and key aides. Both books can be found in large career centers and libraries and are updated quarterly.

Capital Jobs
Published by Tilden Press
1519 Connecticut Avenue, NW
Washington, DC 20036
(202) 332–1700

Published a while ago, this offers the best guide to what working on the Hill is like. Also offers the closest thing to job descriptions for the various positions.

Congressional Quarterly
House Action Reports (Job Listing)
316 Pennsylvania Avenue, SE, Suite 501
Washington, DC 20003
(202) 546–3900

Another excellent resource for Democrats and moderate Republican members in the House: *The Book of U.S. Government Jobs,* 7th ed., by Dennis V. Damp and Samuel Concialdi (Bookhaven Press, 2000).

6

The United Nations and
Related International Organizations

WITH THE AWARD of the Nobel Prize on December 10, 2001, the United Nations, under the inspired leadership of Secretary-General Kofi Annan, has become even more sought after as a potential employer than before—and it has always been a popular choice among internationalists. While opportunities are competitive and thus limited, there are a number of internship and "young professionals" programs that can provide you with experience in some multilateral organizations.

The UN staff has shrunk significantly in recent years, due to efforts to initiate major reforms and to a contracting budget. A personnel quota system based on nationality, tied to the funds contributed by each member country, adds to the complexity of hiring.

Even without definite nationality quotas, the United Nations—quite appropriately—tries to recruit qualified talent from developing nations that are currently underrepresented. For these reasons, if you are a qualified national from an underrepresented country, you have a better chance for a UN job than if you are from a country that has ample representation. Support from your government can be critical. Gender also plays a role, as the United Nations has a shortage of women in the middle and top ranks, and it has made a strong commitment to rectify this imbalance. Thus, while the skills and background you offer are critical, other factors like nationality, gender, work background, contacts, and initiative in locating job opportunities also play an important role in getting hired.

One option for employment may be through a short-term or fixed-term consultancy, either at UN Headquarters in New York, Geneva, a peacekeeping mission, or with an agency abroad. A master's degree is required for the majority of professional positions, as is significant relevant prior experience. The bottom line: Don't think of the United Nations as a training ground, except for internships.

Courses on the United Nations may be interesting and informative, but don't expect them to lead to a UN job. The United Nations values, in particular, M.A.s and Ph.D.s in economics, economic development, public administration, and political science, often combined with a regional expertise with fluency in French and Spanish in addition to English. Work experience is critical. An academic specialization in the UN system is nice to have, but it's not what gets you hired.

THE UN SECRETARIAT

The UN Secretariat comprises an international staff that services the UN Secretary-General, who is the chief administrative officer of the entire system: the General Assembly, the Security Council, the Economic Social Council, and the Trusteeship Council. Much of the research, public relations, and administrative work in the Secretariat is generated by resolutions of the General Assembly. The Secretariat staff administers peacekeeping operations and mediates international disputes, in addition to surveying economic, political, and social trends and problems and preparing studies on subjects such as human rights, disarmament, and sustainable development. The Secretariat also organizes international conferences and conducts information programs to familiarize the international media with the work of the United Nations. Men and women from some 160 countries make up the global Secretariat staff.

Recruitment

The national competitive exams are currently the only way to enter for permanent Secretariat staff at the P2 and P3 levels. The exams are held annually for underrepresented countries. They are generally required for administrative, public information, political, and economic positions. Each June, the countries currently being recruited for are posted on the UN website (www.un.org). If you have dual citizenship, you may apply if one of your nationalities is listed.

You must have official citizenship in the country in order to take the exam. To prepare for the written exams, see the UN website for sample questions. To qualify for an entry-level (P1/P2) position, a candidate must possess a bachelor's degree or the equivalent and be 32 years of age or younger by December 31 of the year of the exam (no exceptions are given). For P3 positions, a candidate must possess an advanced university degree, four years of professional experience, and be 39 years of age of younger. All candidates must be fluent in either English or French. Interested candidates should contact their country mission or visit www.un.org/Depts/OHRM/examin/exam.htm. For information on the structure and work of the various UN departments, visit www.un.org/Depts/index.htm.

Information on vacant positions is also available on the Internet at jobs.un.org. The Secretariat maintains a computerized roster of qualified candidates for these posts. For vacancy announcements, individuals may apply online or via fax/mail; online applications are strongly encouraged. First, log on to the UN website, register, and you will be given a "My UN" page. You must then fill out a Personal History Profile (PHP). The PHP can be saved and modified to apply for future vacancies.

In addition to the now familiar blue-helmeted peacekeepers (see Department of Peacekeeping Operations, below), the Secretariat employs many different kinds of individuals. Listed below is a summary of some of the professional and general staff jobs, as well as the kinds of skills needed. Remember that this is a broad overview only. For professional staff positions, an M.A. or Ph.D. is required, plus several years of experience.

Salary and Benefits

UN salaries are based upon academic and professional qualifications, which determine the post level. Professional base salaries are set by the General Assembly and follow what is known as a "P scale" (*P* referring to the status of Professional staff). Staff members are expected to serve various overseas tours during the course of their careers; like other international positions, there is an overseas post adjustment allowance based on the cost of living and exchange rate of the local currency versus the U.S. dollar. Staff members living away from their home countries also receive a benefits package and education grants and dependency allowance for each eligible child.

<table>
<tr><td>

A

DAY

IN THE

LIFE

</td><td>

Desk Officer in the Department of Political Affairs, UN Secretariat, New York

</td></tr>
</table>

The main mandate of the Department of Political Affairs (DPA) is "early warning," "preventive diplomacy," and "peacemaking." As a desk officer, then, you monitor the political and other relevant developments in the countries you cover and alert your superiors of potential conflicts, thereby helping them to prevent disputes from escalating into armed conflict. This sounds very logical, but in reality the United Nations often is not encouraged by member states to be active in the field of preventive diplomacy, since many countries do not want the United Nations to interfere in what they consider their internal affairs, and the United Nations can only rarely act without the consent of governments.

Your responsibilities as a desk officer vary depending on the countries that you are assigned. It is similar to being a desk officer in the State Department, except that the United Nations does not have a political representative office in most countries to do firsthand information gathering, so you tend to rely more on secondhand sources; and because of the severe shortage of funds, you rarely get to travel to the countries you cover. Some desk officers end up covering countries to which they have never been. If you handle countries where the United Nations is not involved politically, your daily routine consists of checking the wire services and other sources of news; drafting responses to letters addressed to the Secretary-General or other senior officials on the countries you cover; drafting briefing notes and talking points and taking notes for meetings between senior UN officials and representatives of countries that you cover; and writing occasional papers on salient issues in those countries.

The job is much more stimulating when you cover countries in which the United Nations is involved politically (as opposed to peacekeeping, which is the responsibility of the Department of Peacekeeping Operations, although there is some overlap). As a desk officer for, say, Afghanistan or Sierra Leone, you would be involved in peacemaking, usually assisting and accompanying a special envoy or representative of the Secretary-General in his or her negotiations with the country's various opposing factions.

A Sampling of Major Offices within the Secretariat

The Department of Peacekeeping Operations (DPKO)

The Department of Peacekeeping Operations is housed within the Secretariat. The Security Council sets up UN peacekeeping operations and defines their scope and mandate. An operation can last for a few months or for years. Currently, approximately 35,000-plus military and civilian police personnel work in 15 operations and are provided by 89 countries.

Hiring opportunities have decreased substantially since the boom period of the early 1990s as the number and scale of UN peacekeeping operations has declined (e.g., Sarajevo and East Timor) while the number of qualified candidates with prior peacekeeping experience has grown. The greatest need is for field specialists to fill overseas peacekeeping operations posts, particularly in the areas of finance, human resources, procurement, legal, and information technology. There is also a strong push to hire more women; the department is trying to improve its gender balance. These posts, originally filled by "borrowing" UN staff from other departments, are now recruited through various sources from around the world. Still, the competition is stiff, as the roster of qualified individuals from around the world who have already participated in a peacekeeping mission—and therefore are more qualified to serve in future missions—has grown to many thousands of names. The DPKO external applicant roster is currently being revamped. Fifteen thousand applicants have recently registered! If your application has been pending for more than six months, it is suggested that you reapply. Most applicants have strong resumes: They speak at least two languages, have significant overseas experience, and skills in administration and logistics. Many have prior peacekeeping experience. Budgeting abilities and experience working in difficult country postings abroad are also important, as are relevant languages, depending on the operation. Because peacekeeping operations are "multidimensional," according to the United Nations itself, specialists are needed in a variety of areas, from civilian administration to humanitarian relief, Human Rights, and political/judicial affairs. Visit www.un.org/Depts/dpko/field for more information on employment opportunities, pay, important skills and characteristics needed, and current mission information.

Department of Economic and Social Affairs (DESA)
www.un.org/esa/desa.htm

The Department of Economic and Social Affairs works in the area of sustainable development through a multifaceted approach, taking into account considerations that are social, economic, environmental, population, and gender related.

Department of Disarmament Affairs (DDA)
www.un.org/Depts/dda/DDAHome.htm

The Department of Disarmament Affairs advises the Secretary-General on disarmament-related security matters. In order to effectively do this, DDA professionals monitor and analyze developments and trends in the field of disarmament and support the implementation of current disarmament agreements. They also advise member states in multilateral disarmament negotiation and work to promote an open, transparent approach to military and security affairs.

Department of Political Affairs (DPA)

www.un.org/Depts/dpa

The Department of Political Affairs is one of the most well known parts of the UN Secretariat. Individuals working within DPA analyze and provide information on global political events for the Secretary-General. Within the department, there is work done on electoral assistance and governance, as well as general current events monitoring, country-by-country.

Office for the Coordination of Humanitarian Assistance (OCHA)

www.reliefweb.int/ocha_ol/index.html

The Office for the Coordination of Humanitarian Assistance coordinates the delivery of humanitarian assistance that goes beyond the scope of one particular agency (i.e., UN Development Programme [UNDP] or UN High Commissioner for Refugees [UNHCR]) and advocates for humanitarian relief in global crises. It has headquarters staff in New York and Geneva, as well as field base staff in operations in the following countries (and one region): Afghanistan, Angola, Armenia, Azerbaijan, Bosnia and Herzegovina, Burundi, Democratic Peoples Republic of Korea, Democratic Republic of the Congo, Georgia, Great Lakes, Republic of the Congo, Russian Federation, Rwanda, Sierra Leone, Somalia, Sudan, and Tajikistan. Relief Web (www.reliefweb.int), managed by OCHA, provides up-to-date information on complex emergencies and natural disasters collected from more than 170 sources.

Department of Public Information (DPI)

The Department of Public Information is responsible for a wide range of media-related activities, from public information to media liaison work to conference planning. DPI is also responsible for the UN library, publications, and archival collections. DPI also has 77 centers overseas, called Information Centres, which service more than 185 member countries. These offices are involved in all areas of the press, publications, radio, television, films, graphics, exhibi-

tions, and public liaison. They cover the whole spectrum of UN activities in political, economic, social, and humanitarian matters, and work to reach civil society actors and local youth. Information Centres contact government officials,
educational authorities, and media personnel in order to increase awareness in
that country of UN aims and activities, as well as sponsor conferences and outreach events to raise awareness about important issues like HIV/AIDS, land-
mine eradication, and women and children's issues.

Types of Jobs
Professional Level Staff

Political Affairs.   Individuals in the Department of Political Affairs fulfill a variety of functions—analyzing and reporting on current governmental and political events for certain countries and regions; providing valuable information
to the Secretary-General; assisting and supporting overseas peacekeeping operations; and providing technical electoral assistance to newly democratized
countries.

Economic Affairs.   Positions in this field include a wide variety of specializations,
such as designing and conducting research in various economic areas; development of economic models for long-range forecasting and development
strategies; and planning, developing, and monitoring technical assistance projects. An increasingly prominent area of activity is the field of sustainable development and capacity building.

Social Development.   These positions are concerned with a variety of social and
humanitarian areas, such as crime prevention, criminal justice, narcotics control, institutional development and political participation, sustainable development, social integration and welfare, promotion of equality of men and
women, and rural development, as well as issues of importance to youth, the
aging, and the disabled. Demography and population science are other important areas is this field.

Finance.   Positions in the field of finance relate to a wide range of specializations, such as accounting, auditing, financial analysis, and treasury.

Public Information.   Positions involve a wide range of activities related to the production of UN press releases and information materials. Professional posts in this office call for substantial experience in journalism, publications, radio, films, and visual media.

Human Resources.   A variety of human resources positions exist, from recruiting to staff development and training, to benefits and compensation.

Additionally, there are positions in **Information Systems and Technology**, **Science and Technology**, **Statistics**, **Library Science**, and **Conference Services**.

General Service Staff

Most vacancies in this category are for administration assistants; therefore a knowledge of word-processing software and computers is valuable. Staff are involved in the management of human and material resources and a broad array of financial, logistical, and administrative matters. Applicants should be bilingual (English plus French or Spanish).

Language and Related Work

Positions are found in the following areas: translation, interpretation, editing, verbatim reporting, and proofreading in the six official UN languages (Arabic, Chinese, English, French, Russian, and Spanish). Recruitment for these positions is by competitive exam and interview, usually held annually. There is no nationality requirement for language work. Candidates for translator positions are required to translate from at least two of the six official languages. Candidates for interpreter positions are required to interpret simultaneously into one of the six official languages and must have full auditory comprehension of at least two other official languages. Interested candidates should visit www.un.org/depts/OHRM/examin/exam/htm. There you will find information on exams, dates, and which languages are currently in demand, along with sample examinations to help you prepare.

Internships at the Secretariat

Approximately 120 students participate in the formal UN internship program each semester and summer—three times annually. The program consists of three two-month periods throughout the year: mid-January to mid-March, mid-May to mid-July, and mid-September to mid-November.

The positions are competitive, so interested students should send applications early; the United Nations recommends applying 4–12 months prior to an anticipated starting date. Applications for formal summer internship programs must be received by the end of November.

All internships are unpaid and generally last two to three months, though they may sometimes be extended for up to six months with a supervisor's request. Interested students should visit www.un.org/Depts/OHRM/examin/internsh/intern/htm for more information and application details.

Applicants for UN internships must be enrolled in a master's or Ph.D. program at the time of application and while doing the internship.

The UN Secretariat: Outside New York

Geneva Office and Regional Economic Commissions

The UN office in Geneva is the only regional office of the UN Secretariat. The Office of the High Commissioner for Human Rights, for example, is located at the United Nations Office at Geneva (UNOG). The United Nations High Commissioner for Refugees, the United Nations Conference on Trade and Development, and the International Trade Center (ITC) are also located on the premises of the Palais des Nations. In addition, there are five regional commissions aimed at economic and social development of the area in which they are located:

1. Economic Commission for Europe (ECE), Geneva, Switzerland
2. Economic and Social Commission for Asia and the Pacific (ES-CAP), Bangkok, Thailand
3. Economic Commission for Latin America (ECLA), Santiago, Chile
4. Economic Commission for Africa (ECA), Addis Ababa, Ethiopia
5. Economic Commission for Western Asia (ECWA), Amman, Jordan

Aside from administrative personnel, who are either locally hired or provided through the reassignment of existing staff from headquarters or one of the other offices, UN regional offices are staffed primarily with professionals who have significant experience in economics, statistics, sociology, and various aspects of administration and technology. Secretariat staff in New York and Geneva are strongly encouraged to rotate through at least one of the regional commissions to learn more about the work being done in a particular region.

UNITED NATIONS ORGANIZATIONS

The following organizations were created by and report to the General Assembly. In terms of hiring opportunities, these agencies look for very specific technical backgrounds—in health and education, for example, the main areas of their focus and institutional mission. Americans are generally in the same position as they are in the Secretariat—that is, often overrepresented. However, consultancies are easier to get, overall, in some of these agencies that do direct fieldwork.

United Nations Children's Fund (UNICEF)
3 UN Plaza
New York, NY 10017
(212) 310–7000; fax: (212) 303–7984
www.unicef.org

UNICEF, one of the most well known UN organizations, is involved with the needs of children on a global scale. It is the only organization of the United Nations dedicated exclusively to children. In 2000, the total UNICEF expenditure was $1.1 billion. UNICEF works with other UN bodies, governments, and NGOs to improve children's lives through community-based services in primary health care, basic education, and safe water and sanitation in more than 160 developing countries. Recent projects have focused on child labor, HIV/AIDS, sexual exploitation, poverty, and malnutrition. As a follow-up to the 1990 World Summit on Children, UNICEF recently worked closely with the UN Secretariat to assemble the 2002 Special Session on Children, an unprecedented meeting of the UN General Assembly completely focused on the world's children and teens.

The UNICEF Secretariat is headquartered in New York and has seven regional offices and 126 country offices. Approximately 85 percent of UNICEF's

5,500-plus posts are located in the field. UNICEF has a formal, year-round internship program at its headquarters in New York. Internships are a minimum of six weeks in duration but can be held for up to four months. Generally, it is recommended that you apply two to three months in advance of the time you wish to begin. UNICEF maintains a website at www.unicef.org/employ/Intern.htm with application information, procedures, and necessary forms. UNICEF also takes UN Volunteers (UNVs); for more information on the UNV program, see the section on UNVs later in this chapter.

Background Desired.   A graduate degree in social work/social welfare, health, nutrition, teaching, education, economics, international affairs, and languages. Fluency in a second UN language, developing country experience, and relevant work experience are all important. Rarely are entry-level staff recruited into UNICEF: Generally, individuals have several years of relevant experience in health, nutrition, and international development.

UN Conference on Trade and Development (UNCTAD)
United Nations Office
Palais des Nations E-Building
1211 Geneva 10
Switzerland
www.unctad.org

The UN Conference on Trade and Development, established in 1964, is the principal organ of the General Assembly that works in the fields of trade, investment, and development. Its main task is to accelerate economic growth and development, particularly in developing countries. UNCTAD's budget, as of 2002, was U.S.$45 million annually from the United Nations, as well as an additional U.S.$24 million in extrabudgetary funds. UNCTAD analyzes issues in international trade and investment, which it views as important instruments for economic development, and assists developing countries with integrating into the world economy. UNCTAD focuses on the following areas: globalization and development; international trade, investment, enterprise development and technology; services infrastructure, transport and trade efficiency; human resource development; and least developed, landlocked, and island developing countries.

UNCTAD does have an internship program and recruits entry-level candidates through the National Competitive Exam program described above under the UN Secretariat. Midlevel and more senior level posts require a minimum of six years of full-time professional experience; these positions are posted on the UNCTAD website, along with application instructions.

Background Desired.   A knowledge of and experience working within developing countries. An academic and professional background in economics, economic development, and trade are highly desired.

United Nations Development Program (UNDP)

Recruitment Section
Division of Personnel
1 UN Plaza
New York, NY 10017
(212) 906–5597; fax: (212) 906–5282
www.undp.org/; for jobs: www.undp.org/mainundp/jobs/index.html

The United Nations Development Program is the world's largest multilateral source of grant funding for development cooperation. Its activities are directed toward helping developing countries throughout Asia, Africa, Latin America, the Middle East, and parts of Europe in their efforts to achieve sustainable human development. UNDP helps developing countries provide their citizens with adequate nutrition, housing, human development, employment, education, health care, and public services. Currently, UNDP focuses on the following six major strategic areas: democratic governance; poverty reduction; crisis prevention and recovery; energy and environment; information and communications technology; and HIV/AIDS. For complete historical background on UNDP, visit www.yale.edu/unsy/UNDPhist.htm

UNDP staff numbers approximately 7,000 and it works throughout a global network of more than 136 country offices. It is headquartered in New York and has an annual budget of more than U.S.$1 billion. Because of the UNDP's global representation, other UN organizations doing business in foreign countries are sometimes housed in UNDP offices. UNDP also coordinates operational development activities undertaken by the entire UN system. They include special purpose funds such as: **United Nations Capital**

Development (UNCDF), **United Nations Sudano-Sahelian Office (UNSO)**, **United Nations Development Fund for Women (UNIFEM)**, and the **United Nations Volunteers**.

Each year, UNDP recruits a competitive small group (approximately 20) of outstanding young graduates for its professional staff through its Leadership Development Program (LEAD; visit www.undp.org/ohr/lead), placing individuals abroad in a UNDP field office for a two- or three-year term. Preference is given to candidates under 35 years of age, and applicants must have a graduate degree in development, economics, business, public administration, international affairs, or related field *as well as* two to three years of development or relief experience. Successful candidates serve at any of the UNDP field offices throughout the world and usually spend the greater part of their careers overseas. The program is quite competitive; in 2001, there were approximately 1,000 applicants for 20 spots.

UNDP also has a **Junior Professional Officer Program (JPOP)**, which trains young officers sponsored by 20 participating donor governments. These young professionals join for one- or two-year assignments, generally at a field office; after their JPO assignment, individuals are expected to return to their countries. Although the United States sponsors JPOs with other UN agencies (UNHCR, for example), it does not sponsor JPOs with UNDP, which is unfortunate because the JPO program provides an excellent service to UNDP as well as an outstanding training opportunity for an individual interested in a development career. Some industrialized countries have signed agreements with UNDP to sponsor JPOs from developing countries that are not able to afford the expense of subsidizing their own nationals. More than 250 JPOs are in the field at any one time (as of July 2001, 258 JPOs were chosen, with 74 percent of them at UNDP). Graduates of this program sometimes become full-fledged UNDP employees, although candidates are warned from the beginning that the "JPOP is emphatically not a backdoor to a UNDP career." Information about JPOs, including application information and timetables for hiring, can be found at www.jposc.org/html/ie.html.

Background Desired.   Because of the nature of the development work, candidates in this highly competitive program are expected to have a thorough grounding in international economic development. Graduate academic work in this field is expected; JPOs must have completed a master's degree or equivalent. Courses in sociology, business, and public administration are helpful, as are strong information technology skills. Prior work experience (one to two years, minimum) in developing countries is requested, along with a strong commitment to the work of the UN Charter, cultural sensitivity, and strong interpersonal skills. As with most UN organizations, fluency in French and Spanish is usually required. Individuals are generally 32 years of age or younger.

The UN Development Program (UNDP) also has an internship program that provides training for a limited number of graduate students, either at UNDP Headquarters or in an overseas field office. Candidates should be enrolled in a graduate program in international affairs, economics, international development, anthropology, business, or a related field; show a demonstrated interest in development; and ideally have full working knowledge of two of the official UN languages. Interested students should visit www.undp.org/ohr/Interns/intern.htm for information about the program and instructions regarding how to apply.

United Nations Development Program Country Offices.   For internships, and occasionally for consultancies, it makes sense to apply through UNDP Headquarters in New York so that there is an official record of application; you should also fax or e-mail a resume and letter directly to the mission in the country in which you would like to work. For example, if you are interested in going to Sierra Leone, send a letter of inquiry to the Head of Mission at the UNDP office in Freetown, Sierra Leone. If your letter arrives at a time of need, you may be snatched up, particularly for an internship (which is officially unpaid). This rule holds true for UNICEF, UNIFEM, and other overseas offices as well.

How do you get the fax number or e-mail address for an overseas mission office? Good luck—it is not an easy task. You can call the main number for the UN office you're interested in and attempt to get a regional bureau or desk officer for that country, but prepare to be transferred from line to line, as you might in any large bureaucracy. It is usually not a good idea to say why you are asking, just say that you are faxing correspondence to Kenya (or wherever) and would like to obtain the appropriate number.

United Nations Development Fund for Women (UNIFEM)

304 East 45th Street, 6th Floor
New York, NY 10017
(212) 906–6456; fax: (212) 906–6705
www.unifem.undp.org

The United Nations Development Fund for Women promotes the economic and political empowerment of women in developing countries. It supports the implementation of the agenda for women's empowerment adopted in 1995 at the UN Fourth World Conference on Women. UNIFEM has an autonomous association with the UNDP; it is a much smaller agency and therefore hires fewer entry-level employees. For employment information, use the address listed above.

A division of UNDP, UNIFEM offers a limited number of year-round internships in New York and in some of its regional field offices in Africa, Asia, and Latin America. The internship program targets graduate students pursuing development-related and/or women's studies. There are no formal deadlines, and applications are accepted on a rolling basis. Interested students should send a detailed resume and cover letter explaining their interest, availability, expected duration of internship, and field of expertise.

United Nations Volunteers (UNV)

Postfach 260 111
D–53153 Bonn
Germany
(49 228) 815–2000; fax: (49 228) 815–2001

Headquartered in Bonn, Germany, United Nations Volunteers enrolls individuals from many countries in a collective effort to help developing nations. Primarily, UNV's work is in affiliation with UN agency operations at the country level and in peacekeeping operations. The title "volunteer" is somewhat ambiguous. Volunteers are paid, though not at the rate of full-time, permanent employees. But don't let the "volunteer" title fool you—UNV is quite competitive. In 2000, UNV received 10,000 informal inquiries, 9,000 preliminary applications, and 5,300 formal applications for international assignments. About 25 percent made it into the current database. The average age of the UN Volunteer is 39; you must be 25 or over to apply, with five years of work experience and a bachelor's degree or equivalent. Volunteers must also have a good working knowledge of one or more of the following languages: Arabic, English, French, Portuguese, Russian, or Spanish.

About 5,000 qualified men and women from more than 150 countries currently serve as volunteer specialists with the UNV program. Volunteers work in more than 115 professional categories including agriculture, health, education, industry, transportation, and population. For more information, including applications, visit www.unvolunteers.org.

UNVs currently work in a multitude of countries; some locations with large numbers of volunteers include: Yugoslavia (including Kosovo), East Timor, Guatemala, Mozambique, Bosnia-Herzegovina, Tanzania, Sierra Leone, and Cambodia.

Background Desired.   Economics, business administration, teaching, health services, community development, information technology, elections monitoring, human rights, engineering, and more. U.S. citizens may also apply for the UNV through the Peace Corps. Contact www.peacecorps.gov for more information.

United Nations Environment Programme (UNEP)

Chief of Recruitment
Classification and Recruitment Section
Human Resource and Management Service
United Nations Office at Nairobi
P.O. Box 67578
Nairobi
Kenya
254–2–623567; fax: 254–2–623789
e-mail: doreen.munene@unon.org

2 UN Plaza
New York, NY 10017
(212) 963–8210; fax: (212) 963–7341
www.unep.org

Recognizing that environmental problems at the international level required a special approach, the UN General Assembly established the United

Nations Environment Programme in 1972. Since the environment is the logical concern of many different UN organizations, it was considered unwise to make environmental problems the province of one agency. Thus, in contrast to the concept that shaped other UN organizations, UNEP was created as a small co-ordinating body to give leadership and direction to international initiatives—not to do the work itself, but to see that it gets done.

UNEP is headquartered in Nairobi, Kenya, and has regional offices in Paris, Geneva, Osaka, The Hague, Washington, New York, Bangkok, Mexico City, Manama, Montreal, and Bonn. There are ad hoc domestic internships at the liaison office in New York and structured internships in the field offices overseas. Job vacancies are posted on the organization's website. For domestic internships, contact the New York liaison office. For overseas internships, send a resume and detailed cover letter indicating area of interest in environmental studies to the Nairobi address (details and specific requirements are on the UNEP website). Internships are unpaid and begin each year in January, June, and October.

For an internship in New York, write to UNEP at:

UNEP—Regional Office of North America
United Nations Room DC2–803
New York, NY 10017

Background Desired.   Economics, economic development, and significant work experience in world resources, population studies, energy studies, and environmental studies.

United Nations High Commissioner for Refugees (UNHCR)

Case Postale 2500
CH–1211 Geneva 2
Switzerland
Tel: (41–22) 739–8111
www.unhcr.ch

UNHCR has two main functions: (1) encouraging the practice of asylum and then safeguarding the rights of refugees concerning employment, education, residence, freedom of movement, and security against being returned to a country where their lives may be in danger; and (2) helping governments and private organizations in countries of asylum in their task of enabling refugees to become self-supporting.

In recent years, the UNHCR has helped not only refugees but also those forced to live in refugee-like situations. Increasingly, refugees are victims of civil war. In such situations, the UNHCR provides protection and assistance to large groups of refugees fleeing persecution, conflict, and widespread violations of human rights. It also negotiates with governments to ensure the smooth resettlement and repatriation of refugees. The UN Secretary-General has designated UNHCR to coordinate several major UN programs. The UNHCR was the lead UN humanitarian agency in the former Yugoslavia and coordinated emergency provisions to assist the 1.8 million Iraqi Kurds displaced after the Gulf War. It also responded to one of the largest concentrations of refugees in the world when it aided the displaced populations in Rwanda and Burundi.

UNHCR has offices in some 115 countries. More than 80 percent of UNHCR's 5,000-member staff work in the field, often in isolated, dangerous, and difficult conditions. Field staff are required to rotate every three years.

Background Desired.   An advanced university degree in law or a degree (B.Sc./ B.A./L.L.B./M.A.) in international relations, international public or private law; humanitarian studies; public administration or social sciences; or logistics, transport, and telecommunications. Three to four years of relevant working experience in one of the same areas, preferably in a developing country (other than the candidate's) and demonstrated ability to work under tough conditions and poor infrastructure are necessary. Excellent knowledge of English and French is mandatory in addition to good working knowledge of any of the other UN official languages. Candidates can submit applications together with a UN P11 Personal History Form to hqpe92@unhcr.ch.

Americans may apply for a (very competitive) JPO position with UNHCR through the U.S. Department of State's International Organization Bureau (see the website address for the Department of State in Chapter 5).

United Nations Institute for Training and Research (UNITAR)
Palais des Nations
CH 1211 Geneve 10

Switzerland

+(41–22) 917–1234; fax: +(41–22) 917–8047

e-mail: info@unitar.org

www.unitar.org

The UN Institute for Training and Research is an autonomous institute established in 1963 within the UN framework to provide improve the UN staff through training and research. The training function involves individuals primarily from the developing nations who need to improve their qualifications for UN work or for work in their own countries. Research performed is "related to the functions and objectives of the UN," thus allowing wide latitude for the studies undertaken. Current projects include diplomatic training, economic and social development, and training UN employees in new information technologies.

UNITAR accepts a few interns for work in research, training, or administration for periods of between two months and a year.

Background Desired. Applicants should have demonstrated research and/or training ability. While specific courses like economics, economic development, area studies, world resources, international affairs, and foreign policy may be helpful, the staff is extremely small and rarely entry-level.

United Nations Fund for Population Activities (UNFPA)

Chief, Personnel Section

220 East 42nd Street, 18th Floor

New York, NY 10017

(212) 297–5351; fax: (212) 297–4908

www.unfpa.org

The Population Fund, as it is popularly called, was set up in 1967. It helps developing countries improve their reproductive health and family planning services on a voluntary basis and formulates population polices to support efforts toward sustainable development. This UN organization is recognized as the focal point for the promotion and coordination of international population programs. The fund assists national efforts by: (1) promoting government awareness of the consequences of a high population growth rate; (2) providing assistance to countries seeking relief from their population problems; (3) building the knowledge and the capacity to implement population projects; and (4) assuming the leading international role in developing global population strategies. In 1995, UNFPA provided support to 150 countries. Since 1969, the Population Fund has provided a total of $3.4 billion to developing countries.

The Population Fund participates in the Junior Professional Officer program and offers a limited number of unpaid summer internships at its headquarters in New York. Students must be involved in a master's program with a concentration in population studies or development. Written and spoken fluency in English is imperative. Preference is given to students with fluency in French, Spanish, or Arabic. There is no set deadline, but students should apply between January 1 and May 1 for the summer internship program. Students should submit a resume and detailed cover letter describing areas of interest and reasons for wanting to work with UNFPA, or fill out an online application at www.unfpa.org/about/employment/summer.htm. Send information to the following department at the address above:

Summer Internship Program
UFPA Personnel Branch
DN 1802

Background Desired.   The fund often prefers an advanced degree with studies in demography, public health, or population. Also useful are economics, economic development, and developing area studies, with significant related work experience. Applicants should be ready to work in field duty stations, and fluency in languages is also important.

UN Relief and Works Agency for Palestine Refugees in the Near East (UNRWA)

HQ Gaza
P.O. Box 140157
Amman 11814
Jordan
(+972–8) 677–7333 or (+972/08) 282–4508; fax: (+972–8) 677–7555
www.un.org/unrwa

Liaison Office
1 United Nations Plaza, Room DC1–1265

New York, NY 10017

(212) 963–2255 or (212) 963–1234; fax: (212) 935–7899

The UN Relief and Works Agency has existed as a temporary UN agency since 1950, with its mandate renewed periodically by the General Assembly. It provides services to Palestinian refugees, specifically those persons (or their descendants) who were residents of Palestine for the last two years before the 1948 Arab-Israel conflict and who then lost their homes and means of livelihood.

UNRWA operates more than 600 schools for refugee children and employs more than 22,000 staff, virtually all Palestinians, including 11,000 teachers to staff its schools. The educational program is run jointly with the UN Educational, Scientific, and Cultural Organization. UNRWA's health program for refugees is also run jointly—in this case with the World Health Organization. Its other major program is a relief and social services program, staffed mostly with local personnel. The agency's areas of operation are Lebanon, Syria, Jordan, the West Bank, and the Gaza Strip. Vacancy notices are posted through the UN/International Civil Service system, and senior positions are sometimes advertised publicly. The agency does not usually accept interns.

Background Desired.   UNRWA's international staff is limited in number, and the organization sometimes requires the following specializations as well as significant field experience: law, accounting, information and public relations, administration, personnel, and information systems technology.

An excellent source of information about the United Nations is the United Nations Association, or UNA-USA, a nonprofit, nonpartisan organization headquartered in New York, with offices in most major U.S. cities. The website is www.unausa.org. There is also an active Canadian association. The UNA is dedicated to enhancing U.S. participation in the UN system and therefore holds conferences, produces papers and reports, and generally serves as an information source to the public.

UNITED NATIONS SPECIALIZED AGENCIES

UN specialized agencies are autonomous intergovernmental organizations—each with its own charter, budget, and staff—related to the United Nations by special agreement.

Food and Agriculture Organization (FAO)

Via delle Terme di Caracalla
00100 Rome
Italy
(39–06) 570–51; fax: (39–06) 570–53152

2175 K Street NW, Suite 300
Washington, DC 20437–0001
(202) 653–2400; fax: (202) 653–5760

1 United Nations Plaza
Suite DC1–1125
New York, NY 10017
(212) 963–6036; fax: (212) 963–5425
www.fao.org

The purpose of the Food and Agriculture Organization is to raise nutrition levels and improve the efficiency of production and distribution of food and agricultural products. FAO is the largest autonomous agency within the UN system, with 183 member nations plus the European Union. A specific priority of the FAO is to encourage sustainable agriculture and rural development.

The **World Food Programme** is an agency set up by the FAO to provide food aid to all developing countries. The program is supported by voluntary pledges from participating countries in the form of commodities, cash, or services such as shipping. Food aid has been given by the program for a diversity of projects, recipients, and reasons: dairy and livestock improvement, community development, land improvement schemes, victims of natural disasters, and refugees and displaced persons. FAO has about 4,000 employees spread through various offices. Qualifications desired: development-related disciplines, preferably economics, agriculture, nutrition, international affairs; public or business administration; and finance or accounting. Openings are listed on the FAO website; send replies to the Rome address above.

The Associate Professional Officer (APO) program at the FAO allows citizens of donor or developing countries to gain experience by advising on technical and institutional issues. Details and application information are at www.fao.org/tc/Apo/index.html. The FAO also accepts volunteers on a less formal basis.

International Fund for Agricultural Development (IFAD)

Personnel Division
107, Via del Serafico
Rome 00142
Italy
(39) 065–4591; fax: (39) 065–043–463
e-mail: ifad@ifad.org

Room S 2955
United Nations
New York, NY 10017
www.ifad.org

The International Fund for Agricultural Development was established in 1977 as a specialized international financial institution within the UN system. With an annual budget commitment of $450 million, its primary purpose is to help increase agricultural production and strengthen policies and institutions related to the rural poor in developing countries. To this effect, it disburses loans on easy terms to these impoverished countries.

The agency has an Associate Professional Officer (APO) Program that offers training and experience for young professionals who seek careers in international development. APOs must be sponsored by their governments and work as IFAD staff for one year. Application details can be found on the IFAD website.

IFAD's internship program accepts current graduate students with studies in relevant areas. It runs on an ad hoc basis, with internships lasting up to six months. Address your application to the personnel division address above.

Background Desired.   Economics (primarily agricultural economics), economic development, finance, sociology, world resources with an emphasis on food, and development studies.

International Labour Organization (ILO)

Personnel Department
4 route des Morillons
CH–1211 Geneva 22
Switzerland

(41–22) 799–6820 or (41–22) 799–6584; fax: (41–22) 788–4739
Regular vacancies: recruit@ilo.org; Young Professionals Career Entrance Programme (YPCEP): recruit@ilo.org; internships: internship@ilo.org

Washington, DC, office:
1828 L Street, Suite 801
Washington, DC 20036
(202) 653–7652; fax: (202) 653–7687
www.ilo.org

The International Labour Organization's main purpose is to improve labor conditions, raise living standards, and promote economic stability throughout the world. A UN specialized agency, the ILO is distinct from all other international organizations in that a tripartite body representing government, workers, and employers from each member country shapes its policies. The standards developed by the annual international labor conference, while not obligatory, are guides for countries to follow and form an international labor code covering employment, hours of work, protection of women and young workers, workers' compensation, trade unionism, and related matters.

The ILO maintains a Young Professionals Program for advanced students in labor-related fields. Successful candidates spend one year in Geneva and two years in one of the ILO's 40 field offices. The program includes training courses in the ILO's International Training Centre in Turin, Italy. At time of writing, this program was being reevaluated. Visit the agency's website for up-to-date details.

The ILO takes about 130 current undergraduate and postgraduate students as unpaid interns each year. Interns may work at headquarters or at a field office, with duties depending on the intern's experience and abilities. For student internships you must apply online at least three months in advance. Applications to intern at a field office should be sent to the relevant office. The ILO has one or two graduate internships available each summer in the Washington office. Interns generally work with either the director or deputy director to monitor World Bank activities or write reports on issues concerning the ILO. (Other positions are available in the research library.) For internships in the Washington office, resumes/cover letters are accepted on a year-round basis. All internships are unpaid, but the ILO may reimburse local transportation costs. To apply for an internship in Washington, D.C., write to the Internship

Coordinator at the Washington address above. For Geneva, contact the Human Resources Development Branch.

Background Desired.   The type of work undertaken by the ILO points to the following optimum background for employment: economics (particularly labor economics), industrial relations, statistics, area studies, social security and conditions of work, management development, small industry development, occupational safety and health, vocational rehabilitation, vocational training, gender and development studies, elimination of child labor, social protection, information technology, human resources, financial and budget studies, and some experience in trade unions or the U.S. Department of Labor. The ILO's working languages are English, French, and Spanish, and candidates must be fluent in one of these with a working knowledge of at least one of the others. You can apply online for all types of vacancies.

United Nations Educational, Scientific, and Cultural Organization (UNESCO)

Chief of the Recruitment and Staffing Section
Office of Human Resources Management
7, place de Fontenoy
F–75352 Paris 07 SP
France
(33 1) 45.68.10.00; fax: (33 1) 45.67.16.90

UNESCO New York Liaison Office
2 United Nations Plaza—Suite 900
B.P. 20, Grand Central
New York, NY 10017
(212) 963–5995; fax: (212) 963–8014
www.unesco.org

The UN Educational, Scientific, and Cultural Organization, a specialized UN agency, works to promote collaboration among nations through education, science, mass communications, and cultural matters to further the objectives of international peace and the common welfare of humankind.

One of UNESCO's priorities is the eradication of illiteracy. To this effect, UNESCO recognizes the need for educational innovation and works with countries individually and in regional groupings to improve the quality of education offered.

UNESCO also seeks to advance the cause of science globally and helps countries build up their scientific capabilities. It has set up special funds for research, established an international exchange of information on the application of science and technology to development, and organized regional conferences of ministers of science and technology. UNESCO is charged by its constitution to promote "the free flow of ideas by word and image." To this end, it aims to increase each country's access to information. UNESCO's best-known effort in this area has been its international campaigns to save the great monuments of the world. Artistic, engineering, and archeological skills have been mobilized globally to launch cultural rescue operations, such as for the Egyptian temples that were almost submerged by the waters of the Aswan Dam.

Some unpaid internships are available at UNESCO headquarters in Paris and with the liaison office in New York. Qualifications are dependent upon specific project needs at the time. Apply 3–6 months in advance to your country's permanent delegation to UNESCO. For more information, contact either the New York liaison office or headquarters in Paris or visit www.unesco.org/general/eng/about/interne.shtml.

Background Desired.　　Because of the variety of UNESCO activities, you should determine in advance which parts or functions interest you, since qualifications will differ according to section and division. The professional category groups specialists in the fields of education, science, culture, communication, and administration. For lower graded posts in the professional category (P1 to P2) the minimum requirements generally are: a university degree; two or three years of professional experience; and fluency in either French or English and a working knowledge of another UN language. UNESCO also employs many interpreters, translators, and revisers; these posts are filled internally or through organized public exams. Young graduates and citizens of non- or underrepresented countries who have professional experience may apply to the Young Professionals Program through the UNESCO mission offices in their home countries. Qualified nationals of developing countries may also apply to the Associate Experts program; see the website for details. UNESCO also offers fellowships in certain cases.

United Nations Industrial Development Organization (UNIDO)

Vienna International Center
P.O. Box 300
A–1400 Vienna
Austria
(43–1) 26–026; fax: (43–1) 269–2669

UNIDO New York Liaison Office
2 United Nations Plaza
Room DC2–0900
New York, NY 10017
(212) 963–6890; fax: (212) 964–4116
www.unido.org

The UN Industrial Development Organization was established in 1966 to "promote and accelerate the industrialization of the developing countries." During the past 20 years, UNIDO has fielded some 16,000 projects and generated investment for nearly 2,000 industrial ventures. Since 1993, UNIDO has carried out reforms aimed at redefining its relevance in a changed global economic environment. UNIDO has six divisions, five of which are substantive, dealing with human resources, enterprise, and private-sector development; industrial sectors and environment; investment and technology promotion; country programs and funds mobilization; and research and publications. The technical assistance activities of UNIDO are financed mainly by UNDP and voluntary contributions from donor countries and contributions. UNIDO's current membership numbers 169 countries. It is headquartered in Vienna, with 35 country and regional offices and 13 investment and technology promotion offices.

Background Desired.   Courses in area studies, business administration, economics, economic development, engineering, information science, industrial relations, international relations, and language fluency are necessary qualifications. UNIDO participates in the UN's Associate Expert and Junior Professional Officer programs and runs an ad hoc internship program for current graduate students generally lasting 3–6 months. Details are on its website, and applications should be addressed to the Staff Planning and Development Section, Room D1669, at the above address.

World Health Organization (WHO)

Central Human Resources Services
Avenue Appia 20
CH–1211 Geneva 27
Switzerland
(41–22) 791–2111; fax: (41–22) 791–3111
www.who.int/en

The World Health Organization is a special UN agency that plans and coordinates health action on a global basis. It helps member countries to carry out health programs, strengthen their health services, and train their health workers. It also promotes medical research and exchange of scientific information, makes health regulations for international travel, keeps communicable diseases under surveillance, collects and distributes data on health matters, and sets standards for the control of drugs and vaccines.

WHO has six regional offices throughout the world and has numerous projects and divisions including: the Office of HIV/AIDS and Sexually Transmitted Diseases, the Division of Child Health and Development, the Division of Emergency and Humanitarian Action, and the Nutrition Program.

Background Desired.   The type of work performed by WHO defines the type of personnel needed: medical officers, nurses, sanitary engineers, entomologists, bacteriologists, health educators, and occasionally economists and statisticians. Experience in developing countries is desirable, as is fluency in the languages of the area applied for. Non–health-related positions exist in finance, legal, human resources, administrative services, and informatics. The WHO also employs consultants. The WHO's Associate Professional Officer program for younger candidates is open only to nationals of Austria, Belgium, Denmark, Finland, France, Germany, Italy, Japan, Netherlands, Norway, Sweden, and Switzerland. Unpaid internships for up to three months at headquarters or regional offices are also available to students of health-related disciplines.

International Atomic Energy Agency (IAEA)

Division of Personnel
IAEA
Wagramer Strasse 5

P.O. Box 100
A–1400 Vienna
Austria
(43–1) 260–00; fax: (43–1) 260–07
www.iaea.org/worldatom

The International Atomic Energy Agency, an intergovernmental agency, assists governments in ensuring the safe and peaceful global development of nuclear energy and related technologies. Through an international safeguards system, it also tries to ensure that its assistance to any country is not used for military purposes. Technical assistance to developing countries is provided by the IAEA in the form of fellowships, training courses, and study tours. The IAEA maintains its headquarters in Vienna and also maintains field and liaison offices in Canada, Geneva, New York, and Tokyo. It operates laboratories in Austria and Monaco and supports a research center in Italy that is administered by the UN Educational, Scientific, and Cultural Organization.

The IAEA has about 2,000 staff from 80 countries with expertise in a variety of scientific, technical, managerial, and professional disciplines. Most work at headquarters in Vienna, with others at regional offices in Toronto and Tokyo, and liaison offices in New York and Geneva.

Background Desired.   Although a scientific background in engineering, nuclear sciences, and safeguards is of major interest to the IAEA, there may be opportunities for those trained in economics, administration, public relations, and general international relations. Vacancies are posted online. For more information write to:

Recruitment Unit
Division of Personnel, IAEA, P.O. Box 100
A–1400 Vienna
Austria

Other UN Agencies

Three other specialized UN agencies, whose names are self-descriptive, follow:
International Maritime Organization (IMO)
4 Albert Embankment
London SE 1 7SR

England
fax: (44 20) 7587–3210
www.imo.org

International Telecommunication Union (ITU)
Place des Nations
CH–1211 Geneva 20
Switzerland
(41–22) 730–5111; fax: (41–22) 733–7256
e-mail: personnel@itu.int
www.itu.ch

World Meteorological Organization (WMO)
7 bis Avenue de la Paix
CP 2300–1211 Geneva 2
Switzerland
(41–22) 730–8111; fax: (41–22) 730–8181
www.wmo.ch

OTHER INTERNATIONAL ORGANIZATIONS

The following multilateral organizations generally have a particular regional or functional emphasis.

International Bank for Reconstruction and Development (IBRD)

The World Bank Group
1818 H Street, NW
Washington, DC 20433
(202) 473–1000; fax: (202) 477–6391
www.worldbank.org

Commonly known as the World Bank, the IBRD's goal is to reduce poverty and improve living standards by promoting sustainable development and investment. It makes loans from its own funds when private capital is not available on reasonable terms. It also promotes private foreign investment by offering guarantees on loans and investments made by private investors.

The World Bank system encompasses five institutions:

1. *IBRD.* This is the oldest and largest international organization providing development finance. In addition to loans, the World Bank helps developing countries evaluate projects and draw up national programs.
2. *International Development Association (IDA).* The IDA lends on exceptionally easy terms (zero interest) to very poor countries that cannot afford conventional borrowing to meet their needs for development capital.
3. *International Finance Corporation (IFC).* The IFC is the World Bank Group's investment bank in developing countries. It invests in private or "mixed" ventures (i.e., joint ventures between private enterprise and government). Unlike the World Bank and the IDA, the IFC neither seeks nor accepts government guarantees. It is one of the few international development organizations that makes both equity investments and loans. IFC predominantly hires individuals with an M.B.A. degree.
4. *International Center for Settlement of Investment Disputes (ICSID).* The ICSID provides a mechanism for solving disputes between governments and investors.
5. *The Multilateral Investment Guarantee Agency (MIGA).* MIGA was created in 1988 to facilitate the flow of private foreign direct investment to developing member countries. It provides insurance to private foreign investment against political risks in developing countries.

Entry into the World Bank structure is formalized through the **Young Professionals Program (YPP)**, a mechanism for hiring talented individuals for junior professional posts. Upon entry, you receive on-the-job experience and exposure to the Bank Group's operations and policies, starting with two twelve-month rotational assignments in different departments. Upon completion of the rotational assignments, Young Professionals can apply for a regular position within the Bank Group.

To be eligible, candidates must possess a master's degree or the equivalent in finance, economics, public health, education, or natural resource management and a minimum of two years of relevant work experience or continued academic study at the doctorate level. Applicants also must be under 32 years of age, speak English fluently, and be proficient in one of the six official languages. Competition is intense. There are more than 5,000 applications received for each year's 30 positions. Qualified candidates should apply by submitting a resume or curriculum vitae no later than October 31 (specifying your nationality, date of birth, and gender) to: Young Professionals Program, The World Bank. For information regarding employment opportunities for applicants outside the YPP age limit, please contact the staffing center at the same address above.

Participants in the program are selected on a highly competitive basis. Applications are sought from all member countries. Qualifications are screened and interviews arranged for the most promising applicants. Final selection is made by a panel of senior staff members "on the basis of professional merit." Approximately one-half of the accepted candidates hold Ph.D.s in economics. Offers of appointment are made annually, usually in March, and candidates then have up to six months to join the program.

The World Bank recently introduced a new Junior Professional Associates Program offering two-year work terms for recent graduates under age 28 with top grades, relevant studies, and experience. The program is not a direct path to work at the World Bank, but it does provide access to an alumni network and the possibility of future employment after a two-year ban. Recruitment is ongoing, and you can apply online.

The majority of internships with the World Bank require training in economics, finance, accounting, human resource development, social sciences, agriculture, environment, private sector development, and other related fields. All candidates must be enrolled in a full-time graduate study program with plans to return to school full-time after the internship. The World Bank pays a monthly salary and provides an allowance toward travel expenses. Students are responsible for their own housing accommodations. All summer and winter positions are in Washington, D.C., and are a minimum of four weeks in duration. Interested students should apply online at lnweb28.worldbank.org/hrs/careers.nsf.

International Monetary Fund (IMF)

Economists Program
Recruiting and Training Division
700 19th Street, NW

Washington, DC 20431
(202) 623–7422; fax: (202) 623–7333
e-mail: recruit@imf.org
www.imf.org

The International Monetary Fund is the foremost international organization involved in global monetary issues. Established at the 1944 Bretton Woods conference along with the World Bank, it provides technical assistance and financing to countries that are experiencing balance-of-payments problems. The IMF has been especially busy during the past decade helping Russia and the countries of the former Soviet Union and Eastern and Central Europe make the shift from centrally planned economies to market economies. It also participated in bailouts during the East Asian financial crisis in 1998 and has long been heavily—and controversially—involved in Latin America, where it has granted emergency loans to Mexico, Argentina, and other states. In 2002, it made its largest loan ever when it extended $30 billion to Brazil.

With a current membership of 184 countries, the IMF promotes international monetary cooperation, facilitates the expansion and balanced growth of international trade, and promotes exchange rate stability. It also keeps informed of member countries' economic problems, and it often provides financial assistance to help them overcome balance-of-payments difficulties. The IMF has also established a system of special drawing rights to supplement existing reserve assets of its member countries.

The IMF has 2,650 staff from 140 countries. Most work at IMF headquarters in Washington, D.C., though a few are assigned to small offices in Paris, Geneva, and the United Nations in New York or represent the IMF on temporary assignment in member countries. The IMF hires about 200 people each year. It continuously accepts applications for experienced economists with 5–15 years of work at the national level, and support-level positions (such as researchers, librarians, and office staff). Specific vacancies are posted on its website.

Additionally, the IMF has a fiercely competitive two-year **Young Professionals Program (YPP)** primarily to recruit entry-level economists. Note that entry level in this program means that you have recently graduated with a Ph.D. in economics and are under 33; in some cases a lesser degree may be accepted with relevant experience. Successful applicants will normally have assignments in one area department and one functional department at the

Washington headquarters and will also take part in a mission overseas. The assignment given a candidate after this two-year stint depends on his or her background and interests. The deadline is usually November for an assignment starting the following summer. Applications must be made online.

The IMF has summer internships for only 34–40 graduate students in economics currently pursuing Ph.D.s. There are no field positions abroad; all internships are at headquarters in Washington. This program is also highly competitive and is designed as an entry to the Economist Program. You must apply online by January 31.

Background Desired.   Because of the specialized and technical nature of IMF work, Ph.D.s in economics, finance, and statistics are normally hired. The majority of the successful candidates are recently graduated Ph.D.s with little work experience, but the IMF is slowly broadening recruitment to include those with significant, specialized work experience that would be valuable to the IMF. However, in the near-term, job prospects at the IMF are slim to nonexistent for those without a Ph.D.

World Trade Organization (WTO)

Human Resources Section
Centre William Rappard
154 Rue de Lausanne
CH–1121 Geneva 21
Switzerland
(41 22) 739–5111; fax: (41 22) 739–5772
e-mail: humanresources@wto.org
www.wto.org

The World Trade Organization is the legal and institutional foundation of the multilateral trading system. It administers and implements multilateral and plurilateral trade agreements, which make up the WTO, and seeks to resolve trade disputes and expand international trade and economic development. The WTO is the successor to the General Agreement on Tariffs and Trade (GATT). The organization is served by a small secretariat, and the professional staff consists primarily of economists and lawyers specialized in international trade policy.

The WTO has a competitive internship program for postgraduate university students between 21 and 30 who have completed undergraduate studies in a relevant area. Applicants must be from one of the WTO's member nations. The internships last up to 12 weeks; there is no set deadline for applying. Details can be found at nwww.wto.org/english/thewto_e/vacan_e/intern_e.htm

Background Desired.   Economics, international affairs, law, and statistics, with an emphasis on trade issues.

Asian Development Bank (ADB)

Human Resources Division
P.O. Box 789
Manila
Philippines 0980
(632) 632–4444; fax: (632) 636–2550, (632) 636–2444
e-mail: jobs@adb.org
www.adb.org

The Asian Development Bank's function is to promote economic and social progress in member countries of the Asia and Pacific region. The United States became a member in 1966 and provides significant funding for the organization.

The ADB offers a very competitive three-year Young Professionals Program. Candidates must hold a master's degree in a related field, be 30 years of age or younger, have relevant experience (see background desired below), and be from a member country of the ADB. The program can lead to a full staff position.

Summer internships at the ADB are open to graduate students from accredited universities with studies in relevant fields. Details can be found on the ADB website.

You can apply for all vacancies online or at the above address. Appointments are at headquarters in Manila and often involve business travel or missions to member countries.

Background Desired.   Advanced degree and experience in banking and finance, economics, economic development, business administration, and Asian studies.

European Bank for Reconstruction and Development (EBRD)

Human Resources Department
EBRD
1 Exchange Square
London EC2A 2JN
United Kingdom
(44–20) 7338–6015; fax: (44–20) 7338–6097
www.ebrd.org

The European Bank for Reconstruction and Development was established in 1991 after the fall of communist regimes in Central and Eastern Europe. Its mandate is to help build healthy democratic market economies in 27 countries stretching from Central Europe to Central Asia. The EBRD does this by investing directly in projects, often jointly with private-sector companies, and by encouraging other companies to invest in the region.

Positions with the EBRD may be in London or at representative offices in any of its client countries. The EBRD employs only nationals of its 60 member countries, as listed on its website. In addition to posted vacancies, the EBRD encourages unsolicited applications from experienced professionals.

Internships are often available, for example, in the EBRD's Treasury Risk Management department, to graduate students with backgrounds in finance and economics. Vacancies are posted on the EBRD website.

Background Desired. As a development bank, the EBRD is mainly interested in candidates with advanced degrees and experience in banking and finance, especially emerging markets finance, economics, economic development, business administration, and regional knowledge. It also has openings for support staff in areas such as communications and information technology.

Inter-American Development Bank (IDB)

Human Resources Department
1300 New York Avenue, NW
Washington, DC 20577
e-mail: Jobs@iadb.org
www.iadb.org

The purpose of the Inter-American Development Bank is to promote economic and social development in Latin America and the Caribbean. The IDB and its 46 member nations finance high-priority economic and social development projects in the private and public sectors; it provides technical cooperation, research, and training in the development field; and it acts as a clearinghouse for the exchange of information on economic and social questions in Latin American countries. Current leading priorities include poverty reduction, social equality, modernization and integration, and the environment. The IDB is headquartered in Washington, D.C., and has country offices in each of its borrowing countries and in Paris and Tokyo.

The IDB runs a two-year Junior Professionals Program for candidates from member countries. Applicants must possess a master's degree, be 32 years of age or less, and have work experience. Apply to the above address, including a personal history form downloaded from the IDB website.

Academic scholarships are also awarded to students from member countries. For more information visit www.iadb.org/int/eng/japan_scholarship.htm or contact:

Inter-American Development Bank
Japan-IDB Scholarship Program
1300 New York Avenue, NW, Stop B–200
Washington, DC 20577

Students from one of the IDB's 46 member countries and under 30 years of age may apply for professional-level internships. Students should ask for the IDB's personal history form and the skills/school form. Internships are offered in summer and winter. Each position has specific requirements; visit the website for details.

Background Desired.   Finance and banking, economics, economic development, engineering, business, management, law, education, health, public administration, trade, labor, the environment, Latin American studies, Spanish, and Portuguese.

European Investment Bank
100, boulevard Konrad Adenauer

L–2950
Luxembourg
(352) 43.79.31.22; fax: (352) 43.79.31.89
www.eib.org

The European Investment Bank is the European Union's financing institution. It finances capital projects in accordance with the objectives of the European Union and also implements the financial components of agreements concluded under European development aid and cooperation policies outside the European Union. A related agency, the European Investment Fund (www.eif.org), specializes in venture capital, guarantees for small and medium enterprises, and technology investment. To work at either agency, you must be a citizen of an EU or accession candidate country.

Background Desired.   Finance and banking, economics, engineering, business, information technology, management, law, and public administration.

It is not the European Investment Bank, but there are unpaid internship positions available with the Delegation of the European Commission in Washington, D.C., and New York City. Interns typically work in the departments of audio/visual, agriculture, economics and finance, and public information. Students must apply by April 1 for summer internships. The delegation's website also provides useful information on working and interning in Europe at www.eurunion.org/infores/Employment/employ.htm. For internships, send resume, cover letter and current transcript to:
Internship Coordinator
Press and Public Affairs Section
Delegation of the European Commission to the United States
2300 M Street, NW
Washington, DC 20037
Telephone: (202) 862–9500; fax: (202) 429–1766
www.eurunion.org/

Organization for Economic Cooperation and Development (OECD)

2 rue Andre-Pascal
F–75775 Paris
France

(33–1) 45.24.82.00

www.oecd.org

The Organization for Economic Cooperation and Development is the successor to the Organization for European Economic Cooperation, which administered the Marshall Plan for European recovery after World War II. The OECD is an international organization composed of 30 member countries from North America, Europe, and the Asia-Pacific area. The OECD tries to achieve the highest sustainable economic growth, employment, and standard of living in member countries while maintaining financial stability. Another purpose of the organization is to expand world trade. It employs about 2,000 people at its Paris headquarters.

Increasingly, OECD projects cut across sector lines: how policy affects the way economies operate, and how globalization will change the world's economies through intensified competition or trigger resistance manifested in protectionism. The OECD also is changing the scope of operations. Traditionally focused on its own members, OECD is now building relationships with other countries, with the ultimate objective of encouraging those countries to embrace the market economy. OECD engages in policies geared toward economics: trade, enterprise, financial, and fiscal matters; science, technology, and industry; education, employment, and social policies; agriculture; the environment; development; public management; statistics; territorial development; and energy.

The OECD administers a Young Professionals Program (YPP) for candidates from member countries. The YPP is open to nationals of OECD member countries, aged between 26 and 33, with a relevant advanced university degree and work experience. YPP is a two-year appointment as a junior administrator. Candidates have two assignments on different sectoral activities. Applications are usually due in November for a program starting the following year. For more information contact:

OECD Human Resource Management

2, rue Andre-Pascal

75775 Paris Cedex 16

France

The OECD does not offer a formal internship program but does periodically accept graduate students whose fields are directly related to the OECD's work as unpaid trainees. To apply send a cover letter and resume at least three months in advance. For information e-mail hrm.trainee@oecd.org.

Background Desired.　The specialized economic nature of this organization puts a premium on doctorates in economics, development economics, industrial relations, statistics, and finance. Candidates with master's degrees in the same subjects and international affairs, business administration, and related areas and at least two years of relevant experience also are sometimes accepted.

Organization of American States (OAS)

General Secretariat

17th Street and Constitution Avenue, NW

Washington, DC 20006

(202) 458–3519 or (212) 458–3000

www.oas.org

The OAS is the world's oldest regional organization. It unites the countries of the Western Hemisphere "in a community of nations dedicated to the achievement of peace, security, and prosperity for all Americans." The OAS is often thought of as a regional agency of the United Nations. In fact, the only connection is a shared purpose: the maintenance of peace and the peaceful settlement of disputes. It has a membership of 35 countries as well as the European Union and 37 permanent observer states. In other fields—economic, social, legal—the OAS operates independently. The **Council of the OAS** is the executive body of the organization and functions with eight permanent committees. Vacancies are posted on the organization's website.

The OAS has from 30 to 50 internships available through the Student Internship Program in Washington, D.C., during the fall, winter/spring, or summer sessions. Interns generally serve as researchers for senior specialists in one of the OAS departments (economic and social affairs, regional development, education science and culture, inter-American fellowships and training, and the inter-American commissions on drug abuse, women, and human rights). To be considered for an internship, students must have a "good command" of two of the four official languages (English, French, Portuguese and Spanish— English and Spanish preferred). All internships are unpaid but competitive, so get your application in early. Deadlines are June 15, November 15, and March

15 for the fall, winter/spring, and summer sessions, respectively. Interested students must fill out an OAS Student Intern Program application, provide two letters of recommendation, and a copy of a current transcript. For applications and inquiries contact:

OAS Student Intern Program Coordinator
1889 F Street, NW
Washington, DC 20006
(202) 458–3519

Consultative Group on International Agricultural Research (CGIAR)

CGIAR Secretariat
The World Bank
MSN G6–601
1818 H Street, NW
Washington, DC 20433
(202) 473–8951; fax: (202) 473–8110
www.cgiar.org

This group was organized by the FAO, the World Bank, UNEP, and the UNDP. Its purpose is to promote sustainable agricultural for food security in developing countries. It tries to achieve this aim through research programs and the training of scientists and specialists in the developing world. CGIAR's 8,500 scientists and scientific staff conduct research to make tropical agriculture more productive, protect the environment, and preserve biodiversity.

CGIAR's website functions as a hub for several agencies with international vacancies in fields related to agriculture and the environment.

Background Desired.   Agricultural and environmental sciences, forestry, economics, and political development.

International Organization for Migration (IOM)

17, Route des Morillons C.P. 71
CH–1211 Geneva 19
Switzerland
(41–22) 717–9111; fax: (41–22) 798–6150
www.iom.int

The International Organization for Migration, formerly the Intergovernmental Committee for European Migration, has three major objectives: the processing and movement of refugees to countries offering them permanent resettlement; the promotion of orderly migration to meet the specific needs (e.g., employment) of emigration and immigration countries; and the transfer of technology through migration to promote the economic, educational, and social advancement of developing countries.

IOM has a membership of 59 countries and 42 observer countries. Operational offices are located in 72 countries. It uses the UN classification system for its positions. Unpaid internships are available for students with relevant studies. They include work and training at an IOM office. The organization also runs an Associate Expert program for qualified young professionals. For information on both programs visit www.iom.ch/en/who/main_vacancies.shtml#howto.

Background Desired.   Administration, computer science/information technology, economics, education/training, finance/accounting, fundraising, human resources management, humanitarian and emergency operations, languages, management, medical services and public health management, migration, movement and travel management, program management, public international law, and public relations.

Organization for Security and Cooperation in Europe (OSCE)

OSCE Secretariat
Personnel Section
Kärntner Ring 5–7, 4th floor
1010 Vienna
Austria
(43–1) 514–360
fax: (43–1) 514–3696
www.osce.org

The Organization for Security and Cooperation in Europe is the world's largest regional security organization, including 55 countries from Europe, North America, and Central Asia. It works to maintain regional security through early warning systems, conflict prevention, crisis management, and postconflict rehabilitation. The OSCE also deals with arms control, preventive diplomacy, confidence- and security-building measures, human rights, democratization, election monitoring, and economic and environmental security.

Based in Vienna, the organization has offices in Copenhagen, Geneva, The Hague, Prague, and Warsaw and employs about 4,000 staff in 19 missions and field postings in Southeastern Europe, the Caucasus, Eastern Europe, and Central Asia. These field employees work to facilitate elections, prevent conflicts, and promote civil society and the rule of law.

The OSCE has an internship program for current and recent university graduates aged 30 or under who are nationals of a member country. Interns work in one of the organization's many offices. To apply, download an application from the OSCE website.

Background Desired. Depending on the post, international affairs, public affairs, governance, election monitoring, engineering, communications, security policy, human rights, international law, conflict resolution, regional studies, economics, accounting, finance, and related disciplines. For some field postings, demonstrated ability to survive in a challenging environment (e.g. the Balkans, the Caucasus) can be crucial.

HELPFUL RESOURCES

Information about the structure and function of the United Nations system used to be difficult to obtain, but with the advent of the Internet it has become much easier. Each organization has a site, contained in the information above, and the general United Nations website is excellent, up-to-date, and very user-friendly.

The United Nations maintains a bookstore at UN Headquarters in New York and in Geneva. It also has an excellent website listing UN publications and an online ordering mechanism (go to www.un.org/Pubs/index.html). One popular book is entitled *Basic Facts about the U.N.* (New York: United Nations); it provides detailed information on international agencies and their functions, organization, and personnel. There are also many annual reports, including the popular *Trade and Development Report*, *Yearbook of the United Nations* and *The State of the World*. There are also periodicals, academic textbooks, and K–12 curriculum materials for educators.

7

International Business and Banking

DAVID, A FORMER student of mine, was looking for a change. After working for more than eight years in development and education in Southeast Asia, he decided to pursue a career in international finance. The economies of the Southeast Asian "tigers" were beginning to take off, and he wanted to be a part of increasing investment in those countries. Although he had had a wealth of work experience, he knew that he needed a graduate degree to be taken seriously by financial institutions. So after careful consideration, he chose to get a master's degree in international affairs and to focus his academic program on international banking and finance. David considered M.B.A. programs but preferred the flexibility and array of international coursework he could get in an international affairs school. He took courses in central banking, international economics, accounting, portfolio management, and money and financial markets.

Internships, David feels, were a critical part of his success. He did three in graduate school, including one in a major financial institution in New York, and a summer in Bangkok in the research division of a brokerage house. After several months of competitive interviewing in the fall of his second year, David accepted a position with the American financial institution for which he had interned, though in a different division. David now manages a group responsible for overseeing the company's international expansion, a job that involves providing bankers with training and working with senior management to develop new product lines from the existing base.

David's transition from teaching and refugee work to the world of international finance is very instructive. As you will see in this chapter, experience and demonstrated expertise is becoming more critical in the world of business and banking. David's prior work experience gave him a sound base from which to begin—leadership, overseas experience and language fluency, and strong project management skills. Combining the technical coursework of his graduate program, and his several internships, David became an ideal candidate.

ACADEMIC PREPARATION

An M.B.A. or an M.A.?

Simply stated, it is the technical business curriculum, the accounting, marketing, and finance courses, that the M.B.A. brings to the job hunt. Additionally, because of its reputation, an M.B.A. commands immediate respect from most businesses—it is a "known commodity." However, your international experience will be a solid asset when you apply for jobs. Joint M.A./M.B.A. degrees are becoming quite popular and may expand your options.

You don't have to have an M.B.A. to receive serious consideration from some internationally oriented businesses, but you do have to have technical knowledge, courses (five or six, focused in an area), and relevant work experience, which can be either domestic or international. M.B.A.s definitely have the competitive advantage in the job market, particularly for new hires out of graduate programs. For example, if you have done marketing for two years for a domestic firm, a company will assume that you know the basics, and this, combined with your international experience, will make you a strong candidate for an international marketing position.

For a *marketing* track the following courses, or their equivalent, are recommended: one course *both* in basic accounting and basic marketing; two in advanced marketing, such as international and foreign marketing, marketing research, and product management; one in international business; and one or two in finance, especially business finance, money and financial markets, or international investments.

A *finance* track is a bit more specialized, but it has one great advantage. Not only can it be used on the financial side of business, but it will also qualify you for international banking jobs. Recommended courses are basic accounting and four or five different courses in finance, such as international finance, business finance, money and financial markets, monetary policy, corporate financial reporting, financing international transactions, intermediate accounting, or international banking.

Don't be sidetracked into other business courses unless you have special reasons for taking them. Courses in industrial relations, managerial behavior, and the like, while interesting and beneficial, will not necessarily help you get a job in international business. One international business professional I know added, "I would recommend adding specific skills, not simply general courses—in finance, operations, marketing, [and] project management. Also, Six Sigma [a management training tool used to help eliminate mistakes and defects in a process or product] is emerging as a job requirement in many organizations, which essentially involves applying statistical methods to business management. Significant study or certification in this area is highly recommended."

Note: Accounting skills are important for finance and marketing. No one wants to turn you into an accountant (unless you want to be one), but for a successful career in business you will find an understanding of accounting vital for the insight it will give you into overall company policy and prospects.

What Role Does International Economics Play?

Economics is the science—often theoretical—that investigates the laws affecting production, distribution, and consumption. Understanding how the economy works is always useful; for a beginning job, however, employers often want business courses *and* an economics background.

Training Programs: Pros and Cons

Training programs in business can vary considerably. These are usually the best way into the big corporations. You will begin to build a resume that looks more like senior management. Sometimes there is no specialized training for a new employee. He or she is ushered into an office, shown the rudiments of a job, and expected to produce; this is more often the case in small businesses.

Where training programs exist they may be small and individually tailored or more structured and elaborate, with each stage of training well defined and organized. Generally, it can be said that the largest companies have training programs and that recruits entering them are considered to have executive potential.

The length of training may vary from several weeks to several years. In some companies, coursework at school is mixed with on-the-job training. Because of the diversity of the training provided, the only typical program is the atypical one.

You may decide on a business career when you have insufficient or unrelated academic and professional credentials. In that case, you may find it advisable to take one of the special business certificate programs offered at a number of universities. New York University, for example, has an excellent business curriculum for redirecting those with Ph.D.s in nonbusiness fields.

INTERNATIONAL BUSINESS

The globalization of many businesses has prompted recruiters to hire candidates who have combined their business knowledge with international finance, investment, trade, or marketing skills. A strong technical background, quantitative abilities, and language skills will make you a more attractive job candidate in this growing and competitive field. The first decision most of you will have to make is: Do you want to work in an international company—either a large multinational or a small business—or do you want to be a consultant who works with several different companies, often helping to fine-tune their international operations? (As mentioned before, I would steer a student preparing for an international career to add specific skills, e.g., accounting, finance, marketing, etc.) People with particularly strong backgrounds in business are desirable for global assignments because they will be more experienced with problems associated with international situations, such as integrating acquisitions, a job in which project management, change management, and operational skill are very important. It should be noted also that, despite the talk dying down about a second language, it is a skill not to be underestimated. While English is spoken and understood worldwide, I will bet on the success of the person who speaks Portuguese in Brazil before that of one who doesn't, simply because he or she is able to build deeper, more personal relationships. This is from a recent discussion with a Brazilian colleague who notes that every meeting he attends actually involves two meetings: the formal one with the boss who speaks no Portuguese, then the important one that takes place in Portuguese when he leaves the room. Both types of jobs will be discussed in further detail here.

Multinational Corporations

Many multinational corporations (MNCs) are highly autonomous international organizations with only a small staff in the United States. This is similar to the General Electric (GE) model, which maintains highly decentralized operations with a relatively small headquarters staff. For example: GE Consumer Finance is a headquarters operation that supports 36 autonomous country markets. These corporations generally look for those with academic and professional backgrounds in international finance and economics. If you don't

---

Special Target: Foreign Companies in the United States

Whether these companies are businesses or banks, you will be better able to compete with an M.B.A. if you have international training plus business-banking courses. Also look at the *Directory of Foreign Companies Operating in the United States,* published and updated every two to three years by Uniworld Business Publications (50 East 42nd Street, New York, NY 10017) and available at any large reference library.

---

have a traditional business background, there are still many career options within MNCs. For instance, those with backgrounds in marketing, advertising, public relations, legal studies, or human resources will also be attractive candidates. While there are a large number of positions in MNCs, the majority of entry-level positions are in marketing or finance. I would also emphasize the growth of new disciplines, project management and Six Sigma in particular. And though an undergraduate is not likely to have this and a graduate not much more likely, it would be a significant complement to a marketing or finance person to have Six Sigma skills. Thus, it would enhance your qualifications to obtain either formal certification or significant, dedicated study, and practice that one could speak to in an interview.

Special Tip for Individuals Interested in Technology

Check out the website www.techweb.com/careers for a vast amount of information on the information technology job market, including a job bank, resume posting service, and hundreds of company profiles.

If you are hired for international work with a multinational corporation, you will probably begin at the U.S. headquarters of the company, with occasional travel abroad for conferences, negotiations, or consultation. There is definitely a trend of fewer expatriates being hired, due in part to the current economic downturn but also because they are a huge expense for a company when there is a growing candidate pool of foreign nationals who are educated in top business schools, here and abroad. Such individuals are bilingual or multilingual, have demonstrated cross-cultural living skills, are technically trained, and are eager to assume positions of responsibility in their own countries. They may also cost the company less, as salaries are paid in local currency and thus tend to be lower than in the United States; there are additional savings in not having to pay the cost of relocation for the employees and their families. This explains why fewer Americans are now being sent abroad for long-term assignments.

In a few cases, language ability may lead directly to a job; for example, a Japanese language expert may be hired by an American export firm dealing with Japan, but these are definitely exceptions and generally occur in-country. The rule still is that you rarely get hired for your international background alone—you need something more, and the "more" is generally a strong business background, academic and professional.

Sometimes, however, assignments to company offices overseas can be arranged for several years at a time, despite the trend of hiring foreign nationals for overseas jobs. Additionally, some companies now use what is called short-term international rotation (STIR), which involves going from one market to another for a period of approximately six months to install a specific competency or best practice. Students might want to ask about this possibility in interviews.

A midcareer executive with whom I spoke notes,

The STIR phenomenon is a less intensive version of what I see as a new trend in international hiring which involves moving past the priority to foreign nationals toward the placement of people with specific technical or managerial skills anywhere in the world. For example, I know a Japanese person recently hired to head up marketing in a German operation.

The Top 15 U.S. Multinationals

The 2002 ranking that follows below was compiled by *Forbes* magazine. It was chosen because these companies have extensive overseas operations and recruit regularly from both bachelor's and master's programs. It is important to remember, however, that they represent only a small fraction of the international corporate opportunities that exist. These multinationals tend to cluster around a few sectors like oil, finance, automobiles, and computers. There are many other industry areas to choose from, including everything from fashion to agribusiness to service industries like the hotel business. Some people have a passion for an industry, like entertainment, whereas others are more interested in a function, like marketing, and don't care if they are involved in marketing toothpaste or computer software. Other individuals care more about work environment and culture, including such concerns as corporate social responsibility, commitment to diversity, and family-friendly work policies. For example, one student of mine refused to work for Procter & Gamble because of its controversial animal-testing policies; another declined an interview with Philip Morris over concern for the tobacco industry. Once you've found a multinational you're interested in, try visiting Hoover's Online (www.hoovers.com), which offers company capsule descriptions that include lists of competitors. It's a quick way to find similar potential employers.

Note: We have omitted from the list below Fannie Mae and Freddie Mac, which are among the top 15 companies on the *Forbes* list, because they don't have significant international operations. Top U.S. financial services multinationals such as Citigroup and Bank of America appear later in the international banking section.

American International Group
Berkshire Hathaway
Boeing
ChevronTexaco
ExxonMobil
General Electric
IBM
Johnson & Johnson
Merck

Microsoft
Pfizer
Philip Morris Companies
Procter & Gamble
SBC Communications
Wal-Mart Stores

International 500

Forbes also produces an "International 500" list of non-U.S. companies ranked by 2001 revenue. These include energy giants BP, Royal Dutch/Shell, and Total Fina Elf; automakers DaimlerChrysler, Toyota, and Volkswagen; financial services providers like ING and Allianz; manufacturers such as Siemens; and Japanese conglomerates Itochu, Marubeni, Mitsubishi, Mitsui, and Sumitomo. Many of these global mega-corporations recruit staff from around the world and offer interesting opportunities for foreign work. The top 15 of these companies are listed below including their countries of origin and web sites.

1	BP	United Kingdom	www.bp.com
2	DaimlerChrysler	Germany	www.daimlerchrysler.com
3	Royal Dutch/Shell Group	Netherlands/UK	www.shell.com
4	Toyota Motor	Japan	www.global.toyota.com
5	Mitsubishi	Japan	www.mitsubishi.co.jp
6	Mitsui & Co.	Japan	www.mitsui.co.jp
7	Total Fina Elf	France	www.totalfinaelf.com
8	Nippon Telephone & Telegraph	Japan	www.ntt.co.jp
9	Itochu	Japan	www.itochu.co.jp
10	Allianz Worldwide	Germany	www.allianz.com
11	ING Group	Netherlands	www.ing.com
12	Volkswagen Group	Germany	www.volkswagen-ir.de
13	Siemens Group	Germany	www.siemens.com
14	Sumitomo	Japan	www.sumitomocorp.co.jp
15	Marubeni	Japan	www.marubeni.co.jp

American International Group (AIG)

70 Pine Street
New York, NY 10270
(212) 770-7000
www.aigcorporate.com

Started in 1919 as American Asiatic Underwriters, this once-small insurance agency represented American insurance companies in Shanghai, China. AIG, as it is now called, has become one of the largest insurance companies in the world. The company's main services include domestic and foreign general insurance and financial services. It is the largest commercial and industrial insurer in the United States and number two in life insurance. Global businesses also include aircraft leasing, trading and market making, consumer finance, asset management, and retirement savings. AIG had 2001 sales of more than $62 billion and employs close to 77,000 people in 130 countries. Over half of its revenues are supplied by foreign operations.

AIG recruits undergraduates and graduates for Summer Associate, Professional Training (in underwriting, claims, accounting, and actuarial), and Management Associate programs. It also offers other positions in insurance, general business, and systems to more experienced candidates. Qualifications vary depending on the program or position, but in addition to business skills, AIG stresses languages and international experience.

Berkshire Hathaway

1440 Kiewit Plaza
Omaha, NE 68131
(402) 346-1400
www.berkshirehathaway.com

Directed by Warren Buffet (the "Oracle of Omaha") and his partner, Charles Munger, Berkshire Hathaway is a mammoth holding company with subsidiaries in a range of industries. Its main business is property and casualty insurance, both directly and through reinsurance subsidiaries including GEICO, the sixth biggest U.S. auto insurer, and General Re, among the world's leading reinsurers. Most famous for its market-beating investment portfolio, Berkshire Hathaway has used the cash from its insurance business to buy large stakes in firms such as American Express, the Coca-Cola Company, the Gillette Company, H&R Block, Moody's, the Washington Post Company, and Wells Fargo. Its directly owned subsidiaries include FlightSafety International, Executive Jet, Nebraska Furniture Mart, R.C. Willey Home Furnishings, Star Furniture, and Jordan's Furniture; jewelers Borsheim's, Helzberg Diamond Shops, and Ben Bridge Jeweler; and manufacturer Scott Fetzer. Berkshire Hathaway had 2001 sales of $37.6

billion and assets of $162.7 billion. Including direct subsidiaries, it has 110,000 employees at various locations; a very few work at the Nebraska head office. Berkshire doesn't recruit online, but its website has a list of links to its subsidiaries, some of which have international operations, where you can apply directly. A strong finance and business background will be necessary for most jobs.

Boeing
100 North Riverside Plaza
Chicago, IL 60606-1596
(312) 544-2000
www.boeing.com

   Boeing has been building airplanes for 40 years. With $58 billion in sales for 2001, it is the world leader in commercial jets (a nose ahead of Airbus) and the third largest U.S. defense contractor after Lockheed Martin and Northrop Grumman. Boeing also builds launch vehicles for NASA, makes satellites, is an e-commerce leader, and is introducing digital cinema transmission systems. If you're looking for an American company with international business interests, you've found it: Boeing is the biggest exporter in the United States, with more than 15,000 suppliers in 80 countries and customers in 145 countries. It employs more than 170,000 people in 60 countries and at operations in 26 states. Now headquartered in Chicago, the firm has key operations in Washington state, California, Kansas, and Missouri. Major units at Boeing are Air Traffic Management, the Boeing Capital Corporation, Commercial Airplanes, Connexion by Boeing (broadband for airplanes), and Integrated Defense Systems; its Shared Services Group and Phantom Works R&D unit support the other units. To work at Boeing you'll need a strong science or business background: The firm looks for candidates with qualifications in biology, business administration, computer science, engineering (aerospace, chemical, civil, electrical, industrial, mechanical, and metallurgical), chemistry, economics, law, marketing, mathematics, medicine, physics, psychology, physiology, and statistics. Internships are available for students with studies in the above areas at various Boeing offices in the United States.

ChevronTexaco
575 Market Street
San Francisco, CA 94105

(415) 894-7700

www.chevrontexaco.com

Formed by the 2001 merger of Chevron and Texaco, this is one of the world's biggest energy companies and, by some measures, the fifth largest company in the world, with 68,000 staff and close to $100 billion in sales. ChevronTexaco's businesses encompass every area of oil and gas: exploration and production; refining, marketing, and transportation; chemicals manufacturing and sales; and power generation. It also owns the Chevron Phillips Chemical Co., has an interest in Dynegy Inc., investments in 47 power projects around the world, and is developing advanced energy technologies. Active in more than 180 countries, it has production facilities in Argentina, Angola, Australia, China, Indonesia, Kazakhstan, Nigeria, the Republic of Congo, Papua New Guinea, Thailand, Venezuela, the North Sea, and the Middle East. ChevronTexaco offers career opportunities in accounting, earth sciences, engineering, finance development, human resources, information technology, marketing, management, technical positions, operations, maintenance, research, and retail sales. It also has internship programs in many of the above areas.

ExxonMobil

5959 Las Colinas Boulevard

Irving, TX 75039

(972) 444-1000

www2.exxonmobil.com/corporate

The world's largest energy company, ExxonMobil was formed by the 1999 merger of Exxon and Mobil, two industry leaders in oil, gas, and petrochemicals. The company had 2001 revenue of $213 billion and employs more than 100,000 people across 200 countries on six continents. ExxonMobil's main business lines are oil and gas exploration and producing, supplying, transporting, and marketing oil and gas around the world. It is a leading petrochemical manufacturer and also mines and distributes coal and other minerals and produces electricity. Outside the United States it is well known for its Esso and Mobil gas stations. More than half of ExxonMobil's invested capital and foreign sales are outside the United States.

The company has opportunities across the world but typically requires hires to have prior work authorization in the country where they want to work. It hires graduates from a broad range of disciplines with a variety of degrees. As an energy company, it employs many engineers (chemical, civil, electrical, mechanical, and petroleum) and people with training in chemistry, geosciences, accounting and finance, marketing, computers, human resources, management, law, and public affairs. Even more than most companies, it has need of professionals with experience in dealing with governments.

General Electric (GE)

3135 Easton Turnpike
Fairfield, CT 06431
(203) 373-2211
www.ge.com
HR Contact:
GE Recruiting Support Services SSI
P.O. Box 25
Findley, OH 45839

The General Electric Company is a diversified technology, manufacturing, and services conglomerate. It has twelve business sectors: aircraft engines, broadcasting (NBC), appliances, capital services, electrical distribution equipment, electric motors and industrial systems, information services, lighting, locomotive, major appliances, medical systems, and plastics. The company employs more than 311,000 people in 100 countries. About 40 percent of GE's total revenue of $126 billion comes from its foreign operations. GE offers opportunities in international manufacturing and sales and, through GE Capital, specialized positions in finance. The corporation offers internships and co-ops for those interested in engineering, finance, human resources, and information management. GE also sponsors professional development programs in financial management, human resources, audit staff, and information management and technology, which often lead to full-time employment. Other career paths within GE include communications, marketing, operations, quality control, and sales. GE recruits on university campuses and via its website.

International Business Machines (IBM)

IBM Corporate Headquarters
New Orchard Road

Armonk, NY 10504

(914) 499-1900

www.ibm.com

Big Blue is the world's biggest computer hardware manufacturer and business and technology services consultancy, the second-largest software maker after Microsoft, and provides thousands of related products and services, including information technology (IT) rental and financing. This IT juggernaut had 2001 sales of almost $86 billion. Its workforce of 318,000 resides in more than 165 countries. IBM's most significant growth has been in the Asia-Pacific region, and it is the leading computer company in China. Over half of the company's revenue comes from foreign sources. Though IBM looks most extensively for those with engineering degrees or computer science skills, employment opportunities also exist for people with degrees in finance, business, marketing, and mathematics. On the service side, IBM Global Services has many international positions. For those interested in finance, IBM Global Financing is the top IT financier, serving 125,000 clients in 40 countries. If you have a research bent, IBM Research is the largest IT research organization, employing 3,000 scientists and engineers in six countries, at locations including Beijing, Delhi, New York, San Jose, Austin, Haifa, Tokyo, and Zurich.

IBM recruits on college campuses, maintains HR sites for several countries, and sponsors an internship and co-op program where college students can get on-the-job experience and development career skills. Visit www-1.ibm.com/employment for details.

Johnson & Johnson

1 Johnson & Johnson Plaza

New Brunswick, NJ 08933

(732) 524-0400

www.jnj.com

Health care titan Johnson & Johnson has three business lines: consumer products such as its trademark Band-Aids, pain relievers, and personal hygiene tools; medical devices and diagnostic equipment, where it leads world markets for some products such as contact lenses; and prescription drugs. A truly global firm, Johnson & Johnson is a family of 37 affiliate companies with 197 operations in 57 countries and distributes its products in a further 118 countries.

It has over 100,000 staff (more than half work outside the United States) and racked up sales of $33 billion in 2001. Johnson & Johnson hires scientists, medical professionals, researchers, and all manner of corporate staff. Most openings for U.S. jobs are posted online, but if you want to start working immediately for a subsidiary in another country, you should contact that office directly. When hiring university students, the company looks for studies and experience in engineering, finance and accounting, human resources, information management, operations, quality assurance, research and development, sales, and marketing. Johnson & Johnson recruits actively on university campuses and offers part-time and full-time internships.

Merck

1 Merck Drive
Whitehouse Station, NJ 08889-0100
(908) 423-1000
www.merck.com

Merck & Co. is a global health care giant that bases its business on researching and developing pharmaceutical products and services for humans and animals. Its nearly 70,000-person staff work to discover, develop, manufacture, and market a wide range of medicines and vaccines including cholesterol drugs Zocor and Mevacor. Based in New Jersey, Merck has operations and subsidiaries throughout the world. In European countries, the company is often better known as MSD. It had sales of close to $50 billion in 2001. Merck offers career paths in corporate operations, finance, legal affairs, information services, manufacturing and engineering, pharmacy, research, sales, marketing, and public relations. The company has an Intern/Graduate Associate and Co-op Program for university students.

Microsoft

1 Microsoft Way
Redmond, WA 98052-6399
(425) 882-8080
www.microsoft.com

Microsoft is the world's leading software company with $28 billion in annual sales from products such as Windows and Office. It also produces video game consoles, interactive television, and web content and offers Internet access. Though already large, Microsoft is continuing to grow: Its staff numbers have doubled since 1997, and it now has close to 50,000 employees, of which about 16,000 work outside the United States. International operations supplied 27 percent of the company's revenue in 2002, and it has subsidiary operations in 78 countries. Beyond Washington state, Microsoft's main operations centers are in Dublin, Humacao (Puerto Rico), Reno (Nevada), and Singapore. With three-quarters of its people under 40, Microsoft has a fairly youthful work environment. Douglas Coupland's book *Microserfs* offers a witty look at life on the company's Redmond campus. While Microsoft obviously employs scores of computer programmers, there are many other potential career avenues with the firm. Its consultants and technical strategists work with customers in the United States and 35 other countries to design and deploy systems and applications. Other staff work in sales and support, marketing, management, and finance or as attorneys, designers, recruiters, business analysts, and real estate managers. M.B.A.s are particularly in demand. For university students, Microsoft offers the chance to intern as a program manager, software design engineer, or software test engineer at its Redmond or Silicon Valley offices. Many interns are computer science majors; others are expected to at least have some technical expertise. Microsoft has extensive information online about careers and job openings.

Pfizer

235 East 42nd Street
New York, NY 10017-5755
(212) 573-2323
www.pfizer.com

Pfizer is a global leader in health care with $32 billion in sales from drugs such as cholesterol fighter Lipitor, the antidepressant Zoloft, and Viagra, the blue pill that helps men with erectile dysfunction. It also makes numerous over-the-counter remedies and health products for people and pets. Among its subsidiaries are Goedecke, Parke-Davis, and Warner-Lambert. Pfizer employs some 90,000 people and sells its products in 150 countries. Headquartered in New York, it has various U.S. offices and major subsidiaries in England, France, and Japan. Pfizer's main divisions are global research and development, global manufacturing, pharmaceuticals, pharmaceutical sales, consumer health care, and animal health. Within these divisions you might find work in business technology, biology, chemistry, engineering, finance, marketing, market research, pharmacology, or public relations. Pfizer maintains a global job-posting system online. The firm does hire international affairs graduates, particularly for positions in global marketing, marketing research, and strategy. It actively recruits on campuses and runs internship programs for graduate and undergraduate students in its R&D, finance, marketing, human resources, production, sales, and legal departments. To apply for internships, contact the Global Manufacturing Internship Coordinator.

Philip Morris Companies (Altria Group)

120 Park Avenue
New York, NY 10017
(917) 663-5000
www.philipmorris.com

With worldwide sales of $73 billion and about 170,000 staff, Philip Morris is the biggest tobacco company in the world. It controls almost half of the U.S. market and owns Marlboro, one of the world's most recognizable brands. It's not all cigarettes, either. Philip Morris gets almost half of its revenue from food and beer subsidiaries such as Kraft Foods, Nabisco (now part of Kraft), and SABMiller PLC. Other operations include financial services, investment, and real estate. Subsidiary Philip Morris International operates in 180 countries. Philip Morris Capital Corporation is America's number-two industrial leasing firm. International tobacco and food sales supply over 40 percent of total revenues, a ratio likely to increase as smoking continues to decline in the United States. Philip Morris recruits extensively for international positions and has opportunities in business development and planning, corporate affairs, finance, human resources, information services, law, marketing, operations, R&D, and sales. The company's shareholders decided on a name change to the less smoky Altria Group in 2002.

Procter & Gamble

1 Procter & Gamble Plaza
Cincinnati, OH 45202
(513) 983-1100
www.pg.com

Chances are you've got a few Procter & Gamble products in your home: The company is the leading household products maker in America. P&G has close to $40 billion in global sales of its detergents, diapers, soaps, beauty products, foods, and drinks. It also makes pet food, and it added hair-care company Clairol to its stable in 2001. Altogether, 106,000 staff members helped put Procter & Gamble's 250 brands on store shelves in 160 countries from Albania to Uzbekistan. Brands and R&D are key at P&G. *Wall Street Journal* reporter Alecia Swasy offers a critical view of the company in her book *Soap Opera: The Inside Story of Procter & Gamble.*

Recruiting at P&G is atypical: The company follows a "promote from within" philosophy, which means it offers relatively few opportunities for experienced professionals. Most new hires begin at entry level, often straight out of university, and advance within the company. P&G recruits from about 100 schools each year, sourcing candidates based on their degrees, training them, and only later placing them into business units such as Fabric and Home Care, Family Care, and Health and Beauty Care (you can apply online as well). Procter & Gamble takes about 500 interns annually in the United States alone; about a quarter go on to become full-time staff.

SBC Communications
175 East Houston
San Antonio, TX 78205-2233
(210) 821-4105
www.sbc.com

Formerly Southwestern Bell, SBC is one of the Baby Bells hived from AT&T in 1983. The company is now a world leader in telecommunications, offering local and long-distance telephone service, wireless communications, Internet access, network solutions, and data communications. It serves 20 of the largest U.S. markets and has international operations in 28 markets, including Mexico, France, South Africa, Switzerland, Israel, and Taiwan. It is also active in Africa and South America. In the 1990s, SBC acquired other regional bell operating companies: Ameritech, Pacific Telesis, and Southern New England, and it bought stakes in Télefonos de México and West Midlands Cable Communications in the United Kingdom. With about 200,000 employees, SBC has a range of opportunities, particularly for engineers and those with backgrounds in technology or international business. It recruits online and via college campuses and runs a Student Management Program of paid internships in business, marketing, networking, engineering, and IT.

Wal-Mart Stores

702 Southwest 8th Street
Bentonville, AR 72716
(501) 273-4000
www.walmartstores.com

You'll be one in a million if you work for Wal-Mart. With over 1.3 million employees, the consumer juggernaut has some serious global staffing needs. The world's biggest retailer, with 2001 sales of $217 billion, has over 4,600 stores, about 1,200 of them outside the United States. Wal-Mart leads the market in Canada and Mexico and is expanding globally with over 282,000 staff working abroad. Other countries Wal-Mart operates in are Argentina, Brazil, China, Germany, Korea, Puerto Rico, and the United Kingdom.

Wal-Mart recruits extensively at universities and colleges and runs paid, 20-week management training programs. Career options with the company include asset protection, quality assurance, realty, operations, claims administration, finance, information systems, logistics, marketing, merchandising, communications, and general management at the company's various divisions.

SMALL BUSINESS AND ENTREPRENEURSHIP

Obviously, the companies listed above are only a drop in the bucket, and the number of small companies involved in international work is growing day by day. These companies are often more difficult to identify, and they rarely recruit through universities or executive search firms. This puts the responsibility on you to identify and approach such companies. How to begin? Look into an industry area of interest, such as multimedia or fashion, and do some computer searches into active companies in these areas. For example, if you are looking for a job in fashion, type the word "fashion" into one of the Internet search engines, and see what comes to the screen. If you have a particular interest in a region, research which industries are booming; business professionals with a knowledge of how to do business in the region will be in demand.

You can also review periodicals for articles. Begin a clippings file of companies that are active globally and seem interesting to you. If you can, approach them for an informational interview to begin a dialogue.

For the more adventurous among you, starting your own international business may be the answer. Although many business schools have created entrepreneurship concentrations within the M.B.A. program, it usually helps to have some amount of experience under your belt, either in a multinational or as a consultant, before you take the leap. In addition, there are numerous resources on the web about starting and working in a small business. Some sites of interest include: The website for the U.S. Small Business Administration at www.sba.gov; and www.thevine.com, a website of information for entrepreneurs.

INTERNATIONAL TRADE

The loosening of trade restrictions has enabled companies to import and export products more freely, thereby increasing the opportunities for those with interests in business, trade policy, and international affairs. In addition, the Internet provides a global marketplace for those hawking everything from Indian saris to New Orleans–style barbecue sauce. Opportunities in international trade exist both in the private and public sector. In the private sector, you might focus your career search on banking and financial services, advertising and marketing, consulting, tourism, transportation, or publishing. In the public sector, opportunities can be found with the U.S. government, foreign governments, and international agencies. The U.S. Department of Commerce, the Export-Import Bank, Overseas Private Investment Corporation, World Bank, International Monetary Fund, and the International Trade Center have departments that assist, regulate, and monitor international trading activities. Increasingly, states and cities heavily involved with international trade have agencies that perform the same functions.

The following are some directories and websites that deal with international trade:

Exhibitions and trade shows (www.tradegroup.com)
Trade Compass (www.tradecompass.com)

U.S. Council for International Business (www.imex.com/uscib)
U.S. Department of Commerce (www.ita.doc.gov)
U.S. Trade and Development Agency (www.tda.gov)

Another way to capitalize on your background is to try export-import companies, whose work is nothing if not international. These companies usually do not recruit on campus since they are small and have relatively few openings, and M.B.A.s do not usually seek them out.

Import-export companies may either serve as direct retail sellers, such as Pier 1 Imports or Cost Plus, or may sell wholesale to businesses. Beginning salaries are often less than those offered by the conglomerates, and the initial work may be in the stockroom acquainting yourself with shipping forms, bills of lading, and other documentation you should know about. But promotion comes rapidly for the talented, and long-term career opportunities exist.

To prepare for a career in international trade, you'll want a strong economics, international affairs, or business background. Language fluency, experience abroad, and trade knowledge are keys to obtaining jobs in this field.

For directories of exporters and importers, consult the *American Register of Exporters and Importers*, a directory of some 30,000 manufacturers and export-import buying agencies, broken down by product class. It is published by Thomas International Publishers. Other publications of interest are *Bergano's Register of International Importers* and the *Directory of United States Importers and Exporters*. More information about them can be found at:

www.cftech.com/BrainBank/INTERNATIONAL AFFAIRS/ImpExptDir.html
Tradeport (www.tradeport.org), funded partly by the Department of Commerce, offers comprehensive trade information and global import-export directories.

MANAGEMENT CONSULTANTS

The number of management consultants is growing by leaps and bounds. And little wonder: For those with a bachelor's degree, starting salaries in consulting positions range from $45,000 to $60,000. Graduate with an M.B.A., and your salary will probably start somewhere in the six-figure range! "Sign me up!" you might say. But wait a minute, just what is management consulting?

Actually, there are numerous types of consultants. The function common to all consultants, big or small, general or specialized, is to provide advice on how to improve a company's performance, and to formulate new business strategies or ideas for an organization or individuals. As the need for advice and help has grown with the increasing complexity of global competition, technological advances, and business restructuring, so have the number, size, and functions of consultants. The services of consultants are now sought by a wide range of clients, from government agencies and nonprofit organizations to advertisers and accountants, banks, and businesses.

A management consultant may work in a variety of areas, including strategic projects such as mergers and acquisitions, global competition, or market research. Other consultants work with the financial or human resources divisions of their clients. Information systems consultants update and streamline operating systems. According to a consultant currently studying at Columbia University's Business School, most of the large consulting firms have practice groups servicing banks and securities firms, and some even specialize in strategic and operational issues of the financial industry.

The world's largest corporations often have divisions that act as consultants in different industries. For example, General Electric's financial wing, a sizable segment of the huge GE empire, serves as a consultant on financial services to clients. Some large companies have their own in-house consultancies (e.g., Siemens Management Consulting). Large accounting firms like PricewaterhouseCoopers, in addition to auditing, offer accounting and administration services to companies. However, this has been rapidly diminishing in importance as auditors providing consulting advice to the same client create a potential conflict of interest. The future of the consulting arms of auditing firms is shaky, and some voices suggest mandatory spin-offs. Advertising firms offer public relations advice to companies having a problem with their image. The size of consulting firms ranges from hundreds of employees working in a huge glass-and-steel skyscraper to a single figure in a one-room office of a private home.

For a career in management consulting, an international affairs background is generally not sufficient to get you hired. In the first place, other areas of expertise may be required. If, for example, a management consulting firm contracts with a foreign government to revise its tax structure, it will form a team of experts to do the job. Experienced economists, taxation specialists, and financial experts will form the core of the team, often with the addition of a regional specialist. But in almost all cases these people have to be immediately productive. To weed out those who are unprepared to work as consultants, many firms use the case interview method, in which you are presented with a business situation and asked to walk the interviewer through the process of preparing a solution. So as you may imagine, consulting firms often hire business majors who have studied this method and have acquired strong analytical skills. Still, management consulting firms often look for people who are creative, strategic thinkers. The large consulting firms also hire a limited number of industry experts, in which case they look for specialized knowledge. For example, as foreign investment and business in the developing world increases, so does the need for consultants who can bring solutions and ideas to firms in these countries. If you are interested in working in this type of consulting, it is advisable to also take courses in development economics, trade, and international finance. Firms may hire students with Ph.D.s or lawyers or engineers and give them business training. McKinsey, for example, offers a 30-day mini-M.B.A. course for its new non-M.B.A. recruits. Nonetheless, jobs with the top firms are highly competitive. In addition to the advanced degrees required for higher level consulting jobs, 2–5 years prior work experience (in computer technology, energy, or finance, for example) is usually desired.

The top consulting firms generally recruit at the top M.B.A. schools, including Harvard Business School, Wharton, Stanford, Sloan (MIT), and Kellogg (Northwestern). Others, such as Accenture (Andersen Consulting), the largest management consulting firm, hire thousands of recent college graduates each year.

Management consulting can be lucrative, but you're often left with little free time to spend your paycheck. The hours are long, the work can be exhausting, and you're expected to travel frequently. Thus, lifestyle is a huge issue for individuals choosing consulting as a career: Long days, significant hotel stays, and many frequent flyer miles are the norm. Entry-level consultants are sometimes hired to recruit and manage a team of experts. It may be a while before you stop coordinating travel arrangements and actually begin consulting. That

Are you qualified to become a management consultant? According to John Helding, manager of worldwide recruiting at Booz Allen Hamilton, "A good candidate is someone who likes to solve problems (tough, one-of-a-kind problems), work with teams, and develop mentoring and counseling relationships with clients. A good candidate is also someone who can build relationships, both within their professional service firm and with the client and within the client's organization. In terms of credentials, we're looking for people at the top of their class and discipline. People who have a record of accomplishment. Business, engineering, and economics backgrounds are good, but people like I've described above can be found in any discipline. Cases seem to work well for us in the hiring process because they pose a problem and then allow us to see how the candidate approaches problem solving. How do they structure an assessment? What questions do they ask? What hypotheses do they propose? Are they tenacious? Do they get sidetracked? Can they keep a sense of humor through it all and keep pushing forward no matter how difficult? Studies have shown that structured interviews such as case interviews are more reliable indicators of future performance. That makes sense to me because they have identified the right kinds of people for us in the past when combined with assessment of resumes, the candidate's interest, their academic record, and their record of leadership and group activities."

said, the field is strong, and opportunities exist for those willing to make a serious commitment to the lifestyle and academic preparation necessary for such a career; top business schools are typical feeders into the firms that are leaders in the field.

For additional information, research the various kinds of management consulting and the client lists of the particular firms that you are interested in. You might also want to contact the Association of Management Consulting Firms (ACME) (www.acmeworld.org), the nonprofit organization whose members include domestic and international consulting organizations. Formed in 1929, it serves as a watchdog for the consulting profession, promulgating standards of practice and a code of ethics. They can be reached at 521 Fifth Avenue, New York, NY, (212) 697-9693.

The Alliance of Consultants (www.allianceofconsultants.com) is a group of independent business consultants, and the Institute of Management Consultants (www.imcusa.org) represents management consultants around the world. In addition, the Journal of Management Consulting (www.mcninet.com/jmc) is an independent, not-for-profit, educational organization for management consultants.

Professor Tim Opler and students in the Management Consulting Club of the Fisher School of Business at Ohio State University have compiled a comprehensive website for those interested in pursuing a career in management consulting (www.cob.ohio-state/~fin/jobs/mco). Another excellent source for information on the leading management consulting firms is the Vault (www.vault.com). Vault sells profiles to all of the major consulting firms that are quite detailed and provide insider information about corporate culture and hiring practices. It also recently published the *Vault Career Guide to Consulting*, available through their website for $29.95.

Top-Tier Consulting Firms

A.T. Kearney Inc.
222 West Adams
Chicago, IL 60606
(312) 648-0111
www.atkearney.com

A.T. Kearney, an EDS Company, assists industrial, commercial, and government clients in more than 30 countries. It earned $1.34 billion in gross fees during the year 2001. Its areas of practice include benchmarking and marketing strategy, executive search, environmental policies, organization effectiveness, and litigation support. The firm has a strong focus on what they call "CEO-level concerns," which include areas like leadership, globalization, and product strategy. Its merger with EDS, a leading technology firm, strengthened its ability to deliver information management and technology solutions. Kearney has more than 5,000 employees with broad industry experience and recruits from top business schools.

Bain & Company
2 Copley Place
Boston, MA 02116
(617) 572-2000
www.bain.com

Bain's new hires are trained as generalists. The company has a reputation for hiring young, energetic, and creative graduates, many with a business background. As they gain experience, they may decided to remain generalists or to develop expertise in a specific field like competitive strategy, marketing, mergers and acquisitions, information technology, telecommunications, health care, transportation, or retail. Bain employs approximately 2,800 people and maintains 26 offices globally.

Booz Allen Hamilton

Allen Building
8283 Greensboro Drive
McLean, VA 22102
(703) 902-5000
www.bah.com

Founded in 1914, this firm is one of the largest management and technology consulting firms. It serves senior management of business and institutional organizations by developing strategies and action plans for all management functions critical to the success of an enterprise, in particular, strategy, systems, operations, and technology. Booz has over 100 offices worldwide and more than 11,000 staff, making it one of the largest consulting firms that exists globally. It is not a pure strategy firm; one of the hallmarks of its business is helping clients implement its recommendations. In fiscal year 2002, Booz Allen Hamilton recorded $2.1 billion in annual sales.

Booz Allen is composed of two major business sectors: Worldwide Commercial Business and Worldwide Technology Business. Commercial Business is based in New York and works with strategy, organizational development, and change management. The Technology Business is based at corporate headquarters in McLean, Virginia, and deals primarily in the public-sector (government) market and has a strong defense-related orientation.

Boston Consulting Group (BCG)

Exchange Place, 31st Floor
Boston, MA 02109
(617) 973-1200
www.bcg.com

Boston Consulting Group is an elite strategic and general management consulting firm working to help clients develop products and business strategies and select investment practices to improve their effectiveness. It is recognized as the first consulting firm to specialize in pure strategy. Despite its name, BCG is very international and has more than 50 offices worldwide. A positive thing about the BCG culture is that there is attention paid to balancing work and life, not a common thing at many consulting firms. The work is intense, individuals are recruited from top schools, and employees work quite hard. However, it is not a "night and weekend" kind of organization—at least not as much as some other firms. However, the more senior you become in the organization, the more hours you end up spending at work—again, fairly common in the consulting sector.

McKinsey and Company

55 East 52nd Street
New York, NY 10022
(212) 446-7000
www.mckinsey.com

McKinsey is perhaps the most influential and well-respected international consulting firm in the world. It specializes in problem-solving, strategy, and program implementation for corporate and, to a lesser extent, government institutions. Founded in 1926, it now has offices in 44 countries and employs more than 7,000 professionals, serving organizations in both industrial and developing nations. Its clientele consists of organizations in all industries: manufacturing, automotive, transportation, banking, energy, healthcare, insurance, retailing, media and entertainment, telecommunications, public utilities, and public and nonprofit sectors.

McKinsey has the distinction of being the company where M.B.A.s would most like to work for the sixth year in a row, according to a 2002 Universum survey. It draws undergraduate and graduates from top universities and business schools and is known for its strong corporate culture. Most undergraduates leave within two years to attend business school—again, a common thread with other consulting firms.

The Monitor Group

25 First Street
Cambridge, MA 02141
www.monitor.com

Founded in 1983 by Harvard Business School professors and alumni, Monitor is a more recent, but powerful, addition to the list of top management consulting firms. The Monitor Group contains a variety of businesses, but its Action Company and Innovation Management practice are of most relevant interest to aspiring consultants. Monitor's consultants help managers reach and implement integrated management solutions in core business areas that affect their companies. It focuses on much of the same sector activities as many of the other consulting firms and has an incredible international reputation with offices around the world, from Moscow to Manila. Monitor has also worked with foreign governments. Its employees are young, and the firm has a very dynamic reputation.

Big Five

Accenture

1345 Avenue of the Americas
New York, NY 10105
(917) 452-4400
www.accenture.com

In December 1997, Accenture—then Andersen Consulting—famously petitioned to break away from Andersen (then Arthur Andersen), its sibling under the Andersen Worldwide umbrella. The case was resolved in August 2000, and Accenture was officially born. Accenture employs over 75,000 people in 47 countries and is recognized as a global leading provider of management consulting and technology services.

PricewaterhouseCoopers (PwC)

1177 Avenue of the Americas
New York, New York 10036
(646) 471-4000
www.pwcglobal.com

PricewaterhouseCoopers became a megafirm when Price Waterhouse merged with Coopers and Lybrand in 1998. This merger resulted in a firm with nearly 125,000 employees worldwide—mammoth in size, with offices in nearly 150 countries. Although its reputation was somewhat tarnished by scandal in 2000, it has bounced back and maintains a strong global presense. PwC hires both at the college graduate level and at the M.B.A. level, and its business areas are quite broad. The firm maintains a strong accounting service business, but also does consulting. It was named one of the top-ten best companies for working mothers by *Working Mother* magazine.

Deloitte & Touche Consulting

General Practice
2 World Financial Center
New York, NY 10281
(212) 436-2000
www.dttus.com

This consulting firm has been listed in *Fortune* magazine's 100 Best Companies to Work For for several years' running and has been named by *Working Mother* magazine as "One of the Best Companies for Working Mothers" for the past seven years; it proudly asserts its work-friendly policies and broad, flexible career paths. Deloitte & Touche operates in the following fields: information technology, financial information management, health care, manufacturing, financial services, public utilities, and federal, state, and local government. It maintains 700 locations worldwide and employs 15,000 professionals. Deloitte is proud of its multinational client base. There is a comprehensive career opportunities section on its website.

Cap Gemini Ernst & Young

5 Times Square
New York, NY 10036
(917) 934-8000
www.cgey.com

One of the largest professional service organizations, Cap Gemini Ernst & Young has over 56,500 employees in some 130 countries. Areas of practice include management and technology consulting, systems transformation, systems management (outsourcing), and local professional services. It works in a wide array of industries, including (but not limited to) health care, energy, financial services, manufacturing, and travel and tourism.

Bearing Point

1676 International Drive
McLean, VA 22102

(703) 747-3000

www.bearingpoint.com

Bearing Point (known until October 2002 as KPMG Consulting) works with clients in financial services, consumer and industrial goods, high-tech (a large focus within the firm), and communications. It has a very strong public sector/government practice as well. Bearing Point is another huge firm, with over 16,000 employees in 39 countries around the world. It expects its employees to travel a fair amount, especially if it is working with a client that has offices around the country or world. Compared to other firms, it tends to hire consultants with a fair amount of experience already, but because of its size, there are career opportunities at every level.

Government Contractors

Known in Washington, D.C., as "Beltway bandits" because of their proximity to the capital city and their dependence, in some respects, on the government system for survival, government contractors keep much of the wheels and cogs of certain government agencies in operation. Essentially, government agencies like the U.S. Agency for International Development, the Environmental Protection Agency, the Department of Energy, and the Department of Defense contract a large portion of their projects to consulting firms known as government contractors.

Each year, hundreds of multimillion-dollar contracts are awarded to these firms to carry out a vast array of projects in line with the objectives of the particular government agency. Projects range in scope from economic development in Eastern Europe and privatization in Africa to public health projects in Asia and environmental cleanup.

A number of these contractors place people overseas for medium-term consultancies (6–12 months). Remember, too, that all of these contracts are won by these consulting firms through competitive bidding. Aside from very experienced professionals with technical skills relevant to the project activities, there is a need for managers, marketers, and proposal writers.

Some of the large consulting firms that were previously profiled maintain strong public sector practices: Booz Allen Hamilton, Bearing Point, and Deloitte & Touche, to name a few. Other Beltway bandits are smaller firms like SAIC and Pacific-Sierra on the defense/security side of things, and Development

Alternatives, DAI, Chemonics, or Management Systems International in the international development sector.

There are some entry-level administrative positions that you can obtain with a B.A.; these provide excellent exposure to the consulting process and valuable experience with government contracts, as they are based in the D.C. metro area. Unfortunately, there is not really a "middle level" for M.A.s; the senior staff tends to have significant (7–10 years) of experience, and many have Ph.D.s.

A Note on Political Risk Analysis

In the 1980s, international crises in Iraq, Central America, Eastern Europe, and almost everywhere on the globe provided impetus for the growth of political risk analysis consultants. Many of these companies were started by and staffed with former American military and government officials.

The general function of these firms was to assess the risk to business ventures in various parts of the world. It was an important service to many corporations because of the access it often provided them to foreign leaders and to sensitive—possibly secret—information that the firms hoped to gain from consultants formerly employed in government service.

Many international affairs students express an interest in this field; unfortunately, it began shrinking in the late 1980s, and much of the work formerly done by risk analysts has been assumed by the emerging markets divisions in commercial and investment banks (see the banking section of this chapter for more information on emerging markets careers). As such, the work still involves political analysis, but it also demands a strong economics and financial background. Today, the work may be performed for a company by an outside consulting firm or by an in-house analyst. Sometimes a single individual (often a retired high-level Foreign Service officer) performs the functions. Some of the prominent consultants in this field include Control Risks Ltd., International Business-Government Counsellors, Kissinger Associates, and Kroll Associates.

INTERNATIONAL BANKING

The internationalization of banks and the growth of emerging financial markets in the capitalist world system translates into numerous career opportunities for those interested in international banking and finance. Career options range from corporate finance with an investment bank, public finance, sales and trading, to retail brokerage and asset management. Employers generally hire people with technical backgrounds in finance, economics, and politics who have international work experience and foreign language fluency. In many instances, it is not necessary to hold an M.B.A., but prior work experience is very relevant and often required.

Many banks offer summer associate programs that enable students to work on many of the same projects as permanent employees. Positions may be in U.S. offices or in an overseas branch. Recruitment for these summer positions generally begins in late fall or early spring. Note that job availability is subject to the unpredictability of the market. Competition for these positions is fierce, so apply early and be patient and persistent.

Commercial Versus Investment Banking

Commercial banks are usually more flexible about the background required of applicants than are multinational corporations or consulting firms. This flexibility extends beyond the conventional accounting and finance courses to include economics and expertise in international affairs—depending on the bank. Associate positions, which are entry-level jobs in major banks for those with an M.B.A. or M.A. in international affairs, pay $70,000–80,000 or more.

Investment banks are increasingly involved in the provision of global financial services by negotiating international financing through mergers and acquisitions, joint ventures, equity participation, and debt issues. These banks provide financing for businesses by floating their stocks and bonds. Most, if not all, U.S. investment banks have some international presence, be it international subsidiaries or affiliates. Many European investment banks, like Deutsche Bank and Union Bank of Switzerland, have long held an international presence and have become increasingly involved in Eastern Europe as the markets have opened to Western European, American, and Asian investment. If you are interested in the investment side of banking, include investment banks such as Goldman Sachs, JP Morgan Chase, Morgan Stanley, Merrill Lynch, and Lehman Brothers in your job search.

It is important to note that investment banks traditionally hire more M.B.A.s than M.A.s, for several reasons. First, there is a strong value placed on a very high level of quantitative and analytic skills. Many new recruits have engineering or computer science undergraduate degrees and/or two years of prior experience as an analyst at a commercial or investment bank out of college. The competition, therefore, is stiff, and so you can't expect to get by with merely graduate coursework in finance.

The emerging markets area, growing by leaps and bounds a decade ago, has come to a near standstill due to the economic events in the late 1990s. Latin America, in particular, has been hard-hit, but Eastern European and South Asian investments have suffered as well, taking with them not only dollars but also jobs. Other types of institutions that might have more of an appetite for emerging-markets investing are hedge funds and mutual funds, who either specialize in global-macro investing or have a small allocation to that asset class. For this field, besides strong technical skills and banking experience, economics coursework and a background in the politics of the region are especially helpful as you analyze the risks involved for potential investment. Fluency in an appropriate language is a requirement, and actual experience in the region can give you a strong advantage. The positions that do still exist are based around the world; Latin American emerging markets positions tend to be based in New York, and most banks have placed their Eastern European operations in London; Asia is researched from a variety of places including New York, California, and Hong Kong, or Singapore.

M.A.s and M.B.A.s are hired in the emerging markets area; however, remember that business school graduates often have had more intensive training in finance and investment and more related work experience (in general, at least two years as an analyst in a bank before attending graduate school). Economics majors may find work in economic research at the bigger banks.

There are some alternatives for those interested in the general concept of country risk work. Ratings agencies such as Standard & Poor's, Moody's, and Fitch work in this area, as do research firms including the Economist Intelligence Unit and the Eurasia Group. According to one finance professional, "I think some interesting areas for candidates to explore in this type of economy are risk-related functions like country credit risk or market risk management which can be more counter cyclical." Country credit risk is the risk of devaluation, debt default, and systemic banking crises. Market risk is systematic risk—it is the risk that broad market moves will result in losses on individual positions (irrespective of security-specific risk issues). For more information on these and other terms, check out the financial glossary at www.amex/com/dictionary.

| A DAY IN THE LIFE | ***An Associate in a Major New York Investment Bank*** |

I typically enter the office around 7:30 A.M. and spend around an hour familiarizing myself with current events. I read the *Wall Street Journal*, *New York Times*, *Reuters*, *Bloomberg*, *Asia/Latin America Watch*, and *FX* rates/stock indices for covered countries. Most of my days are spent doing country credit reviews to establish and maintain ratings and set or change country credit limits. This involves a good deal of macroeconomic research and conversations with our regional credit officers. In addition, I aggregate the firm's exposure to particularly high-risk countries through unsecured lending to counterparties (banks usually) in those countries and through margin clients who may be trading those countries' currencies. My day is often interrupted by questions from members of the firm's credit committee about various countries in which we may be interested in doing business. One day not long ago, I met with representatives from Lehrman Bell Mueller in the morning to discuss content and cost of economic forecasting data. For the remainder of the morning, I reviewed Mexico and Brazil economic forecast revisions (new current account/cpi numbers), then did a credit review of the Korean banking system for an upcoming meeting. Before lunch I assisted a colleague with Russia GDP numbers and then spent a working lunch with another colleague discussing joint country rating systems. After lunch I did more research on the Korean credit review by doing a Lexis-Nexis search and Onesource/Bankstat search on Korean banks for banking sector review. My day ended—as it usually does—around 6:30 P.M.

Overseas Assignments and Languages

If you are an American, it is unusual (but not unheard of) to be assigned immediately abroad. As we have seen in several instances, the trend is to hire foreign nationals to staff offices in their home countries; however, if you prove yourself successfully, then after a few years you may be in an excellent position to negotiate an assignment abroad, particularly if you are fluent in a language and have prior experience in that country or region. Language skills are always helpful but will not get you the job unless you have the professional skills and some experience to back your languages up. It is helpful to examine this from the bank's perspective; sending an expatriate abroad costs several times the amount as hiring a qualified foreign national; thus, expat assignments are generally reserved for training and management development opportunities, "rewards," and for high-profile, large-scale operations in which the bank wants a senior individual familiar with the corporate culture and strategy of the institution.

What Kinds of Banks Offer the Best Chances for International Work?

Major money center banks like Citigroup and JP Morgan Chase are all heavily involved in international business. In addition to commercial functions, they have taken on investment functions, mainly through mergers with other institutions. They tend to have fairly large expatriate staffs compared to other banks. U.S. branches of foreign banks also offer a growing source of jobs, as an increasing number of these banks, among them BNP Paribas and the Bank of Tokyo, take advantage of legislative changes that make it easier for foreign banks to do business in New York. They are also benefiting from an increase in investments by foreign companies in American manufacturing.

Entry-Level Jobs

In an initial training program, you might be first involved in full-time academic coursework, though academic work mixed with on-the-job training and rotations has become more of the norm.

In either case, the thrust of your training will be to acquaint you with procedures and problems in the evaluation of applications for loans. Since credit analysis is the heart of much commercial banking, there will be stress on accounting procedures, problems of finance, and money and banking practices.

Many large banks publicize their interest in finding the best "all around" individual rather than the graduate with the best technical background. Still, when you look at the statistics of those hired by these banks, you will find that the large majority of successful candidates have had not only coursework in finance and accounting but also experience in the field, whether domestic or international. Two to three internships may allow you to compete successfully with candidates who have completed a two-year analyst program. Sometimes banking internships are more difficult to obtain than full-time slots, particularly if you have no prior related experience; therefore, you need to be aggressive and use all of the contacts you can to obtain such an internship.

The following is a list of the top 10 international banks ranked by total assets in 2001. Other financial services firms of lesser size you may want to consider include Credit Suisse Group, ABN-Amro Holding, Morgan Stanley, Merrill Lynch, Crédit Agricole, Goldman Sachs, Wachovia, ING, and Wells Fargo. All of them are still significant global players.

Citigroup
Mizuho Holdings
Deutsche Bank Group
Sumitomo Mitsui Financial Group (SMFG)
UBS
HSBC Group
BNP Paribas
JP Morgan Chase & Co.
HVB Group
Bank of America

Citigroup

399 Park Avenue
New York, NY 10043
(212) 559-1000
www.citigroup.com

With more than $1 trillion in assets, Citigroup is the world's second-largest financial services corporation. It provides retail, commercial, and investment banking; asset management; and insurance. Over 250,000 Citigroup employees work at 2,600 offices and branches in the United States and over 3,000 locations in 100 countries across the globe, handling 200 million customer accounts in total. The current corporation was created by the 1998 merger of Citicorp and insurer Travelers Life and Annuity. Its other major brands include Citibank, CitiFinancial, Primerica, Salomon Smith Barney, and Banamex. Citigroup has five business divisions: a global corporate and investment bank created through the merger of Citibank and Salomon Smith Barney that offers financial products and services to companies, governments, and institutional and individual investors; Citigroup International, which oversees business outside North America; Citigroup Investment Management, which melds life insurance, annuities, private banking, global asset management, and pension plan management; the Global Consumer Group, providing retail banking, credit cards, insurance, and loans to individuals; and the Smith Barney Global Private Client Group, which offers wealth management and financial services to all comers. It is a leader in the development of risk management products, enabling customers to manage interest rate, currency, commodity, and equity risk.

Citigroup offers management associate programs, training programs, and internships for those with strong quantitative and analytical skills, financial aptitude, excellent academic records, and leadership potential. Its corporate website has a feature (Job Agent) that lets you search for specific positions. Some divisions also recruit separately.

Mizuho Holdings

1–6–1 Marunouchi
Chiyoda-ku, Tokyo 100-8208
Japan
(81–3) 5224-1111
www.mizuho-fg.co.jp/eng

The biggest bank in the world by assets ($1.28 trillion), Mizuho Holdings was created by the 2000 merger of Dai-Ichi Kangyo Bank, Fuji Bank, and the Industrial Bank of Japan. The group is a full-service bank that combines operations at Mizuho Bank, which leads Japan's retail market; Mizuho Corporate Bank, a huge lender to businesses; Mizuho Securities; and other subsidiaries (including a number that operate outside Japan). Its activities include managing trusts, securities, asset management, derivatives, credit cards, leasing, and venture capital, as well as running Japan's Takarakuji public lottery. At time of writing Mizuho—the name means "a fresh harvest of rice"—was engaged in extensive restructuring and trimming its 32,000 staff. Foreign operations are limited, but Mizuho Trust & Banking has offices in New York and Luxembourg and a small office in London. Mizuho Corporate Bank has subsidiaries in Dusseldorf, Paris, Manama (Bahrain), Hong Kong, and Singapore. The retail bank has offices in Hong Kong, Toronto, and Zurich. Mizuho Securities USA is based in Hoboken, New Jersey, and has about 100 employees.

Deutsche Bank Group

Taunusanlage 12
D–60325 Frankfurt am Main
Germany
(49) 69–910-00
www.deutsche-bank.com or www.db.com/careers

Deutsche Bank is Germany's largest financial services group, with over $800 billion in assets under management. Although its home market is Europe, it has branches in 75 countries and serves over 12 million customers. More than half of its 82,000 staff work outside Germany and over 50 percent of its shares are owned by non-German entities. About 18,000 employees work in the Americas and 6,000 in Asia. A universal bank, Deutsche Bank is organized into three divisions: Corporate and Investment Banking, Private Clients and Asset Management, and Corporate Investments. Recent U.S. acquisitions include Bankers Trust and asset management firm Scudder Investments. Deutsche Bank hires graduates in business administration, economics, mathematics, information management, physics, law, and liberal arts, and it values international work experience. A graduate degree is not always necessary. It recruits online, has entry-level programs in various areas, and offers specialist internships starting in Germany and subsequently at foreign offices.

Sumitomo Mitsui Financial Group (SMFG)

1–2 Yurakucho 1-chome
Chiyoda-ku, Tokyo 100-0006, Japan
(81–3) 3501-1111 or (81–3) 5512-3411
www.smfg.co.jp/english or www.smbc.co.jp/global
In the United States:
Manufacturers Bank
515 South Figueroa Street
Los Angeles, CA 90071
(213) 489-6200
www.manubank.com

Following the merger of Sakura Bank and Sumitomo Bank in 2001 and the creation of the Sumitomo Mitsui Financial holding company in 2002, SMFG became Japan's second-largest banking group, with assets of $770 billion. It offers an array of financial services including leasing, securities, credit cards, investment, mortgage securitization, and venture capital through various subsidiaries. The group has nearly 25,000 employees at 545 branches in Japan and 21 overseas offices throughout East Asia and in India, Australia, Canada, Brazil, the United Kingdom, Germany, Belgium, France, Spain, Ireland, Bahrain,

Iran, Uzbekistan, Egypt, and South Africa. It also has branches in the United States and owns Manufacturers Bank, which serves businesses in California. Companies under the Sumitomo Mitsui Banking Corporation umbrella include Bank of Kansai, Minato Bank, Wakashio Bank, Japan Net Bank, Sakura Guarantee Co. and Guarantee Company in Japan, Banco Sumitomo Mitsui Brasileiro, Sumitomo Mitsui Banking Corporation of Canada, PT Bank Sumitomo Mitsui Indonesia, Sumitomo Mitsui Finance Australia, SMBC Capital Markets, and Daiwa Securities SMBC abroad.

UBS

Bahnhofstrasse 45
Postfach
Switzerland
(41) 1–234-1111
www.ubs.com

Headquartered in Switzerland, UBS (Union Bank of Switzerland) is the world leader in private banking services and among the top banking groups in asset management (it has over $745 billion), investment banking, and securities. It comprises five business groups: UBS Wealth Management & Business Banking (private and retail banking); international securities and investment banking firm UBS Warburg; UBS Global Asset Management; American wealth management company UBS PaineWebber; and UBS Corporate Center, which coordinates all operations. UBS is highly globalized, with 70,000 staff at 1,500 offices in 50 countries. For M.B.A.s, UBS offers opportunities around the world; graduates with other degrees may find positions in accounting, client advisory or relationship management, finance, human resources, information technology, legal services, management support and specialized functions, marketing and communications, equities, fixed income and foreign exchange, investment banking, logistics, operations, risk control, and treasury. Its divisions offer internships in many of the same areas. Consult the group website for details.

HSBC Group

8 Canada Square
London E14 5HQ
United Kingdom

(44–207) 260-0500

www.hsbc.com

HSBC was born in East Asia in 1865 as the Hongkong and Shanghai Banking Corporation but is now incorporated in the United Kingdom and based in London. It's the biggest British bank on the block with assets of $746 billion and 177,000 employees, and it offers a full range of banking and financial services. HSBC has a global network of 8,400 offices in 81 countries in all regions. Hong Kong and the United Kingdom account for over half of its assets, with most of the rest coming from the Americas and the rest of Asia-Pacific. HSBC Bank USA has 450 offices. In 2002, it established a new headquarters at Canary Wharf and unified its diverse international operations under the HSBC name. Its subsidiaries operate around the world, providing personal and commercial banking, investment banking, asset and investment management, private banking and trustee services, securities, finance, insurance, retirement benefits, actuarial and personal financial services, property services, and shipping. For candidates with undergraduate degrees, HSBC recruits for commercial banking (mainly in the United Kingdom) and has trainee programs for executives, managers, branch banking, information technology, international management, corporate, investment banking and markets, group private banking, and asset management. These programs are open to students from all fields, but fluency in a second language and skill with numbers is important. In certain areas a C.F.A., securities, foreign exchange, or accounting diploma is desirable. For current students HSBC offers summer internships in its Corporate, Investment Banking and Markets, Group Private Banking, and Asset Management departments and in Commercial Banking. Detailed recruitment information is available online.

BNP Paribas

16 boulevard des Italiens

75009 Paris

France

(33–1) 4014-4546

www.bnpparibas.com or http://careers.bnpparibas.com

France's largest bank, with $726 billion in assets, BNP Paribas deals in all major areas of financial services, including corporate, investment, retail, and private banking. The product of a merger between Banque Nationale de Paris and

Paribas, it has operations in over 85 countries and 85,000 employees; 65,000 of these work in Europe. BNP Paribas Capital handles private equity. The group also owns BancWest in the United States, which operates Bank of the West and First Hawaiian Bank. The bank has several departments. Corporate Finance has 400 employees, most in Europe but in the Americas and Asia at BNP Paribas Peregrine. The Equities Department has 1,600 staff in 26 cities serving 35 countries. Fixed Income employs 1,100 in 30 countries, International Trade Finance has 300 people, Commodities and Energy financing 750, and Corporate Banking 1,400 in 40 countries around the world. It has opportunities in all these areas and others such as business advising, branch management, funds management, project management, research, and auditing. The majority of professional recruits have master's degrees. You can apply to positions online or to the human resources department in your preferred location; the procedure for internships is similar.

JP Morgan Chase & Co.

270 Park Avenue
New York, NY 10017-2070
(212) 270-6000
www.jpmorganchase.com

JP Morgan Chase is one of the top global financial services firms in the world. It manages assets worth over $700 billion and has operations in 50 countries, with offices in cities from Adelaide to Zurich. The firm was formed in 2000 when the Chase Manhattan Corporation and J.P. Morgan & Co. merged; Chase previously fused with Chemical Bank in 1991. JP Morgan Chase's 100,000 employees work in such financial areas as investment banking, research, private equity, investment management, private banking, treasury and securities services, consumer banking, small business services, auto finance, education finance, credit cards, home finance, investments, and insurance. For university students, it offers summer internships with its corporate groups and in wholesale and consumer financial services.

HVB Group

Am Tucherpark 16
D–80538 Munich
Germany

(49) 89–378-0

www.hvbgroup.com/english

Formerly known as Bayerische Hypotheken und Vereinsbank, HVB is Germany's number-two universal bank with $630 billion in assets and is the top mortgage lender in Europe. HVB operates 2,000 branches in 30 countries and in recent years has been expanding aggressively in its core Central European market through acquisitions such as Bank Austria. It offers the standard range of retail, corporate, and investment banking at its Germany and Austria and Central and Eastern Europe business segments, and further financial services through its global business segments HVB Real Estate, HVB Corporates & Markets, and HVB Wealth Management. It is active across Europe and has branch offices in the United States, Argentina, Australia, Brazil, China, Hong Kong, India, Iran, Japan, Mexico, Singapore, South Africa, South Korea, United Arab Emirates, and Vietnam. HVB has 66,500 employees; about half work in Germany, and less than 1,000 are outside Europe. Job and internship opportunities exist across all its divisions, but most new recruits and interns begin at an office in Germany. Fluency in German is nearly always required.

Bank of America

Corporate Center, 100 N. Tryon Street

Charlotte, NC 28255

(704) 386-5000

www.bankofamerica.com

Bank of America is the third-largest U.S. universal bank by assets ($622 billion in 2001). It has branches in 21 states and the District of Columbia, with offices in 40 countries. Its 143,000 employee provide a full range of banking and credit services to individuals, companies, and governments. The company's subsidiaries include BA Merchant Services, which handles credit cards, and Banc of America Securities, an investment bank. Its Global Corporate and Investment Banking group has offices in 30 countries and clients in over 150 nations. Career paths at the bank include asset management, corporate and investment banking, e-commerce, equities, debt capital markets; global markets sales, trading and research, global treasury services, leasing, and portfolio management. Bank of America's university recruiting and summer associate programs are described in detail on its website.

HELPFUL RESOURCES

The Institute of International Bankers, headquartered in New York, can be reached through their web page at www.iib.org. The institute was founded in the 1960s and acts as a professional association for "over 200 banking organizations operating in [the United States] that have their headquarters in 50 other countries," according to their website.

The U.S. Council on International Banking, also headquartered in New York, can be reached at www.intlbanking.org. It acts as a representative for the international financial services industry in all areas of international banking operations.

Wet Feet Press (San Francisco) publishes a number of helpful resources, including:
Ace Your Case! The Essential Management Consulting Case Workbook.
So You Want to Be a Management Consultant.

Published by Harvard Business School:
Harvard Business School Career Guide to Finance.
Harvard Business School Career Guide to Management Consulting.
Harvard Business School Career Guide to Business.

By Gale Research Company:
Business Rankings Annual. Written by Brooklyn Public Library Press Staff.
Encyclopedia of Business Information Sources.

Other recommended publications include:
Directory of Firms Operating in Foreign Countries. Published by World Trade Academy Press.
How to Find Information about Companies: The Corporate Source Book. Published by Washington Researchers.
International Corporate Yellow Book. Published by Monitor Leadership Directories Inc.
Peterson's Business and Management Jobs. Published by Peterson's Guides Inc.
Price Waterhouse Information Guides. Published by Price Waterhouse.

8

Nonprofit Organizations

WHAT IS A NONPROFIT ORGANIZATION?

Nonprofit organizations occupy a special, growing niche within society because they combine many elements of public enterprises and private corporations. It would therefore be a mistake to think of nonprofit organizations simply as charities, where the rigor and competitiveness of the market are sacrificed for the greater public good. In fact, nonprofit organizations often demand skills and experience on par with private businesses. The main difference is that the products and services they provide—such as knowledge of a certain region, research on the causes of social problems, or support for projects that alleviate poverty—are things that may not necessarily generate a monetary profit.

The variety of issues addressed by nonprofit organizations offers something for almost any individual who is interested in politics, social change, research, and advocacy. Nonprofit organizations fulfill missions as varied as helping refugees displaced by war or disaster; raising awareness of foreign policy issues; facilitating cultural exchange between U.S. and international students; monitoring and reporting human rights abuses; and supporting infrastructure projects or small enterprise in developing countries.

The structure of nonprofit organizations varies with the type of work they do. Many are incorporated under section 501c(3) of the U.S. tax code, and with this status comes a specific set of privileges and constraints. Nonprofit organizations may also be affiliated with the United Nations, with the U.S. government, or with other institutions such as universities. Many operate independently without any such affiliation. Funding for nonprofit organizations is also highly dependent on their function. Nonprofits may draw their resources from a private bequest or trust; corporate or individual donations; consulting arrangements with the United Nations or U.S. government; or grants from private foundations. Some nonprofit organizations also sell publications, reports, or other products to generate a portion of their operating revenue.

In many ways, nonprofit organizations are subject to the same market forces as private businesses. A recession or a drop in the stock market can reduce the flow of contributions from individual or corporate donors. Because the funding of these organizations is often precarious, job possibilities may depend not only on the size of the organization but also on the state of the economy and particularly the state of business. Changes in the political climate of the United States or shifts in political thinking on a global scale often force segments of the nonprofit community to rethink strategies for fundraising and program development. Thus, nonprofits look for creative, adaptable individuals with highly developed technical, management, and leadership skills, just as businesses do. Indeed, as more and more nonprofits establish partnerships with businesses or seek corporate support for their projects, the lines between the sectors are becoming more and more blurred.

For these reasons, job seekers should keep in mind that a strong belief in the mission of a nonprofit organization is only one of many qualifications. While most entry-level positions require only a bachelor's degree, middle- and senior-level positions usually require a professional (i.e., master's) degree in addition to significant work experience and language skills. Fundraising is also a constant concern in most nonprofit organizations, and experience in grant writing or corporate or foundation relations are also highly valuable and often critical for the executive level. Although the nonprofits listed in this section all include some international component, only some involve traveling or working outside the United States. There is a wide variety in the amount of international exposure and travel, depending on the position within the organization.

Because there is such a wide variety of nonprofit organizations, it is important to carefully evaluate your interests and skills before beginning a job search in this sector. Research a field (i.e., human rights, forest conservation), then look for organizations whose missions and areas of activity match your own interests. Consider an internship to get your foot in the door—many, many people secure employment in this sector through internships. You also need to research whether your experience matches the needs of the sector and each individual organization. On a positive note, entry-level positions in nonprofit organizations turn over quickly, so that persistence and research, as with so many other fields, are as important as good timing.

There are several job-search engines specifically focused on the nonprofit community. Two major engines that have both job listings and career information are:

Idealist (www.idealist.org). A project of Action Without Borders, listing non-profits around the world; volunteer, internship, and job opportunities; as well as a wealth of other information relevant to the sector.

Opportunity NOCS (www.opportunitynocs.org). Launched with a grant from the Packard Foundation, Opportunity NOCS was initiated by the Management Center in 1998 as a resource for job seekers interested in the nonprofit community.

In this chapter, we have attempted to segment, or classify, the nonprofit community into different areas that align with either different functions (think tanks, foundations) or issues (health, environment, etc.). Of course, some organizations perform in a variety of areas, so read carefully, as there may be some overlap.

RESEARCH AND THINK TANKS

The world of research and think tanks may be ideal for those who are strongly interested in both the academic and policy aspects of international affairs but who do not wish to pursue an academic career. These organizations are funded primarily by private donations or endowments and may also derive a small part of their income from the sale of journals, reports, or conference proceedings. Although their subject matter varies, most U.S.-based think tanks are focused to some degree on U.S. foreign policy or U.S. political interests.

While none of these organizations are explicitly tied to any political party or ideology, many of them tend to gravitate toward the right or the left of the political spectrum. By reading their publications or mission statements, you will generally be able to discern whether your own beliefs coincide with those of a particular organization. Some institutions sponsor (i.e., employ) only accomplished scholars who conduct their own research under the auspices of a think tank. Other research organizations, particularly the larger ones, also employ recent bachelor's or master's graduates to contribute to larger projects or to assist more established scholars.

If you have a strong interest in politics, public policy, and the theoretical issues in international affairs, and if you enjoy writing research papers and engaging in political debate, a research institute or think tank may be an excellent choice. Without the pressure to teach, think tanks offer an alternative to university research—a venue for research to be applied to the actual policy arena. The flip side, of course, is that for some the ivory-tower element can be stifling, and the work can be somewhat solitary. Some master's-level researchers have voiced frustration with the lack of regard they received from the Ph.D.-level senior researchers. Finally, if you want to see the impact of your work on actual policies, you might prefer a government institution or international organization.

Most think tanks require a Ph.D. for positions that are purely research-oriented. Without a Ph.D., it is likely that available research jobs will include some administrative duties. Because of their research orientation, the work environment of many think tanks tends to be highly intellectual. Obviously, demonstrated writing and research skills are extremely important for job seekers in this field—assisting with publications with a faculty member is a good way to get some initial experience in this regard. Also, many think tanks hire interns—this is an excellent way to try out the research environment to see if it suits your interests and academic skills.

Many policy institutes, naturally, are located in the Washington, D.C., area because of the access to government agencies. However, some well-known ones exist in New York and California.

American Enterprise Institute for Public Policy Research (AEI)

1150 Seventeenth Street, NW
Washington, DC 20036
(202) 862–5800
Jobs and internships: (202) 862–4881
www.aei.org

The American Enterprise Institute is known for its strong conservative bent, promoting limited government, private enterprise, vital cultural and political institutions, and a strong foreign policy and national defense. It fosters research on economics and trade, social welfare, government tax and spending, U.S. politics, international affairs, and U.S. defense and foreign policies. It analyzes public policy proposals and identifies and presents varying points of view on the issues studied. AEI commissions scholars to undertake original research and publishes their findings, sponsors conferences and debates, and makes the proceedings available to the public. Interns aid scholars and managers with research and projects. AEI also hires those with a bachelor's or master's degree for research or staff positions.

The Brookings Institution

1775 Massachusetts Avenue, NW
Washington, DC 20036
(202) 797–6096 or (202) 797–6000
www.brook.edu

Brookings is devoted to research and education in economics, foreign policy, government, and the social sciences. It organizes conferences and seminars on these issues and publishes its findings for the public. Its main purpose is to improve the performance of American institutions, the effectiveness of government programs, and the quality of U.S. public policies. Brookings has a strong reputation for its research and is known for its relatively liberal political views.

Its activities are carried out through three research programs: economic studies, governmental studies, and foreign policy studies. It also has an advanced study program and a publications program. Brookings offers unpaid internships in the above research programs and with education, communications, and information services. Their job hotline at (202) 797–6096 posts current job openings. Those with a bachelor's or master's degree are qualified for research assistant positions. The fellowship program is for doctoral students only. Up-to-date openings are posted online.

Carnegie Council on Ethics and International Affairs

170 East 64th Street
New York, NY 10021
(212) 838–4120
www.cceia.org

The Carnegie Council, formerly the Council on Religion and International Affairs, was established in 1914 by Andrew Carnegie. Since the beginning it has acted to support its strong belief that ethics, as informed by moral and religious traditions, is an integral component of any policy decision. The interrelationship of ethics and foreign policy is thus a unifying theme of all Carnegie Council programs, which include seminars, discussions, lectures, and the publication of books, pamphlets, newsletters, case studies, and the annual journal *Ethics and International Affairs*. The Carnegie Council also maintains education and studies departments and Merril House workshops. The staff is not large, but there are some positions available for those with an M.A., and it does have various openings for interns; see the website.

Carnegie Endowment for International Peace

1779 Massachusetts Avenue, NW
Washington, DC 20036
(202) 483–7600
www.ceip.org

Established in 1910, the Carnegie Endowment aims to promote international peace and understanding through research, discussion, publication, and education in international affairs and U.S. foreign policy. The Carnegie Endowment has a wide-ranging research agenda, which includes economic assistance and peacekeeping issues; nuclear nonproliferation; and the political economy of market reforms. It publishes the quarterly journal *Foreign Policy* and hosts the program *Face-to-Face*, which facilitates dialogue between international leaders and involved Americans. The Carnegie Endowment has a prestigious one-year Junior Fellows Program. The fellows either work as editorial assistants at *Foreign Policy* or as research assistants to senior associates. It is open to graduating college seniors or those who have graduated within one year of application. The application deadline is January 15. Employment opportunities are listed online.

Center for Defense Information (CDI)

1779 Massachusetts Avenue, NW
Washington, DC 20036–2109
(202) 332–0600
www.cdi.org

The Center for Defense Information is an independent research organization that monitors military spending, defense policy, and weapons systems. The director and staff regularly present military analyses on these subjects to the Pentagon, State Department, congressional committees, and the media. The CDI is committed to supporting an effective, but not excessive, military program, eliminating waste in military spending, and preventing nuclear war. The CDI offers full-time paid internships and employment opportunities in its research, television, and military units.

Center for Strategic and International Studies (CSIS)

1800 K Street, NW., Suite 400
Washington, DC 20006
(202) 887–0200
www.csis.org

The Center for Strategic and International Studies is a public policy research institution. Its mission is to advance the understanding of emerging world issues in the areas of international finance, the emerging markets, U.S. domestic and economic policy issues, and U.S. foreign policy and national security issues. The staff generates strategic analysis on the "new world disorder." CSIS publications—there are many—are designed to shed light on a special problem by defining its origins, importance, possible evolution, and policy options. The staff consists of 80 research specialists, 80 support staff, and 70 interns. CSIS accepts interns on a full- or part-time basis. It also offers minority scholarships and leadership awards to undergraduate students who apply as interns.

The Century Foundation

41 East 70th Street
New York, NY 10021
(212) 535–4441
www.tcf.org

Formerly known as the Twentieth Century Fund, the purpose of the Century Foundation is to research and write about economic, social, and political issues. It supports progressive public policy initiatives. The research concentrates on four broad areas: economic policy, governance and policy, media studies, and foreign policy. Many of its papers deal with domestic issues, but international subjects are researched as well, including: strengthening the United Nations; organizing new security arrangements; building democracies and institutions in the former Soviet Union; improving relations with Latin America; and restructuring America's defense and foreign policy institutions. The Century Foundation takes interns and lists employment opportunities online.

The Conference Board

845 Third Avenue
New York, NY 10022
(212) 339–0345
www.conference-board.org

The Conference Board is a leading business membership and research organization, connecting senior executives from more than 2,300 enterprises in 60 nations. Major areas of research include corporate citizenship; governance; the environment; health and safety; human resources; economic research and analysis; and quality management. The Conference Board produces the Consumer Confidence Index, a leading economic indicator. It employs economists, researchers, editors, and organizational and administrative staff. Openings are posted online at www.conference-board.org/aboutus/employment.cfm.

Council on Foreign Relations

58 East 68th Street
New York, NY 10021
(212) 434–9400
www.cfr.org

The Council on Foreign Relations aims to increase Americans' awareness and understanding of international issues, nurture experts on foreign policy, and contribute ideas. To this end it conducts meetings of policy experts, produces various publications, organizes events, and maintains a website. It has 3,900 members with special interests and experience in international problems. Since its founding in 1922, it has published the quarterly journal *Foreign Affairs.*

The studies program explores questions of international importance through individual scholarly research by its professional staff and through study groups and conferences involving members and nonmembers.

To encourage the next generation of foreign policy leaders and thinkers, the Council on Foreign Relations has a special membership program for younger Americans though various fellowships. There are 350 younger Council Term members. Numerous internships are offered, most on a rotating spring, summer, and fall schedule. Entry-level positions exist for research assistants, editors, and meeting planners. All senior-level researchers have Ph.D.s and/or many years of relevant policy and academic experience.

EastWest Institute

700 Broadway, 2nd Floor
New York, NY 10003
(212) 824–4100
www.iews.org

The EastWest Institute provides a forum for experts from various disciplines to examine issues such as economic reform and democratization in Eastern Europe and the states of the former Soviet Union, Western assistance to the region, and political, military, and environmental security. Based in New York, the institute has offices in Belgrade, Brussels, Victoria (Canada), Helsinki, Kiev, Moscow, and Prague. Interns are accepted year-round, and there are occasional entry-level positions available.

Foreign Policy Association (FPA)

470 Park Avenue South
New York, NY 10016
(212) 481–8100
www.fpa.org

The Foreign Policy Association strives to develop thoughtful and articulate public opinion on international affairs through informational and educational materials, television programs, and meetings designed to increase American interest in foreign policy issues. Its *Great Decisions* program and briefing book outlines the history and policy options of eight key foreign policy topics. The program involves thousands of people in discussion groups, seminars, and public forums. FPA publishes a quarterly *Headline* series on international issues and produces a useful weekly "Global Jobs" e-mail newsletter. FPA offers unpaid internship programs in development, editorial, events, programming, and public affairs.

The Henry L. Stimson Center

11 Dupont Circle, Suite 900
Washington, DC 20036
(202) 223–5956
www.stimson.org

The Henry L. Stimson Center is a small research and educational institute in Washington, D.C., with a focus on international security issues in which policy, technology, and politics intersect. Current projects include chemical and biological weapons nonproliferation, confidence-building measures in regions of tension, and advocacy of U.S. interests abroad. The Stimson Center offers paid research assistant positions and various internships; details are posted on the website.

Institute for International Economics

1750 Massachusetts Avenue, NW
Washington, DC 20036–1903
(202) 328–9000
www.iie.com

This organization was created by the German Marshall Fund of the United States. It focuses on issues it considers likely to confront policymakers over the medium term. The institute recently published working papers on the effects of U.S. economic sanctions, the political economy of the U.S. Trade Representative, U.S.-Japan relations, and global corruption. Most senior researchers have Ph.D.s in economics, but there are occasionally research assistant positions available for candidates with lesser degrees.

Institute for Policy Studies (IPS)

733 15th Street, NW, Suite 1020
Washington, DC 20005
(202) 234–9382
www.ips-dc.org

The Institute for Policy Studies, known for its progressive politics, is composed of scholars and activists who challenge politicians and prepare alternative directions to achieve real security, economic justice, environmental protection, and grassroots political participation. Through working groups and informal alliances, the institute focuses on themes such as the impact of the new globalized economy on the United States, the special role of women in developing countries, the role of the United Nations in global security arrangements, and new ways of understanding social/economic equity and human rights. The Latin American Program examines hemispheric relations with the goal of establishing an improved relationship between the hemispheres. IPS lists details about its many internships online.

International Center for Research on Women (ICRW)

1717 Massachusetts Avenue, NW, Suite 302
Washington, DC 20036
(202) 797–0007
www.icrw.org

The International Center for Research on Women is a private nonprofit that focuses on the dual economic and family responsibilities of most women in Africa, Asia, and Latin America. Established in 1976, ICRW conducts research and makes policy recommendations, provides technical services, and educates people worldwide about the contributions of women to economic development, the role of women in the family, and environmental and reproductive health issues that are of special concern to women. The center runs a fellowship program for researchers; openings for staff positions are listed online.

International Development Research Center

250 Albert Street, P.O. Box 8500
Ottawa, Ontario K1G 3H9
Canada
+1 (613) 236–6163
www.idrc.ca/en

The International Development Research Center was set up by the Canadian government to initiate, encourage, support, and conduct research into the problems of the developing regions of the world and into the means for applying and adapting scientific, technical, and other knowledge to the economic and social advancement of those regions. Regional offices are located in Singapore, Bogota, Dakar, Beirut, and Nairobi, the areas of greatest interest to the center.

The professional staff is made up of citizens of many countries, including the United States. Vacancies are posted online.

National Bureau of Economic Research (NBER)

1050 Massachusetts Avenue
Cambridge, MA 02138–5398
(617) 868–3900
www.nber.org

The National Bureau of Economic Research is one of the largest economic research organizations in the world. It works on economic problems of domestic as well as international importance. The results of its research are issued in the form of scientific reports entirely divorced from recommendations on policy. In this way, the NBER aims to provide well-researched documentation on important problems, objectively presented as a basis for discussion by policymakers.

NBER associates concentrate on four types of empirical research: developing new statistical measurements; estimating quantitative models of economic behavior; assessing the effects of public policies on the U.S. economy; and projecting the effects of alternative policy proposals. The International Studies Program also analyzes issues of international trade, exchange rates, and capital flows. The NBER does not have an internship program.

Social Science Research Council

810 Seventh Avenue
New York, NY 10019
(212) 377–2700
www.ssrc.org

The Social Science Research Council is a nongovernmental, nonprofit, international association devoted to the advancement of interdisciplinary research in social science. It offers fellowships for predoctoral, doctoral, and postdoctoral dissertation research in the social sciences in regional and topical studies.

United Nations Association of the USA (UNA-USA)

801 Second Avenue
New York, NY 10017
(212) 907–1300
www.unausa.org

The United Nations Association philosophy is expressed in the following quote: "The United Nations is the only institution in the history of man that has become indispensable before it has become possible. Putting its faith in the United Nations, the UNA is not unwilling to admit its weaknesses but emphasizes its strengths and potential." Located a few blocks from the United Nations, UNA-USA seeks to stimulate American public opinion in support of constructive U.S. policies in the United Nations. It tries to develop new ideas on how to make the United Nations more effective and provides American citizens with information on current UN issues through its information, research, education, and community action programs.

UNA-USA conducts a variety of programs. Its Policy Studies Program brings together independent panels of experts in specific fields to apply their knowledge to controversial international programs. The Communications Division provides unbiased information about the United Nations and sponsors a program examining the relationship between the media and the United Nations. It works with the media and Congress, trying to convey to the American public objective information about the United Nations and its activities.

The Model UN and Education Program enables some 60,000 high school and college students per year to participate in authentic simulations of sessions in the General Assembly, Security Council, and other UN bodies.

UNA-USA is the official coordinating body for the annual observation of National United Nations Day, on October 24. Although headquartered in New York, UNA-USA has a Washington office that feeds information on the United Nations to Congress and the executive branch.

UNA-USA offers unpaid internship positions to undergraduate and graduate students with international affairs backgrounds, writing and research skills, and knowledge of the United Nations or other multilateral institutions. Internships are available in communications, corporate affairs, national programs, education, and the Model UN.

World Policy Institute

New School University
65 Fifth Avenue, 9th Floor
New York, NY 10011
(212) 229–5808
www.worldpolicy.org

World Affairs Councils

World Affairs Councils exist in most major U.S. cities. In general, their function is to help Americans gain a better understanding of significant issues in U.S. foreign policy and to stimulate informed citizen participation in world affairs. At one time directly connected with the Foreign Policy Association, these councils are now independent and provide their own funding and programming. Most of the councils depend to a large extent on volunteers, although there are a few paid positions in the largest councils. Still, they can provide a source of networking. If you are new to a city you might want to call or stop by, get a calendar of events, and begin by attending sessions or speakers of interest.

Located at the New School for Social Research, the World Policy Institute is engaged in policy research and public education on critical world problems and U.S. international policy. The purpose of the institute is to develop and implement proposals for stable management of the world market economy, a workable system of international security, and a transnational civil government.

It publishes the quarterly journal *World Policy*, which focuses debate on U.S. international policy. Other projects include research on the arms trade, global change and liberalism, and Cuba-U.S. relations. It has a small staff but accepts interns on a regular basis.

Worldwatch Institute

1776 Massachusetts Avenue, NW
Washington, DC 20036
(212) 452–1999
www.worldwatch.org

Worldwatch seeks to promote an environmentally sustainable society. In addition to publishing research papers, it publishes *World Watch* magazine. Recent topics include stabilizing the global climate and protecting cultural and biological diversity. The small staff is said to be "future-oriented," with strong environmental backgrounds and, often, developing country experience.

AREA INTERESTS

If there is one particular corner of the globe that fascinates you, an area-focused nonprofit organization may be a good career choice. Unlike think tanks, area-centered institutions often encompass much more than just academic research. They may also work to build awareness among the general public of a region, to facilitate cultural or educational exchange, to promote trade with an area, or to advocate for a political issue.

Job seekers should keep in mind that a strong interest in a region is not enough for most positions with area-focused institutions. Employers are looking for the right combination of nonprofit management skills, language ability, academic background, as well as travel, study, and/or work experience in a particular region. Some specialized regional academic training at the undergraduate or graduate levels, as well as relevant language skills, are critical. For many senior positions, a doctorate is required.

The work environment of an area-centered nonprofit can be extremely stimulating and culturally rich. Because of the nature of this type of organization, your colleagues are likely to bring a diverse set of experiences to the workplace. Funding for these nonprofits comes mainly from private donors and foundations; because the climate for funding changes rapidly with changes in political affairs, often, money for regionally focused organizations follows security concerns or corporate interests. Thus, remaining aware and knowledgeable of news and political events in a region, even if it is not covered widely in the U.S. media, is very important.

American Council on Germany

14 East 60th Street, Suite 606
New York, NY 10022
(212) 826–3636
www.acgusa.org

This organization, as might be surmised from the name, seeks to promote better understanding between the United States and Germany. Drawing on resources from both countries, the council sponsors group discussions, personal exchanges, and joint working projects. In addition, it supports efforts by government, academia, and business that may yield benefits to both countries.

The John J. McCloy Fund, which was a gift to the council from the German government, provides fellowships to young Germans and Americans, giving each the opportunity to work in the other country. Fellowships have been in the fields of trade unionism, journalism, state and municipal government, law, and creative writing.

Other council projects include biennial meetings of American and German leaders to examine urgent global issues, biennial meetings of American and German young adults, and workshops, seminars, lectures, and programs for freshman legislators of both countries.

American Jewish Committee (AJC)

165 East 56th Street
New York, NY 10022
(212) 751–4000
Mail: P.O. Box 705
New York, NY 10150
www.ajc.org

In addition to local and domestic goals, the American Jewish Committee is very much involved internationally. It works to strengthen U.S.-Israel relations, build international support for Israel, and promote the Arab-Israeli peace process. The Jacob Blaustein Institute for Advancement of Human Rights works to build a positive relationship between Jews and the countries in which they live. AJC has programs in the former Soviet Union, Eastern and Central Europe, Bosnia, South Africa, Asia, and the Pacific Rim. AJC recently opened an office in Berlin, which will focus on the legacy of the Holocaust and anti-foreign sentiment in Germany.

American-Mideast Educational and Training Services (AMIDEAST)

1730 M Street, NW, Suite 1100
Washington, DC 20036
(202) 776–9600
www.amideast.org

AMIDEAST is what used to be known as American Friends of the Middle East. Formerly a small organization that encouraged cultural exchange between Americans and the people of the Mideast, it is now involved in all aspects of the development of human resources in the Middle East and Africa.

AMIDEAST's newest projects include strengthening private-sector enterprises and their training facilities and building democratic institutions. Programs include advising and testing; institutional membership; education and training; and language training. AMIDEAST does not have a formal internship program but accepts interns as needed. Most are employed at the headquarters in Washington. AMIDEAST occasionally offers employment to former interns. The majority of the staff manages activities at the headquarters; those interested in working at field offices abroad should apply directly to them. AMIDEAST has 11 offices throughout the Middle East.

American-Scandinavian Foundation

Scandinavia House, 58 Park Avenue
New York, NY 10016
(212) 879–9779
www.amscan.org

This foundation advances cultural relations between the United States and the Scandinavian countries. Among its programs are exchange programs; publication of books and periodicals; and cultural projects such as concerts, lecture tours, and exhibitions of art and culture.

Americas Society/Council of the Americas

680 Park Avenue
New York, NY 10021
(212) 249–8950
www.americas-society.org

In a very general way, the Americas Society works toward strengthening understanding between the United States and other nations in the Western Hemisphere. The Public Affairs Program provides seminars and conferences on current political and economic problems of the hemisphere; the Literature Program promotes the publication in the United States of Latin American and Caribbean fiction, poetry, and drama; the Visual Arts Program holds exhibits in the society's art gallery; and the Music Program brings Latin American music and performers to audiences in the United States.

Asia Foundation

465 California Street
San Francisco, CA 94104
(415) 982–4640
www.asiafoundation.org

The Asia Foundation aims to strengthen Asian educational, cultural, and civic activities with American assistance. It makes private American support available to Asian individuals and institutions that are helping to modernize and develop their own societies. It also encourages cooperation among Asian, American, and international organizations working toward these goals.

Asia Society

725 Park Avenue
New York, NY 10021
(212) 288–6400
www.asiasociety.org

The Asia Society is dedicated to increasing American understanding of Asia. It is concerned with the traditional arts and humanities, as well as with contemporary social, political, economic, and cultural issues.

Asia House Gallery, one of the best-known of the society's programs, introduces many Americans to Asian art treasures. The Performing Arts Program brings the finest Asian theater, music, and dance to America. The Education Program seeks to strengthen the study of Asia throughout the curriculum of American schools at all levels.

Its Meetings and Studies Program brings outstanding Asian and Western scholars, politicians, and economists before American audiences, at Asia House and elsewhere in the country. This program depends on the advice and participation of the society's Country Councils, each of which is composed of Asia Society members with special interests in and knowledge of an Asian country or region. There are councils for Afghanistan, Bangladesh, Burma, Cambodia/Laos, China, the Himalayas, India, Indonesia, Iran, Korea, Malaysia/Singapore, Pakistan, the Philippines, Sri Lanka, and Thailand.

Atlantic Council of the United States

910 17th Street, NW, Suite 1000
Washington, DC 20006
(202) 778–4961
www.acus.org

The Atlantic Council seeks to promote ties among Europe, North America, Japan, Australia, and New Zealand. It fosters debate on issues of international security and political and economic problems. The Atlantic Council seeks to identify challenges and opportunities, illuminate choices, and foster informed public debate about U.S. foreign security and international economic policies. Recent publications include *The Twain Shall Meet: The Prospects for Russia-West Relations* and *New Frontiers for U.S.-Japan Security Relations.*

China Institute in America

125 East 65th Street
New York, NY 10021
(212) 744–8181
www.chinainstitute.org

The China Institute in America has a dual purpose: (1) to educate Americans in various aspects of Chinese culture; and (2) to help Chinese-Americans adjust to the life and customs of their new country. The institute operates a School of Chinese Studies that offers courses in Chinese history and culture especially for teachers. The school also offers courses in computer programming for Chinese immigrants. Lectures, seminars, and conferences are held on a wide range of political, economic, and cultural subjects relating to China. Small art exhibitions are presented from time to time at the institute's gallery.

Council of the Americas

680 Park Avenue
New York, NY 10021
(212) 628–3200
www.counciloftheamericas.org

Though it is organized as a nonprofit, the Council of the Americas functions as an advocate for U.S. businesses investing in Latin America. It is directed and operated by its corporate members and seeks to increase cooperation and understanding between Latin American countries and foreign investors. Toward these ends, the council (1) provides for a direct dialogue between Latin American government officials and U.S. corporate executives; (2) coordinates the work of its member companies in sponsoring managerial education and grass-roots self-help in Latin America; (3) encourages direct dialogue between U.S. corporate executives and officials of the U.S. government concerned with Latin America; and (4) exchanges information on Latin American social, economic, and political development among its members.

Council on Hemispheric Affairs

1730 M Street, NW, Suite 1010
Washington, DC 20036
(202) 216–9261
www.coha.org

The Council on Hemispheric Affairs brings together U.S. leaders from the academic, business, professional, and public sectors to analyze policies and problems in inter-American relations. Issues studied include economic inter-relationships, military assistance programs in Latin America, ways to advance respect for human rights, opportunities for women and minorities in Latin America, and the right of Latin American trade unions to organize and function freely. The council publishes the bimonthly *Washington Report on the Hemisphere*. Unpaid internships are available to college and graduate students and recent graduates in the fields of U.S., Latin American, and Canadian relations.

Middle East Institute

1761 N Street, NW
Washington, DC 20036
(202) 785–1141
www.mideasti.org

The Middle East Institute was founded in 1946 to increase understanding between the people of the Middle East and the United States. The institute focuses on the following: a complete library of documents on the Middle East; publication of the *Middle East Journal*; conferences, seminars, and lectures; a business advisory service for businesses interested in trade expansion; and a language training program. The Middle East Institute offers unpaid internships for undergraduates and recent graduates. Interns may be placed with the programs department, *Middle East Journal*, development/fundraising, or the library. It also posts job vacancies online.

National Committee on U.S.-China Relations

71 West 23rd Street, Suite 1901
New York, NY 10010
(212) 645–9677
www.ncuscr.org

The National Committee on U.S.-China Relations believes that increased knowledge of China and U.S.-China relations is essential to the effective conduct of U.S. foreign policy. The committee hopes to promote this knowledge through a program of educational, cultural, civic, and sports exchanges with the People's Republic of China and through educational activities enhancing such exchanges. Conferences, meetings, and information services round out the committee's activities. Many high-level delegations of Americans have been invited for study tours of China, and many Chinese cultural and sports attractions—dance groups, a table-tennis team, an acrobatic troupe, and a gymnastics team—have toured the United States under the auspices of the committee.

Near East Foundation (NEF)

420 Lexington Avenue, Suite 2516
New York, NY 10170
(212) 867–0064
www.neareast.org

The Near East Foundation is one of the oldest U.S. organizations involved in technical assistance and rural development overseas. Although it emphasizes the Near East, it is also involved in other parts of Asia and in Africa. The NEF works to help people escape the trappings of poverty and invests its resources in trained U.S. technicians who set up overseas projects that benefit people in that area.

Among the kinds of work it performs are vocational training for young people, helping farmers by introducing crops suited to special weather conditions and by making available superior breeds of livestock, and helping villages through teacher training and disease control.

North American Congress on Latin America (NACLA)

38 Greene Street, 4th Floor
New York, NY 10013
(646) 613–1440
www.nacla.org

The North American Congress on Latin America is a progressive organization focusing on the region. It publishes the bimonthly magazine *Report on the Americas*, which focuses on political economy. Each issue usually features a single country with the aim of putting U.S. relations with that country into perspective. NACLA takes interns on a year-round basis.

Operation Crossroads Africa

P.O. Box 5570
New York, NY 10027
(212) 289–1949
http://oca.igc.org/web/index.html

Operation Crossroads Africa arranges work camps, study tours, and other projects for North American college students in African countries during the summer months. Eight to ten Americans, an Operation Crossroads leader, and African volunteers live in a rural community in Africa and work on a project that usually requires vigorous physical labor: digging foundations, hauling water, mixing cement. Crossroads offers an intense cross-cultural and educational experience and, at the same time, an opportunity to make a contribution to community development in Africa. Positions are available for those individuals who might be interested in leading study tours on a seasonal basis.

Partners of the Americas

1424 K Street, NW, Suite 700
Washington, DC 20005
(202) 628–3300
www.partners.net

Partners of the Americas fosters a closer relationship between the people of the United States and the people of Latin America by means of self-help projects. The network of volunteers works on nonpolitical, community-based activities. Partners works on technical assistance programs related to agriculture and rural development, cultural exchange, natural resource management, training, and health. Some 60 "partnerships" link a state in the United States with a country or an area in Latin America (e.g., Kansas with Paraguay, or Texas with Peru). One example of how the partnerships work: To build a school, one partner contributes the land and labor, and the other provides the equipment or funds. Job and internship opportunities are posted on the website.

EDUCATIONAL DEVELOPMENT AND CULTURAL EXCHANGE

If the field of education is of interest, but teaching is not for you, consider the nonprofit subsector that deals with international education and cultural/

educational exchange. These two areas are quite distinct: One deals with the development of educational systems in developing countries, while the other promotes educational exchanges (for students and professionals) between countries. Much of the work in both fields is project-based and requires strong project management, writing, and organizational skills. Jobs exist both at headquarters and in the field. If a job is based in the United States, a travel component (to monitor or implement projects) often exists.

In both fields, a master's degree is generally a minimum qualification for professional positions, though there are positions that exist at an entry level with a bachelor's degree; these jobs will largely be administrative in nature but may expand depending on the organization and your skills and motivation. In the field of international education, prior experience in a developing country is essential (usually 2–3 years), and teaching experience is often highly valued.

In international educational development, you might work in curriculum development, girls' education, human resources development, leadership development, or teacher training. The field of girls' education is a particularly big topic now, because of the sheer fact that girls in developing countries are often left behind when it comes to education, and studies have established the link between increased education of females in a society and poverty indicators like lower birth rate, infant mortality, and increased economic advantages for a society.

In educational/cultural exchange, daily work involves developing, managing, and administering programs to send students or professionals overseas or to bring them to the United States. These visits can have many purposes: to learn about a country by experiencing it firsthand, to engage in research of some sort, or to learn through training and visits to another country's top educational and political institutions. The Fulbright program is probably the best known of such programs. There are organizations that might bring a group of journalists to the United States from a recently democratized country to learn about a free press system, or a group of scientists to compare research and approaches to global warming and climate change. Jobs also exist on college and university campuses—in the Offices of International Student Services or International and Study Abroad Programs. One place to begin your research into this field is through the National Association of International Educators (NAFSA) at www.nafsa.org.

Salaries in educational development and exchange are on the lower end of the nonprofit world, mirroring the lower salaries generally attributed to the education sector. Thus, starting salaries are often modest. Obviously, this increases with experience, with midlevel salaries in the $30,000–$60,000 range, depending on credentials and experience.

National Association of International Educators (NAFSA)

1307 New York Avenue, NW, 8th Floor
Washington, DC 20005
(202) 737–3699
www.nafsa.org

The National Association of International Educators is a professional association that promotes the international exchange of students and scholars by supporting research and developmental projects and by conducting workshops and conferences in the field. NAFSA's members come from 50 states and 80 countries. It publishes many resources for the field, as well as monthly job listings.

Academy for Educational Development (AED)

1825 Connecticut Avenue, NW
Washington, DC 20009–5721
(202) 884–8000
www.aed.org

The Academy for Educational Development works with policy leaders; nongovernmental and community-based organizations; businesses; governmental agencies; international, multilateral, and bilateral funders; and schools, colleges, and universities to address human development needs in the United States and throughout the world. The AED provides advisory and staff services to these organizations and conducts in-depth research designed to meet today's social, economic, and environmental challenges through education and human resource development. International projects include advancing basic education and literacy, global training for development, and teaching services through the LearnTech project. Positions range from entry-level to program managers and officers. AED places only officer-level or above overseas. AED also offers paid and unpaid internships and posts intern and job vacancies online.

American Council on Education (ACE)

1 Dupont Circle, NW
Washington, DC 20036
(202) 939–9300
www.acenet.edu

The function of the American Council on Education is to extend the range and enhance the quality of higher education in the United States. It acts as the nation's umbrella for higher education, representing approximately 1,800 members, including accredited, degree-granting colleges and universities from higher education and other education-related organizations.

ACE also helps U.S colleges and universities internationalize. It seeks to enlarge the constituency and resource base of international education, international studies, and foreign language programs through collaboration with South Africa, Mexico, Latin America, Central and Eastern Europe, and a variety of international associations. Other programs include adult learning, business and higher education, and minorities and women in higher education. Teaching experience and courses on education, economics, and international studies are desired. A Ph.D. is preferred.

American Field Service (AFS)

198 Madison Avenue, 8th Floor
New York, NY 10016
(212) 299–9020 or (800) AFS INFO
www.afs.org

The American Field Service first became known for its participation in World War I when it was started as a volunteer ambulance service for the French army in 1914. The American-French understanding that resulted from this association led to scholarships for American students at French universities. From there, AFS broadened its activities to include its current concentration on high school students.

Today, AFS offers an opportunity for students between the ages of 16 and 18 to live for a summer or a year with families of different cultures. American students are sent abroad, and foreign students are welcomed to the United States. AFS also offers opportunities for teachers to come to the United States to teach. More than 10,000 students, young adults, and teachers participate in exchange programs each year. Abroad, AFS works with hundreds of local committees in more than 50 countries on six continents. In addition to the U.S. headquarters in New York, AFS has three U.S. regional service centers located in Portland, Oregon; St. Paul, Minnesota; and Baltimore, Maryland.

American Forum for Global Education

120 Wall Street, Suite 2600
New York, NY 10005
(212) 624–1300
www.globaled.org

The American Forum for Global Education was formed in 1988 by the merger of the Center for War/Peace Studies and the National Council on Foreign Languages and International Studies. Currently, the task of the forum is to promote international education and understanding. It provides consultations to schools wishing to globalize their curricula and offers professional development programs and study tours for educators, students, and administrators. The forum takes interns on a year-round basis.

Council on International Educational Exchange (CIEE)

205 East 42nd Street
New York, NY 10017
(212) 822–2600
www.ciee.org

Since 1947, the Council on International Educational Exchange has been working "to help people gain understanding, acquire knowledge, and develop skills for living in a globally interdependent and culturally diverse world." The CIEE's members are U.S. academic institutions and national organizations that send American students abroad or bring foreign students to the United States. Previously, it operated travel services through Council Travel, which was sold in 2001. Today, CIEE is divided into two interrelated but operationally independent entities: CIEE-International Study Programs and CIEE Exchanges. It also offers faculty development seminars for teachers. The council operates study centers in Africa, Asia, Australia, Europe, Latin America, and the Middle East. CIEE has an intern program and employs those with an interest in international studies, education, and nonprofit administration.

Experiment in International Living (EIL)

Federation International Office
P.O. Box 595, 63 Main Street
Putney, VT 05346
(802) 387–4210
www.experiment.org

Founded in 1932, the Experiment in International Living focuses on cross-cultural communication with the belief that living with foreigners is the best way to understand their culture. Thousands of young Americans "experiment" annually by living with foreign families, and many foreigners live with American families. In addition to hosting, the EIL also offers group travel programs, foreign language training, academic study abroad, au pair homestays, and volunteering. EIL is involved with 24 nations and recently added multinational programs to China, Argentina, and Turkey. EIL also offers programs for adults age 55 and over. Federation EIL is the worldwide network of Experiment in International Living.

Institute of International Education (IIE)

809 UN Plaza
New York, NY 10017
(212) 984–5400
www.iie.org

The Institute of International Education is a leading organization in the field of educational and cultural exchange. It administers scholarships and fellowships for foreign students and arranges for their admission to U.S. colleges and universities. It also serves U.S. students by screening applicants for Fulbright grants for overseas study. Among its other functions are organizing travel, study, internships, and research programs for U.S. and foreign leaders and specialists; providing information and advice on higher education in the

United States and abroad to individuals and institutions throughout the world; planning itineraries and providing hospitality for foreign students and leaders in the United States; and conducting seminars and conferences on major issues in international education.

The IIE activities can vary from the institutional development of a university in an emerging country to multinational corporate staff development, and from short-term training to long-term research on world food needs. Its overseas advising, testing, and training offices are located in Bangladesh, Brazil, China, Egypt, Hong Kong, Hungary, India, Indonesia, Kazakhstan, Mexico, Philippines, Russia, South Africa, Thailand, Ukraine, and Vietnam. Each year 18,000 people from 175 nations participate in IIE programs.

Metro International Program Service of New York

285 West Broadway, Suite 450
New York, NY 10013
(212) 431–1195
www.metrointl.org

Metro International coordinates citywide services and programs for foreign students in the New York area. It organizes programs and publications to help foreign students adjust to the city and learn about contemporary life in America. It also provides students with orientation sessions and opportunities to become involved with the local community and publishes a housing guidebook. Metro has held seminars that focus on business and foreign policy and homelessness. It also organizes a global classroom program and works on the New York City marathon.

Sister Cities International (SCI)

1301 Pennsylvania Avenue NW, Suite 850
Washington, DC 20004
(202) 347–8630
www.sister-cities.org

Sister Cities International aims to foster better international cooperation and understanding by forging relationships between cities in the United States and other nations. The concept of sister cities was launched in the United

States in 1956, when President Dwight Eisenhower called for massive exchanges between Americans and people in other countries.

Today over 650 communities in the United States are said to carry out meaningful exchanges with their affiliates in 121 countries throughout the world. For instance, Sister City relationships connect San Jacinto, California, and Zhukovsky, Russia; Louisville, Kentucky, and Quito, Ecuador; and Rochester, New York, and Waterford, Ireland. Sister City initiatives include creating sustainable economic development in tourism, trade, technology, and supporting municipal offices in newly emerging democracies. SCI offers internships in their Washington, D.C., office in administration, membership and conferencing, and grants/affiliation.

World Education

44 Farnsworth Street
Boston, MA 02210
(617) 482–9485
www.worlded.org

Founded in 1951, World Education uses special techniques developed in India for teaching illiterate villagers in several dozen countries to read and write. Central to the technique is the use of reading materials that help villagers with their work. World Education projects reflect the priorities and needs of their learners and have included promoting economic opportunities for women in Mali, the careful use of pesticides in Indonesia, and nonformal education projects in Thailand and Bangladesh. World Education has worked in over 60 countries in Asia, Africa, and Latin America, as well as in the United States. Job vacancies are posted online.

INTERNATIONAL DEVELOPMENT

International development is a large field, encompassing economic initiatives to alleviate poverty and political and social development projects that focus on democratization, civil society, and institutional strengthening. Development professionals work in the areas of microenterprise, urban planning, health, environment, relief, urban development, private sector development, social development (e.g., health, education), democracy and governance, and the strengthening of civil society. Thus, the field of development overlaps with some of the other sections in this chapter.

Qualifications vary dramatically across subsectors in development, but in general at least two years of field (i.e., developing-country) experience are necessary for a professional position in the field; with some organizations, the fieldwork requirement has increased to three to five years. This presents a Catch-22: How do you get experience in the field if no one will hire you and send you overseas without field experience? The Peace Corps is one of the best ways for American students to obtain substantive field experience, and it has the benefit of insurance, housing, training, and a small stipend. Non-U.S. citizens may look into similar opportunities in their own countries. Internships may be another possibility, or volunteer opportunities with church-related organizations or secular NGOs that sponsor such programs (such as WorldTeach, featured in Chapter 10).

Other desired qualifications for development professionals include some background in economics, fluency in at least one foreign language, project management coursework and experience, and a master's degree. Having an area of expertise—be it health, microenterprise, finance, or one of the others mentioned above—is also becoming more important. This may affect the type of master's degree you choose to pursue (an international affairs degree with a focus on international development or a master's in public health, for example). It is important to research your particular area of interest in development to see what the typical academic backgrounds are for people in the field. In addition, general nonprofit management skills—in financial management, budgeting, grant-writing, and staff management and development—are also highly valued.

The development field has become increasingly competitive as industrialized countries slash foreign aid budgets and as developing country nationals are educated outside their home countries to assume positions of responsibility back home. Hiring local nationals has an added advantage of contributing to the sustainability of projects while supporting local capacity building. All of these factors have resulted in a decrease in positions and a change in the type of position offered. Many organizations are working to enable local partners to implement projects as opposed to being implementers themselves. Thus, facilitation and partnership building skills are important.

An excellent place to start your research into the development field is the website of InterAction (www.interaction.org), the major umbrella group of U.S.-based nonprofits engaged in international development work. InterAction also hosts a major conference, has numerous publications, and posts job and internship listings. It is described in more detail below. The Society for International Development is also a major professional association, hosting an annual conference that is quite well respected and excellent for learning and networking. For a good list of nongovernmental organizations, check out the USAID website entitled "Development Links" at www.usaid.gov/about/resources.

ACCION International and ACCION USA Headquarters

56 Roland Street
Boston, MA 02129
(617) 625–7080
www.accion.org

This organization specializes in research, evaluation, and implementation of development programs in the United States, Africa, Central and South America, and the Caribbean. ACCION focuses on the problems of low-income populations and stresses the need for self-help in local, regional, and national development plans. ACCION provides tools of credit and training to create microentrepreneurs. ACCION has an excellent reputation in the field and thus is a competitive place to seek employment. It is always looking for individuals with experience in banking and microcredit, relevant language skills, and overseas work. ACCION does take unpaid interns from time to time but does not place them overseas. It posts volunteer opportunities and job vacancies online.

American Friends Service Committee (AFSC)

1501 Cherry Street
Philadelphia, PA 19102
(215) 241–7000
www.afsc.org

The American Friends Service Committee was founded in 1917 by American Quakers to provide conscientious objectors with an alternative to military service, such as aiding civilian victims during war. Its work began with relief and medical services during World War I, then broadened to include an emphasis on nonviolent solutions to international conflicts. Conferences and seminars involving individuals of many nations are held frequently in order to increase understanding among all nations. AFSC works in the United States and in various countries of Africa, Asia, Latin America and the Caribbean, Eastern Europe, and the Middle East. AFSC conducts programs of social, peace education, and technical assistance in areas such as reconciliation and community development "to enable people to discover and utilize their own power and resources." The Quaker United Nations office in New York and Geneva work in cooperation with UN delegates and committees. AFSC posts job vacancies and volunteer opportunities online and operates fellowship programs.

Cooperative for American Relief Everywhere (CARE)

151 Ellis Street, NW
Atlanta, GA 30303
(404) 681–2552 or (800) 521-CARE
www.care.org

CARE was established to help millions of people left destitute in Europe after World War II. The founders were 22 American relief, religious, refugee, and labor organizations. CARE's initial efforts were centered around food packages. It has since shifted its focus in the direction of self-help programs around the world to help people live in dignity and security. Among the 340 programs are: nutrition, development, private enterprise development, health, and education. CARE also helps victims of natural disasters, such as famine, floods, or earthquakes, and victims of civil strife in all parts of the world. Today CARE reaches 25 million people in more than 60 developing countries.

Headquartered in Atlanta, CARE has field offices in 14 U.S. cities and in each country where it works. CARE publishes an extensive jobs newsletter on its website. CARE also operates internship programs and, in December 1995, initiated a competitive fellowship program, which places six people biannually in country offices around the world. Most of CARE's regional offices accept volunteers for clerical and staffing duties.

Catholic Relief Services (CRS)

209 West Fayette Street
Baltimore, MD 21201–3443

(410) 625–2220 or (800) 235–2772

www.catholicrelief.org

Catholic Relief Services is an official overseas relief and development agency founded in 1943 by the Catholic bishops of the United States. It works to remove the causes of poverty, provide emergency aid to refugees, channel food to the world's needy, and promote social justice. To help solve the world's food problem, it places high priority on projects designed to assist the small rural farmer, emphasizes consumer cooperatives and rural credit structures, and stresses water resource projects and agricultural training programs. CRS also clearly states that it exists, in part, to serve the "poorest of the poor." An impressive statistic from CRS is that over 90 percent of its support goes directly to the field.

CRS has an international development fellowship program that places 20–25 fellows annually in yearlong assignments in countries around the world; CRS recruits each fall at major international affairs schools to fill the class. While the program does not pay a large amount of money, it is quite competitive, often leads to regular positions with CRS, and is usually filled by people with one to two years of developing country experience and fluency in French, Spanish, or Portuguese. CRS posts fellowships and job opportunities online.

Center for Development and Population Activities (CEDPA)

1400 16th Street, NW, Suite 100

Washington, DC 20036 USA

(202) 667–1142

www.cedpa.org

The Center for Development and Population Activities is dedicated to helping women around the world care for themselves, educate their children, and contribute to their communities. Through partnering with 138 organizations in 40 countries, CEDPA has provided family planning and other life-enriching services to millions of women since it was founded in 1975. CEDPA reaches out to the community, develops women's networks, and advocates at regional and global levels to bring about lasting, positive changes for women. In addition to the main office in Washington, CEDPA has offices in Egypt, Ghana, Guatemala, India, Mali, Nepal, Nigeria, Russia, Senegal, and South Africa. CEDPA posts internship and job vacancies on its website.

Childreach

155 Plan Way
Warwick, RI 02886–1099
(401) 738–5600 or (800) 556–7918
www.childreach.org

Childreach, the U.S. member program of a global child-centered development organization plan, seeks foster parents in developed countries as sponsors for needy children and their families in developing countries. Instead of giving cash handouts directly to families, the money goes to projects that promote safe drinking water, sanitation, children's health care, home improvement, and agricultural projects. Childreach focuses on the domains of building relationships, growing up healthy, learning, livelihood, and habitat. Childreach reports that 77 percent of every dollar raised goes toward implementing programs that benefit sponsored children and their communities. The great majority of the plan's expenditures are for its overseas programs and services, while a small amount also is reserved for development education in the United States and an intercultural communications program.

Food First/Institute for Food and Development Policy

398 60th Street
Oakland, CA 94618
(510) 654–4400
www.foodfirst.org

Founded in 1975, the Institute for Food and Development Policy, better known as Food First, is a think tank and action center supported by members. It is dedicated to highlighting root causes and solutions to hunger and poverty around the world. Seeking to establish food as a fundamental human right, it conducts research and advocacy related to economic and social human rights and reshaping the global food system. It produces a variety of print and electronic media tools for education and provides training to teachers and students, policymakers, the media, and other interested parties. On the international front, Food First played a role in advocating for fair trade policy at the World Trade Organization's meeting held in Doha, Qatar. Food First posts intern and job vacancies online.

Institute for Sustainable Communities (ISC)

56 College Street
Montpelier, VT 05602
(802) 229–2900
www.iscvt.org

Founded in 1991, the Institute for Sustainable Communities is an independent nonprofit organization that helps communities in emerging democracies solve environmental, economic, and social concerns of sustainable development. ISC provides training, advice, and grants to broad-based groups of people within communities. To date, ISC has managed more than 50 projects in 15 countries. It is based in Vermont and has offices in Bulgaria, Macedonia, Russia, and Ukraine. ISC posts vacancies for internships, consultants, and regular employment online.

InterAction

1717 Massachusetts Avenue, NW, Suite 701
Washington, DC 20036
(202) 667–8227
www.interaction.org

InterAction provides a forum for cooperation, joint planning, and the exchange of ideas and information among more than 160 U.S.-based nonprofit organizations working worldwide. InterAction is organized as a confederation of member agencies and is governed by a board of directors composed of one representative from each member organization. It is supported by its membership.

InterAction publishes *Member Profiles*, which reviews the activities of U.S. nonprofit organizations engaged in agriculture, community development, education, and health. In addition, InterAction publishes a well respectednewsletter (*Monday Developments*), which lists job openings for a variety of development organizations.

Although InterAction is a coalition of private and voluntary organizations working in international relief, migration and refugee assistance, and development education, it does not give grants or place employees with member agencies. It posts job and internship vacancies within InterAction on its website.

Jesuit Refugee Services (JRS)

International Headquarters
C.P. 6139
I–00195 Roma Prati
Italy
+39—06 68 97 73 86
www.jesref.org

Founded in 1980, Jesuit Refugee Services has a mission to accompany, serve, and defend the rights of refugees and displaced people. It is at work in more than 40 countries offering refugees "practical and spiritual support, according to their humanitarian needs, regardless of their beliefs." JRS posts global job vacancies online.

Oxfam-America

26 West Street
Boston, MA 02111
(617) 482–1211 or (800) 77-OXFAM
www.oxfamamerica.org

Oxfam (Oxford Committee for Famine Relief) provides direct relief as well as long-term development assistance around the world. Field directors employed by Oxfam implement projects in which local people do the work, make the decisions, and take charge of their own development. Projects are in the fields of nutrition, health, agriculture, family planning, and poverty and social justice. Oxfam also produces and distributes educational materials on issues of hunger and development in industrialized countries. There are 12 autonomous Oxfam organizations throughout the world. Most full-time positions at Oxfam require prior field experience in a developing country. Oxfam posts job vacancies and volunteer opportunities online.

Save the Children

54 Wilton Road
Westport, CT 06880
(203) 221–4000 or (800) 728–3843
www.savethechildren.org

Since 1932, Save the Children has been dedicated to improving children's lives and works in the area of women and children's development. It operates across the United States and in nearly 50 countries. Working in partnership with families, communities, governments, individuals, corporations, businesses, foundations, and other NGOs, its programs include health, nutrition, education, economic opportunity, and emergency and disaster relief. It requires significant field experience (3–5 years) for the vast majority of its positions. It posts volunteer and internship opportunities and job vacancies online.

Society for International Development (SID)

1875 Connecticut Avenue, NW
Washington, DC 20009
(202) 884–8500
www.sidint.org

Created in 1957, the Society for International Development is a global network of more than 3,000 individual members and 55 institutional members concerned about sustainable development. SID provides a forum for the exchange of ideas, facts, and experiences among professionals from 125 countries concerned with the problems of economic and social development in modernizing societies. To this effect, SID publishes the quarterly journal *Development,* which present opinions and comments of scholars and practitioners in the field, and the biweekly newsletter *Bridges.* It also holds conferences on the regional and international level. The SID secretariat is based in Rome and has chapters worldwide; there are ten chapters in the United States.

Sponsors of SID include many national banks in various parts of the world, and its members include such diverse organizations as Planned Parenthood, the OECD, and banks, development bodies, research organizations, and foundations in many countries. The society's priority for the twenty-first century is to shift the focus of development policy from territorial to individual security and to strengthen civil society to promote a sustainable world.

TechnoServe

49 Day Street
Norwalk, CT 06854
(203) 852–0377
www.technoserve.org

TechnoServe attempts to improve the long-term economic and social well-being of people in the developing world by fostering small and medium-sized enterprises, thereby applying business solutions for rural poverty. TechnoServe works primarily in rural agricultural sectors in Latin America and Africa to provide technical and managerial training. In Ghana, for example, Techno-Serve is helping low-income people build a cooperative business in which they can grow, manage, and export cashews. In places like Kenya, Peru, and El Salvador, TechnoServe works to open markets to rural farmers.

TechnoServe, like Save the Children, rarely accepts entry-level applicants for its professional positions, preferring those with 3–5 years of related experience. TechnoServe has offices in Washington, D.C., the United Kingdom, Mozambique, Nicaragua, Peru, El Salvador, Ghana, Honduras, Kenya, Uganda, and Tanzania, with an affiliate in Poland. It posts job vacancies online.

Trickle Up Program (TUP)
54 Riverside Drive PH
New York, NY 10024
(212) 362–7958
www.trickleup.org

Founded in 1979, the Trickle Up Program creates new opportunities for the lowest-income populations of the world to start or expand their own microenterprises. TUP is committed to empowering the most impoverished people in the United States, the Americas, Africa, and Asia to take their first steps out of poverty by providing conditional seed capital and basic business training. If a group of five or more people in a developing country wishes to invest 1,000 or more hours of their time, they can apply for a TUP grant of $100 to initiate a profit-making enterprise (the amount is $700 for U.S. applicants). TUP has had extraordinary success in helping low-income populations to become self-supporting. Professionals from development agencies who volunteer their services to the organization perform most of the coordination in the field. Trickle Up takes interns and occasionally hires for its small, full-time office staff. Trickle Up posts intern and job vacancies on its website.

U.S. Committee for UNICEF
333 East 38th Street
New York, NY 10016
(800) FOR-KIDS
www.unicefusa.org

The U.S. Committee for UNICEF is one of 37 national committees set up around the world to raise financial assistance for UNICEF, which works around the world to provide health care, clean water, improved nutrition, and education to millions of children. In addition to raising funds, the U.S. organization aims to inform Americans about UNICEF and the problems of the world's children. The committee produces educational material for primary and secondary schools. Major fundraising programs for UNICEF include the "Trick-or-Treat for UNICEF" Halloween collections, greeting card sales, a bike-a-thon and swim-a-thon, recycling for UNICEF, and film benefits. It posts volunteer opportunities online.

Volunteers in Technical Assistance (VITA)

1600 Wilson Boulevard, Suite 710
Arlington, VA 22209
(703) 276–1800
www.vita.org

Volunteers in Technical Assistance makes information and technical resources aimed at fostering self-sufficiency available to individuals and groups in developing countries. It places special emphasis on agriculture and food processing, renewable energy applications, water supply and sanitation, housing and construction, and small-business development. VITA programs in information services and communication technology help field projects around the world by providing low-cost connectivity for remote areas. VITA is implementing long-term programs in Guinea, Morocco, and Ukraine. VITA also supplies disaster-related information to relief agencies around the world.

ENVIRONMENT, ENERGY, AND POPULATION

One of the most interesting jobs that I can imagine belongs to one of my former students, now heading the office of World Wildlife Fund/China, where he oversees a wide range of projects aimed at conserving the diversity of species—plant and animal—in that vast country. His experience in China prior to graduate school, combined with a master's degree in international affairs focusing on economic development and the environment, along with several strategic internships, prepared him well for this challenging position.

Another former student—a returned Peace Corps volunteer—who graduated with a joint master of international affairs and master of public health,

A Development Project Assistant

As a country associate in the Dominican Republic, my areas of responsibility include project and program development and management, project monitoring, institutional strengthening, and program planning and administration. My activities today serve as a pretty accurate example of what my job is like. After arriving at the office, I began my morning activities; as we are currently restructuring our country program, we are in the process of developing a strategic program plan for the next three years, which will state what program areas we will focus on. Although we are advocating a focus on human rights projects working with populations who have traditionally suffered the most social and economic injustices in the country, we also recognize the need for more immediate assistance, like microcredit projects.

Thus, I began the day organizing a debriefing session on an external evaluation that took place last month to determine the viability of implementing a small-enterprise development program. I designed a general scope of work for the evaluation, found and hired evaluators, took care of all logistics, prepared background documentation, arranged translations, etc. Our debriefing reviewed all aspects of how the evaluation took place, discussed lessons learned, and brainstormed strategies for improving the organization of future evaluations.

Then, I met with an external consultant working as a project coordinator for us; we discussed how to implement the final stages of this project and arranged for me to travel to the field to discuss future project monitoring with the local community organization implementing the project. My last morning activity was to prepare for my attendance at workshop tomorrow where NGO representatives will meet to share experiences and plan future collaboration to promote legal and civil rights for the poorer populations in this country. (We are financing this workshop.)

In the afternoon, I worked in the area of program planning and administration by completing a semiannual report on the budgets and progress of all of our country projects to be sent to headquarters. This involved liaising with the project managers and our accountant to provide a current report of our large project portfolio, which includes projects in agriculture, nutrition water, and sanitation, as well as the small project portfolio. I left for home just as daylight was fading away and the usual, hectic traffic jams were springing up all over Santo Domingo.

has spent the last two years in Zaire working on health-related projects in the Rwandan refugee camps.

As you can see from the two careers described above, the fields of environment, energy, and population encompass a wide range of activities. Some are involved in advocacy, some in research, as well as in direct program and project management in other (mostly developing) countries. According to Kevin

Doyle, program director at the Environmental Careers Organization, the area for which most funds and attention are being directed is water. Developing and developed countries are consumed with the important issue of providing safe, accessible drinking water to their urban and rural populations. There are also critical initiatives around sanitation and disease (malaria, dengue fever, etc.). Energy and climate change are two other areas where quite a bit of attention is being paid, and partnerships are being developed among NGOs, the private sector, and multilateral organizations to develop alternative energy sources and to try to combat the negative effects of greenhouse gases.

Qualifications for professional positions usually require a master's degree, but some entry-level administrative positions are available to those with a bachelor's degree, and they can provide excellent exposure to relevant issues such as clean water and air, family planning, wildlife conservation, and forest management. A technical undergraduate background or graduate school degree—in environmental engineering, biology, geology, or a similar area of interest—is ideal, although some positions are available for individuals with a master of international or public affairs or business administration. It is important to do your research carefully to determine what kind of degree is best for you.

As in international development, field experience is also a requirement in many cases, with two years being the minimum. Training in management, project evaluation, and knowledge of regulatory environmental laws, environmental economics, and a technical area of expertise are highly valued. Starting salaries can range from the mid $20,000s to the low $40,000s, depending on the size of the nonprofit organization, your job function, and your level of technical and managerial expertise.

In the area of environment, the Environmental Careers Organization, based in Cambridge, Massachusetts, is a national nonprofit educational organization. Its website (www.eco.org) is an important source for career information related to the environment; through it you can also order their excellent publication *The Complete Guide to Environmental Careers in the 21st Century*.

The field of public health certainly could encompass its own section, but health and environment are closely linked together and thus both will be covered here. The area of international health covers more than population—it includes relief and refugee work, epidemiology, and maternal/infant health, to name a few such areas. This section focuses on the area of population, specifically because of its impact on our global resources.

Conservation International (CI)

1919 M Street, NW, Suite 600

Washington, DC 20036

(202) 912–1000

www.conservation.org

    Conservation International is a nonprofit organization working around the world to protect biodiversity in hotspots, major tropical wilderness areas, and key marine ecosystems. By applying science, economics, policy, and community participation through a diversity of programs, CI works with indigenous organizations, conservation organizations, international organizations, local governments, and the private sector to maintain the Earth's living natural heritage. CI sample program areas include research and science, conservation finance and investment, ecotourism and business, education and awareness, policy and economics, and environmental journalism. CI posts employment and internship vacancies on its website.

Environmental Defense (ED; formerly the Environmental Defense Fund)

257 Park Avenue South

New York, NY 10010

(212) 505–2100

www.environmentaldefense.org

    Environmental Defense, a national nonprofit organization, was founded in 1967 in response to DDT pesticide use. Since then, ED has grown to 300,000 members with a staff of 168 employees. It aims to make the world aware that environmental problems can no longer be limited to one country but must be seen as global. ED links science, economics, and law to create innovative, economically viable solutions to today's environmental problems. It aims to halt ozone depletion, stop acid rain, save tropical rain forests, clean up toxic wastes, create living cities, and safeguard wildlife and habitats. ED advocates using economic incentives as a means to solve environmental problems. It also maintains a 750,000-member action network to alert a community of activists about pending environmental legislation. ED posts job and internship vacancies on its website.

Family Care International (FCI)

588 Broadway, Suite 503
New York, NY 10012
(212) 941–5300
www.familycareintl.org

Family Care International was established in 1987 to develop creative and practical solutions to health and family planning problems affecting women in the developing world. It helps governments and NGOs develop community-based programs, collaborative groups, and networks on topics such as safe motherhood and adolescent sexual and reproductive health. It holds workshops in developing countries. FCI's advocacy messages and materials have reached more than 170 countries, and it is currently active in 15 countries. FCI posts job and internship vacancies on its website.

Friends of the Earth (FOE)

1025 Vermont Avenue NW, Suite 300
Washington, DC 20005
(202) 783–7400 or (877) 843–8687
www.foe.org

Friends of the Earth was founded in 1969 in San Francisco and is now part of the largest federation of environmental groups, Friends of the Earth International, an international network of grassroots organizations in 70 countries. Today FOE campaigns tackle a variety of concerns, including: genetically engineered foods, pesticides, energy policy, corporate responsibility and the public's right to information, tax reform, urban sprawl, transportation, government spending, trade, international finance, clean water, and forest preservation. Working with local organizations, FOE hosts conferences, lobbies Congress, conducts public education and training activities, and publishes a variety of reference materials and reports.

Greenpeace

702 H Street, NW, Suite 300
Washington, DC 20001
(202) 462–1177
www.greenpeace.org

Greenpeace is one of the most well known environmental nonprofit organizations. It was founded in 1971 by a small group of activists who believed a few individuals could make a difference. Today, with national and regional offices in 41 countries and more than 2.8 million members worldwide, Greenpeace is dedicated to preserving the Earth. It uses "nonviolent and creative measures" to stop perpetrators and seek solutions to the threat of nuclear war; nuclear and toxic pollution; global greenhouse warming and ozone layer destruction; and the slaughter of whales, dolphins, seals, and other endangered animals. Greenpeace also aims to restrict genetic engineering and encourage sustainable trade. Its office in Amsterdam coordinates its international campaigns. Greenpeace posts job and internship vacancies online.

International Institute for Sustainable Development (IISD)

161 Portage Avenue East, 6th Floor
Winnipeg, Manitoba R3B OY4
Canada
(204) 958–7700
www.iisd.org

Through policy research, information exchange, analysis, and advocacy, the International Institute for Sustainable Development aims to help societies achieve sustainable development through innovation. IISD prepares policy recommendations on concerns such as international trade and investment, economic policy, climate change, and natural resource management. IISD publishes a quarterly newsletter and other materials addressing subjects such as youth, poverty, security, indigenous peoples, and measurements and indicators. It also offers reporting services covering international negotiations and conferences. IISD has an established international environmental fellowship program. IISD posts job vacancies on its website and provides a link to Sustainable Development Job Bank, which it maintains in collaboration with other members of the Sustainable Development Communications Network.

International Planned Parenthood Federation/
Western Hemisphere Region (IPPF/WHR)

120 Wall Street, 9th Floor
New York, New York, 10005

(212) 248–6400
www.ippfwhr.org

International Planned Parenthood Federation (IPPF)

Regent's College, Inner Circle
Regent's Park, London NW1 4NS
United Kingdom
(+44 171) 487 7900
www.ippf.org

The International Planned Parenthood Federation/Western Hemisphere Region is one of six regional offices of the International Planned Parenthood Federation, whose central office in London links the autonomous family planning associations worldwide. Members are local, grassroots, autonomous associations providing family planning and related health services according to local needs, laws, and customs. Together, the IPPF's members have created the largest network of family-planning services in the world.

The IPPF/WHR was founded as a nonprofit organization in 1954 and is the only region of the IPPF that is a separately incorporated entity. The IPPF/WHR's members include 44 associations in North America, Latin America, and the Caribbean that together provide services to 8 million people each year through more than 40,000 service points.

The IPPF publishes a variety of books, periodicals, and audio/visual materials related to sexual and reproductive health rights. The central and regional libraries of the IPPF are an important source of information on all aspects of human fertility and contraception. The IPPF posts job vacancies on its website.

National Geographic Society

1145 17th Street, NW
Washington, DC 20036–4688
(800) 647–5463; outside U.S. and Canada: +1 813 979–6845
www.nationalgeographic.com

Founded in 1888, the National Geographic Society is one of the largest nonprofit scientific and educational organizations in the world. It aims to increase geographic knowledge and promote research and exploration around the globe. The work of the society is much in evidence through its main publication,

National Geographic. National Geographic also publishes books, television specials, photography specials, *National Geographic for Kids*, *Traveler* magazine, *World* magazine, and National Geographic Interactive. National Geographic sponsors a limited number of internships for students interested in geography, photography, and journalism.

Natural Resources Defense Council (NRDC)

40 West 20th Street
New York, NY 10011
(212) 727–1773
www.nrdc.org

The Natural Resources Defense Council attempts to protect the planet's endangered natural resources and to improve the quality of the human environment. It combines legal action, scientific research, and public education in an environmental program. NRDC's major issues of concern are air and water pollution, energy policy, nuclear safety, natural resource management, and the international environment. Together with the Sierra Club and other environmentally conscious organizations, the NRDC helps to formulate national positions on the environment for use by U.S. policymakers. Owing principally to a series of NRDC lawsuits, all of the loans and grants by the U.S. Agency for International Development (USAID) are now subject to strict environmental requirements to guard against projects that might cause environmental harm.

NRDC's international programs work on rainforests, biodiversity, habitat preservation, oceans and marine life, nuclear weapons, and global warming. NRDC campaigns include: saving the Amazon old-growth mahogany and cedar rainforest in Peru, protecting sturgeon, adopting sustainable coffee systems in Latin America, and working with the African Development Bank on the first debt-for-conservation swap in Africa.

Nature Conservancy

Worldwide Office
4245 North Fairfax Drive, Suite 100
Arlington, VA 22203–1606
(800) 628–6860
http://nature.org

The Nature Conservancy's mission is to preserve plants, animals, and natural communities that represent the diversity of life on Earth and to protect the lands and water that they need to survive. Since 1951, the Nature Conservancy has worked with business, governments, partner organizations, communities, and individuals to protect more than 98 million acres of land and waters world-wide. The Nature Conservancy works on a science-based planning process to help identify priority areas. It has assisted partners in China's Yunnan Province and throughout the Americas, Caribbean, and Asia-Pacific region. While its headquarters are in Virginia, there are several regional offices with employment opportunities. It has a globally diverse workforce of 3,000 staff based in 28 countries and posts job, internship, and volunteer vacancies on its website.

The Ocean Conservancy (formerly the Center for Marine Conservation)

1725 De Sales Street, Suite 600
Washington, DC 20036
(202) 429–5609
www.oceanconservancy.org

The Ocean Conservancy is dedicated to protecting marine wildlife and habitats and conserving coastal and ocean resources. The center also supports major international efforts to protect all wildlife species threatened by international trade. Programs include policy-oriented research, public education, and support for domestic and international conservation programs. For example, the center is working on sea turtle conservation and the designation and protection of marine habitats such as coral reefs.

Population Connection (formerly Zero Population Growth)

1400 16th Street NW, Suite 320
Washington, DC 20036
(202) 332–2200
www.populationconnection.org

Population Connection is the nation's leading grassroots organization concerned with the impact of rapid population growth and consumption. While advocating a world with reproductive rights and the availability of effective contraception, the organization maintains that unlimited population growth is threatening the planet's natural resources and the quality of life of future generations. It also views urban blight, poverty, and the depletion of resources to be additional consequences of uncontrolled population increase. Population Connection publishes *Population Connection Reporter*, operates fellowship programs, and posts job vacancies online.

Population Council

1 Dag Hammarskjold Plaza
New York, NY 10017
(212) 339–0500
www.popcouncil.org

The Population Council has been searching for a better understanding of problems relating to population since John D. Rockefeller III established it in 1952. Its functions are to conduct research and provide professional services in the broad field of population, encompassing development issues and population policies; investigate safe and effective means of birth planning; and design, implement, and evaluate programs to provide birth planning services and information. The council is in contact with institutions overseas having similar interests. Occasionally it provides financial support for the work of institutions and trains professionals in specialized areas of population studies.

The council distributes publications and information on population matters to interested professionals. The council's research and publications cover diverse topics related to population research and policy, such as HIV/AIDS, reproductive health, biomedical research, and gender roles and empowerment. Titles include the journal *Population and Development Review* and the booklet series *SEEDS*, which addresses economic roles and needs of low-income women. The council also operates the Center for Biomedical Research in New York City.

With about half of the staff based in the New York and Washington, D.C., offices, the council's global programs staff projects in Latin America and the Caribbean, Africa, Asia, and the Middle East. Positions exist for interns and first-level degrees, but the Population Council usually hires people with an M.P.H. degree or similar backgrounds. The council also operates fellowship programs for social and biomedical scientists. The council posts internship and job vacancies on its website.

Rainforest Alliance

665 Broadway, Suite 500
New York, NY 10012
(212) 677–1900 or (888) MY EARTH
www.rainforest-alliance.org

The Rainforest Alliance's primary mission is to develop and promote economically viable and socially desirable alternatives to tropical deforestation. These alternatives are designed in concert with local peoples to develop forest products and businesses that offer long-term, stable income for people living in or near tropical forests. The Rainforest Alliance also educates the public about tropical conservation. Current programs include Adopt-A-Rainforest, sustainable agriculture, sustainable tourism, smart wood use, national resources and rights, and a conservation media center. The alliance publishes a searchable electronic almanac of conservation programs and three newsletters (*Eco-Exchange, Canopy,* and *Rainforest Matters*), operates research projects and fellowships programs, and hosts a weekly conservation radio show broadcast from Costa Rica.

The Rainforest Alliance posts internship and job vacancies on its website. Internship positions are available in various programs and departments, mostly in the New York office during the summer, fall, and spring semesters. Interns may research environmental and market issues, environmental policy and law, tropical agriculture and forestry, media surveys, and other special topics or projects.

Sierra Club

85 Second Street, Second Floor
San Francisco, CA 94105
(415) 977–5500
www.sierraclub.org

The slogan of the Sierra Club is: "Not blind opposition to progress, but opposition to blind progress." Founded in 1892, this environmentally conscious organization helped bring the National Park Service and the Forest Service into existence and played a leading role in the establishment of many national parks. Today it conducts programs to help people take action at a local level, tries to keep wilderness in its natural state, protects the world's remaining natural ecosystems, and promotes exploring, protecting, and enjoying the planet. The Sierra Club Foundation funds public education, litigation, and training efforts.

The Sierra Club operates several chapter and field offices across the United States and Canada and conducts projects in Mexico and southern Africa. The international office of the Sierra Club works closely with the UN and USAID on international activities pertaining to the environment. Other programs include responsible trade, global warming, nuclear waste, and population. The organization publishes several books and *Sierra* magazine. It posts available jobs and internship vacancies on its website.

World Resources Institute (WRI)

10 G Street, NE, Suite 800
Washington, DC 20002
(202) 729–7600
www.wri.org

The World Resources Institute, a center for policy research, seeks to address a fundamental question: How can people and nations meet their basic needs and economic requirements without undermining the natural resources and environmental quality on which life depends? The WRI brings together leading thinkers from many fields and nations to study this question and to create policy options for the future. Through its research it provides information about global resources and environmental conditions. In order to increase public awareness, it publishes a variety of reports and holds conferences and seminars. It also maintains the searchable electronic environmental information portal Earth Trends. The World Resources Institute posts job and internship vacancies online.

World Wildlife Fund (WWF)

1250 24th Street, NW
Washington, DC 20037
(202) 293–4800 or (800) CALL-WWF
www.wwf.org

The World Wildlife Fund, which includes the former Conservation Foundation, works to preserve wildlife and their habitats by making modest investments of time and money in the activities of private conservation organizations, international agencies, and national governments. Since its founding in Switzerland in 1961, WWF has assisted more than 13,100 projects in 157 countries. Among its accomplishments are helping to create 500 parks in countries including Kenya, Nepal, and Peru; and pioneering debt-for-nature swaps in Ecuador and the Philippines. In more than 50 countries across five continents, World Wildlife Fund staff teach local people to use alternative fuels and train and equip rangers, guards, and antipoaching teams. WWF posts internship and job vacancies online.

FOUNDATIONS

Foundations are unique in the realm of nonprofit organizations because their mission is to give away money rather than to raise it. While other nonprofits design and implement various programs, it is often foundations that provide the support for their work. The scope of a foundation's activities varies greatly with size. The largest ones, such as the Ford Foundation and the Rockefeller Foundation, may closely monitor and evaluate the projects they fund and may engage in other activities, such as raising awareness of issues that concern them and building organizational capacity of grantees to better address the issues at hand. Smaller foundations, on the other hand, may be less involved and primarily see their role as funding agents.

The types of projects supported by a foundation also vary widely, as do the skills required by them. Some foundations target a specific area of the world, so they look for applicants with language skills, regional training, or international work experience. Others focus on a single issue, such as the environment, and may want applicants with technical expertise.

Because foundations do not have a steady source of income aside from their endowments, they try to keep administrative costs low by minimizing the middle level of management between senior staff and assistants. Most entry-level jobs at foundations require only a college degree, whereas upper-level positions usually require a Ph.D. and 8–10 years of work experience. For

A	
DAY	*A Day in the Life at a Foundation*
IN THE	
LIFE	

A Day in the Life at a Foundation

The goal of a foundation is to support projects and initiatives, through grants, that impact the community and serve the public good. My job within a community-based foundation is in development/donor relations. This role is essential to the organization because I must ensure that the foundation, which depends on contributions from individual donors, always maintains a steady and consistent source of financial resources from which grants can be made into perpetuity.

A typical day at work may include lunch with a donor to discuss their interests—be they in economic development, education, or health—and to bring them up to date with current projects. In addition, I may meet with program staff members to ascertain the types of projects they are planning to support through grants. These kinds of meetings help me to find a match between a donor's interest and a current project that needs support.

In addition, I engage in a tremendous amount of administrative work that is tied to the donor's charitable giving. This includes correspondence and a weekly review of gifts that were made to the foundation and the grantee organizations that benefited from those gifts.

The highlight of my job is that I am always meeting new people and helping the community in which I live. The downside is that I can get bogged in administrative work as in any job. However, I find it rewarding. There is a fair amount of local travel to visit project sites and several conferences in the field of philanthropy, which I attend annually.

job seekers with a master's degree and little work experience, there may be few positions available. However, with a master's and a few years of relevant experience, you might be able to land a job in a smaller family-run or corporate foundation, or a position like that of program associate at the Ford Foundation (see the Ford Foundation entry below for more information on this program).

There are several excellent resources for those interested in seeking information on the field of philanthropy. The Council on Foundations (www.cof.org) has quite a bit of information about the role of foundations and links to many excellent resources, as well as job listings. The Foundation Center (www.fdncenter.org) is an excellent organization with offices across the country. The Foundation Center provides workshops for those interested in the process of grant-making and is there to serve as a resource for philanthropy professionals and those interested in the field.

Carnegie Corporation

437 Madison Avenue
New York, NY 10022
(212) 371–3200
www.carnegie.org

The Carnegie Corporation is a philanthropic foundation created by Andrew Carnegie and is primarily interested in education, international peace and security, international development, and strengthening U.S. democracy. Grants for projects are made to colleges, universities, and professional associations. The corporation awards grants totaling approximately $75 million a year. Job vacancies are posted online.

Echoing Green Foundation

60 East 42nd Street, Suite 2901
New York, NY 10165
212.689.1165
www.echoinggreen.org

A unique venture philanthropy firm, the Echoing Green Foundation provides seed money to individuals who want to work in the field of social change, specifically those individuals interested in creating a new organization or program. To learn more about the application process, visit the organization's website. The two-year fellowship provides a $30,000 annual stipend (for a total of $60,000). The organization also provides training and technical assistance to help ensure that the project or organization will succeed. In addition, the website provides reference materials and resources for potential fellows.

Ford Foundation

320 East 43rd Street
New York, NY 10017
(212) 573–5000
www.fordfound.org

One of the largest foundations in the world, Ford gives funds for educational, developmental, research, and experimental efforts designed to produce significant advances in selected problems of national and international importance such as education, urban and rural poverty, economic development, human rights, and governance. Though the Ford Foundation generally hires only Ph.D.s and/or those well established in their careers, it does offer a semi-annual two-year program assistant position for those with a master's or law degree. Applicants should be interested in public service, philanthropy, and the not-for-profit sector; Ford is looking for a diverse applicant pool.

Kettering Foundation
200 Commons Road
Dayton, OH 45459
(937) 434–7300
www.kettering.org

The Kettering Foundation conducts theoretical and operational research in the practice of politics at the community, national, and international levels. Its founder, Charles Kettering, held more than 200 patents, including the automobile starter. The object of the foundation's work is the development of new ways to address fundamental problems in politics. The foundation's efforts are concentrated in the area of international affairs, public policy, public-government relationships, community politics, and public leadership education. It has sponsored programs of nongovernmental diplomacy among the United States, the former Soviet Union, and China and conducted a national assessment of how citizens, the press, and public officials respond to major policy issues. The foundation's work is carried out by staff, associates, student research assistants, and international scholars-in-residence. Kettering also has offices in Washington, D.C., and New York City.

Phelps Stokes Fund (PSF)
74 Trinity Place, Suite 1303
New York, NY 10006
(212) 619–8100
www.psfdc.org

Established in 1999, the Phelps Stokes Fund creates educational opportunities for African Americans, Native Americans, and needy white youth in the United

States. Similarly, African education is a primary concern, and PSF programs have been broadened to include funding of emerging colleges in the Caribbean. The organization has a small staff but has gained wide recognition for its work.

PSF provides opportunities for Americans to meet with Africans: American scholars are sent to African institutions, and African professors serve as visiting faculty at American colleges and universities. In addition, interest-free emergency loans are given to African students in American colleges. Much of the foundation's research has also centered around the state of African education.

Rockefeller Brothers Fund

437 Madison Avenue, 37th Floor
New York, NY 10022–7001
(212) 812.4200
www.rbf.org

The Rockefeller Brothers Fund makes private grants under the principal theme of global interdependence to counter world trends of "resource depletion, conflict, protectionism, and isolation which now threaten to move humankind everywhere further away from cooperation, equitable trade and economic development, stability, and conservation."

Under this theme there are two major components: sustainable resource use and world security. In addition, the fund focuses on New York City, the well-being of the nonprofit sector, education in the United States, and South Africa. Grants are regularly given to projects in East Asia, East-Central Europe (with a special concern for the Balkans), and countries of the former Soviet Union.

Rockefeller Foundation

420 Fifth Avenue
New York, NY 10018
(212) 869–8500
www.rockfound.org

In addition to involvement in a great number of national projects (this foundation committed $5 million to the September 11 relief effort), the Rockefeller Foundation also funds many projects of an international nature. Among its international concerns are the conquest of hunger, problems of population, the quality of the environment, and university development. Some of its recent projects include increasing female education in Africa; forming a sustainable development plan in Nanking, China, and using the media to build environmental awareness; sponsoring public art projects on border issues by Mexican and U.S. artists; and starting new health training programs in Zimbabwe, Uganda, Ghana, and Vietnam.

The foundation also invites scholars and artists each year to spend four weeks in residence at its Bellagio Study and Conference Center at Lake Como, Italy, to enable them to work on a book or other creative undertaking.

Soros Foundation Network

Open Society Institute—New York
Office of Communications
400 West 59th Street
New York, NY 10019
(212) 548–0668
www.soros.org

The Soros Foundation Network is composed of a group of autonomous nonprofit organizations operating in 29 countries, plus foundations in Kosovo and Montenegro, and two regional foundations: the Open Society Initiative for Southern Africa and the Open Society Initiative for West Africa. The organizations, founded by George Soros, focus on the support of educational, social, and legal reforms. While they are concentrated in Eastern Europe, Central Asia, and the Caucasus, there is also a presence in Guatemala, Haiti, South Africa, and the United States. The Open Society Institute has its headquarters in New York and a sister organization in Budapest, Hungary. It funds a variety of projects, detailed on the website, which is helpful as you try to navigate this complex group of institutions.

Tinker Foundation

55 East 59th Street
New York, NY 10022
(212) 421–6858
www.fdncenter.org/grantmaker/tinker

The Tinker Foundation attempts to "create a climate of better understanding between the peoples of the United States and Ibero-America, Spain, and Portugal." A sampling of subjects for which grants have been given includes the following: a grant to enable the American Field Service to establish a two-way exchange program of high school teachers from Argentina, Brazil, Colombia, and the United States; the purchase of a liberal arts library for the Bilingual Institute of Biscayne College; defraying the travel costs of Latin American participants to a meeting of the Atlantic Conference sponsored by the Chicago Council on Foreign Relations; an award to the Department of Agricultural Economics of Cornell University to work on the economic and social aspects of agricultural development in the Mexican tropics; and an award to Johns Hopkins University to support its Latin American Diplomats Program. Tinker hires individuals with a background in Latin American studies, relevant languages, and experience in education, culture, and the nonprofit sector; advanced degrees are preferred. The foundation was created in 1959 by Dr. Edward Larocque Tinker.

The Echoing Green Foundation

A relatively new foundation that is worth exploring for those interested in nonprofit work is the Echoing Green Foundation. Echoing Green provides seed money to individuals who want to work in the field of social change, specifically individuals interested in creating a new organization or program. To learn more about the application process, visit the organization's website (www.echoinggreen.org). The two-year fellowship provides a $30,000 annual stipend (for a total of $60,000). The organization also provides training and technical assistance to help ensure that the project or organization will succeed.

TRADE AND PROFESSIONAL ASSOCIATIONS

There are thousands of professional associations on the international, national, and regional levels. In the United States, the largest number are located in Washington, D.C., but you will find them throughout the country. Usually, one thinks of joining such organizations for information, education, and to expand one's professional network, but they also supply a myriad of career opportunities.

Professional associations represent different professions, like the American Economics Association or the Association of International Bankers. Trade associations typically provide a service to certain industries, like the U.S. Council for International Business. As a professional in an association, you might arrange conferences and seminars and thus be involved in professional development/education, or do research for your members or lobby for them on a particular issue. The advantages of working in an association are many: The vast network of members is perhaps the greatest, and you'll certainly feel like you are at the center of the action. The downside might be the eventual frustration that comes from servicing organizations that you would actually like to be working for. However, keep in mind that you are well placed to conduct research on future employers and to establish solid working relationships with them. The *Encyclopedia of Associations* is an excellent place to begin researching associations; it is available in most career centers and libraries.

American Economic Association (AEA)

2014 Broadway, Suite 305
Nashville, TN 37203–2418
(615) 322–2595
www.vanderbilt.edu/AEA

Founded in 1885, the American Economic Association encourages economic research and publication. More than 50 percent of the association's members are from academic institutions, and 35 percent are from business and industry. Among the journals that AEA publishes are the *American Economic Review* and *Journal of Economic Abstracts*. Of great interest to readers of this book, AEA also publishes a monthly listing of job vacancies called *Job Openings for Economists*. It's available online and in print.

American Federation of Labor-Congress of Industrial Organizations (AFL-CIO)

Department of International Affairs
815 16th Street, NW
Washington, DC 20006
(202) 637–5000
www.aflcio.org

The AFL-CIO's Department of International Affairs recommends foreign policy positions to trade union leadership and the rank and file. Among the international issues covered by this department are AFL-CIO policy toward the International Labor Organization, the International Confederation of Free Trade Unions, and other international labor organizations; the need for strong national defense, the absence of trade unions, and the exploitation of labor in certain countries; and the Arab-Israeli conflict.

The AFL-CIO is in contact with the embassies of foreign governments in an effort to promote a better understanding of the American labor movement. The Department of International Affairs also furthers AFL-CIO policies through publications, conferences, orientation of foreign visitors, and trade union missions overseas.

American Political Science Association (APSA)

1527 New Hampshire Avenue, NW
Washington, DC 20036–1206
(202) 483–2512
www.apsanet.org

The American Political Science Association is an organization for students and professors interested in the study of government and politics. It publishes *American Political Science Review*, a quarterly journal of scholarly articles and book reviews in political science, including international affairs; and *Political Science and Politics*, a quarterly professional journal in political science. For political science job seekers, APSA publishes the monthly *Personnel Service Newsletter* of employment opportunities. The online version is updated daily; a subscription fee is required for both.

American Society of International Law (ASIL)

2223 Massachusetts Avenue, NW
Washington, DC 20008
(202) 939–6000
www.asil.org

The American Society of International Law fosters the study of international law and promotes the practice of international relations based on law and justice. It is a forum for the exchange of views on current international legal topics and a center for research on issues concerning international law. It publishes books and periodicals on international law and sponsors student activities in this field.

ASIL's website has details about job openings and unpaid internships in sales and marketing, finance, international legal materials, and general research.

Business Council for International Understanding (BCIU)

1212 Avenue of the Americas, 10th Floor
New York, NY 10036
(212) 490–0460
www.bciu.org

The Business Council for International Understanding facilitates dialogue between the U.S. business community and government officials. It tries to improve the climate for international business-government relations at the policymaking level as well as in day-to-day operations. BCIU is best known for it U.S. ambassadorial and senior diplomat industry briefing program, in which U.S. diplomats come to BCIU to discuss political, economic, and commercial issues with senior management of U.S. companies active or interested in issues of a particular country. BCIU has an internship program for college juniors and seniors.

International Management and Development Institute (IMD International)

CH de Bellerive 23
P.O. Box 915
CH–1001 Lausanne, Switzerland
+ 41 (0)21 618 01 11
www02.imd.ch

The purpose of IMD International is to "provide education which will strengthen corporate and government management teams internationally." As a business school and training center, it hopes to increase government and public understanding of the international corporation as a "constructive force" in the domestic and world community. It works to achieve its aims through government-business training programs, executive seminars, Washington briefings, and a general education campaign geared toward government and the public.

National Foreign Trade Council (NFTC)

1625 K Street, NW, Suite 200
Washington, DC 20006
(202) 887–0278
www.nftc.org

Sound economic growth is a widely accepted objective, although the means of achieving such growth may be subject to a great deal of controversy. The National Foreign Trade Council argues that foreign trade and investment are key instruments in achieving this growth; it further believes that close coordination between U.S. domestic and international economic policies is required to establish a favorable climate in which international business can operate. Rules are the NFTC's bread and butter. Specifically, it performs research, issues documentation and policy statements, and holds conferences and seminars to assert its views.

RELIEF, REFUGEE ASSISTANCE, AND HUMAN RIGHTS

The fields of relief and refugee assistance are often interrelated. Countries receive relief aid in the wake of natural or man-made disasters—famine, drought, war, or other sorts of civil strife. They are given food and medical aid and refugee assistance if people or populations are displaced—thus the overlap with refugee work. Somalia, Bosnia, and Rwanda are all recent examples of large-scale relief efforts involving individual countries and the international community. The work is rewarding but very difficult and can involve arduous—and sometimes dangerous—living conditions that are made more difficult by the psychological strain of the harsh realities of human suffering. In relief and refugee work, it is important to understand the distinction between refugees (a legal term) and internally displaced persons (IDPs). For instance, people who are displaced within their own country would receive relief assistance but not refugee assistance per se. Increasingly, in the aid community there is a large discussion/debate over whether IDPs should be formally recognized and protected by the Geneva Conventions in the same way as refugees. It's actually a fascinating discussion of sovereign national rights, and some people in the United Nations and outside are increasingly arguing that nations that do not respect the human rights of their citizens relinquish their sovereignty.

Human rights work certainly may encompass relief and refugee work but is broader, often involving advocacy, education, research, monitoring, and policy. Higher-level professionals travel to different countries to interview and document human rights abuses and/or advocate for broader human rights protections. They often have expertise in international legal systems, and many have law degrees. Human rights professionals work on a variety of issues, including women's and children's rights, health, treatment of minorities, religious freedom, labor issues, and freedom of the press, just to name a few. Recently, there have been efforts to adopt human rights frameworks for foreign policy and development assistance within NGOs and multilateral organizations. The idea is that using human rights as the basis for analysis makes for a more politically savvy development programming perspective. For example, instead of simply offering water projects, some organizations are beginning to put their efforts into the context of what national and local governments are doing (or not doing) in terms of water access.

The field is incredibly competitive, and most jobs are obtained through networking; significant prior experience is a must, as are strong writing and research skills and a demonstrated commitment to the issues at hand. According to one professional in the field, "Given the competitive constraints of the field of human rights, internships are often the best way to break into a real job." Languages and regional expertise may also be valuable.

For more information, check out these human rights websites:

The UN website (www.un.org/english) has an area for human rights issues
UN High Commissioner for Human Rights (www.unhchr.org)
Individual human rights missions have sites with human rights links like
    the Office of the High Representative in Bosnia (www.ohr.int)
National Center for Human Rights Education (www.nchre.org)

American Near East Refugee Aid

1522 K Street, NW, Suite 202
Washington, DC 20005
(202) 347–2558
www.anera.org

This organization was established by Americans concerned about the plight of Palestinians. It provides assistance to education, health services, and community development projects among Palestinians in the West Bank and Gaza Strip, Lebanon, and Israel.

Amnesty International

322 Eighth Avenue

New York, NY 10001
(212) 627–1451

International Secretariat
99–119 Rosebery Avenue
London EC1R 4RE
United Kingdom
(020) 7814 6200
www.amnesty.org

By writing letters, holding publicity campaigns, sending missions and ob-
servers, and publishing special reports, Amnesty International works to gain the
freedom of prisoners of conscience and protect and preserve basic human rights.
It also seeks humane treatment for all prisoners and detainees, opposes the death
penalty, and works to expose disappearances and political killing by governments. Amnesty International won the Nobel Prize in 1977, and today it has more
than 1 million members, subscribers, and donors across 140 countries. Recent
Amnesty International campaigns include refugee rights, the UN Commission on
Human Rights 50 Years Later, the death penalty, women and human rights, and
the e-mail and Internet campaign www.stoptorture.org. Amnesty International
has a strong internship program; most full-time positions are quite competitive
and require prior experience in the human rights field. Like any large organization, it also has openings in administration, finance, and human resources.

Bread for the World

50 F Street, NW, Suite 500
Washington, DC 20001
(202) 639–9400
www.bread.org

Bread for the World, a Christian organization, seeks to eliminate hunger and
successfully lobbied Congress to establish a 4 million ton wheat reserve against
world famine. It mobilizes public support for right-to-food resolutions to be
passed by Congress. Although it does not distribute food, it is an effective lobbying force in alleviating global hunger. Bread for the World also supports progressive welfare reform and economic policies. It lists openings online.

Center for Independent Living (CIL)

2539 Telegraph Avenue

Berkeley, CA 94704

(510) 841–4776

www.cilberkeley.org

The Center for Independent Living calls for an independent lifestyle and civil rights for disabled people. It offers attendant referrals, housing searches, employment services, deaf and blind services, independent living skills, peer support, and advocacy. CIL has helped people from Nicaragua, Jamaica, and the Virgin Islands to establish centers for the disabled in their home countries. It posts openings on its website; in many cases candidates should have experience working with the disabled.

Church World Service (CWS)

28606 Phillips Street

P.O. Box 968

Elkhart, IN 46515

(574) 264–3102

www.churchworldservice.org

The Church World Service, which represents most of the Protestant denominations, has a relief and rehabilitation goal of feeding the hungry and resettling refugees, and a long-range aim of sustainable development and peace "in our time." CWS holds community-wide hunger education and fund-raisers. Its programs operate in all areas of the world, and representatives are stationed on all continents. Its relief work is similar to that of CARE and Catholic Relief Services. Jobs are posted online.

Committee on Migration and Refugee Affairs

c/o InterAction

1717 Massachusetts Avenue, NW, Suite 701

Washington, DC 20036

(202) 667–8227

www.interaction.org/refugees/migrefug.html

This committee, which operates under the auspices of InterAction, is composed of 23 nonprofits that focus on refugee protection, assistance, and resettlement advocacy. Recent concerns include protection and resettlement for refugees from Africa and the former Yugoslavia. Among its international members are the American Red Cross, International Refugee Service of America, and Refugees International. The website includes details on many more refugee-related organizations.

Freedom from Hunger Foundation

1644 DaVinci Court
Davis, CA 95616
(800) 708–2555
www.freefromhunger.org

"Feed a man a fish and he will eat for a day. Teach him to fish and he will eat for a lifetime." This Chinese proverb expresses the philosophy of the Freedom from Hunger Foundation. Instead of providing food for hungry people, it offers programs of education and self-help designed to give them the knowledge and tools to improve their own lives. The foundation looks to implement programs that are cost-effective, sustainable, and replicable. Contact Freedom from Hunger directly for employment and internship information.

Freedom House

120 Wall Street, Floor 26
New York, NY 10005
(212) 514–8040

1319 18th Street, NW
Washington, DC 20036
(202) 296–5101
www.freedomhouse.org

Freedom House was started by Eleanor Roosevelt and Wendall Wilkie to combat totalitarianism and strengthen democratic institutions and the right of individuals to free choice. The organization issues an annual report that evaluates the state and degree of freedom in every country in the world. Freedom House also holds conferences on issues revolving around freedom and publishes the bimonthly magazine *Freedom Review* as well as a number of books. International programs include promoting an engaged U.S. foreign policy, monitoring human rights, and supporting a free press around the world. It is particularly oriented toward Eastern Europe and Central Asia, and outside the United States it has offices in Belgrade, Bratislava, Budapest, Bucharest, Kiev, Rabat (Morocco), Tashkent, and Warsaw.

The Global Health Council (GHC; formerly the National Council of International Health)

1701 K Street, NW, Suite 600
Washington, DC 20006
(202) 833–5900
www.ncih.org

The Global Health Council is dedicated to saving lives by improving health worldwide. One way it does this is by increasing U.S. awareness and response to international health needs. The GHC works in advocacy, alliance building, and communications and spreads best practices in health. Its key concerns are: child health and nutrition, reproductive health, maternal health, HIV/AIDS, infectious diseases, disaster and refugee health, and health systems. In addition to posting its own job and internship openings, the GHC maintains a career network and posts domestic and international jobs for members in the health field on its website.

Human Rights Watch

485 Fifth Avenue, 34th Floor
New York, NY 10017
(212) 972–8400
www.hrw.org

Human Rights Watch monitors the human rights practices of governments and protests against murder, disappearances, torture, imprisonment, psychiatric abuse, censorship, and deprivation of political freedom. It is the largest U.S.-based human rights organization. Annually, it sends out more than 100 investigative missions to gather current information on human rights in more than 70 countries.

This organization links five existing Human Rights Watch divisions: Helsinki Watch, Americas Watch, Asia Watch, Africa Watch, and Middle East Watch. In Kenya, Africa Watch publicized the efforts of lawyers, clergy, and others to challenge the dictatorial government's one-party rule. Human Rights

Watch also sponsors an international film festival that showcases the work of international filmmakers dealing with human rights issues. Areas of special initiative include academic freedom; antinarcotics and human rights; business and human rights; and prison and human rights in the United States. It has branch offices in Washington, D.C., Los Angeles, San Francisco, London, and Brussels. It lists jobs, fellowships, internships, and volunteer opportunities online (www.hrw.org/jobs). A large organization, it often has openings for researchers, field investigators, advocates, administrative support staff, managers, and directors and communications, fundraising, and operations staff. A college degree is sufficient for administrative positions, but for research and professional positions you will need a graduate degree, related work, research, internship and/or field experience, languages, and other skills. Fellowship applicants must have a law degree.

International Federation of Red Cross and Red Crescent Societies

P.O. Box 372
CH–1211 Geneva 19
Switzerland

17 chemin des Crêts
Petit Saconnex, Geneva
Switzerland
+41 (22) 730 4222
www.ifrc.org

American Red Cross National Headquarters
431 18th Street, NW
Washington, DC 20006
(202) 639–3520
www.redcross.org

The International Committee of the Red Cross acts as a neutral intermediary in conflicts to protect victims of war in accordance with the Geneva Conventions. The League of Red Cross Societies, another part of the International Red Cross, coordinates the efforts of member societies in meeting the needs of victims of natural disasters and refugees from war situations. Through special missions, the loan of experts, the hosting of seminars, and the printing of publications, the league helps national societies to expand and improve their programs of disaster relief, nursing, blood donations, and public relations. Current International Red Cross issues include the problem of landmines, the effects of weapons and war, and humane action in armed conflict.

The American Red Cross, one of the most active of the league's members, helps meet emergency needs of disaster victims, assists sister societies in expanding their programs, and provides opportunities for officials from other countries to study American Red Cross programs.

There are several types of jobs available with the Red Cross, requiring such diverse skills as the ability to lead an overseas delegation or providing different types of medical training. U.S. opportunities are listed online (www.redcross.org/jobs).

International Rescue Committee (IRC)

122 East 42nd Street, 12th Floor
New York, NY 10168
(212) 551–3000
www.intrescom.org

Formed in 1933 at the request of Albert Einstein to assist anti-Nazi activists fleeing Hitler's regime, the International Rescue Committee is in the forefront of all refugee crises. IRC has helped victims of racial, religious, ethnic, and political persecution and those displaced by violence. IRC was the first U.S. organization on the ground in the former Yugoslavia and continues to work to resettle thousands of refugees displaced by the ethnic strife. IRC also has refugee projects in Rwanda, Tanzania, Georgia, Azerbaijan, Cambodia, Mozambique, Pakistan, Somalia, the Sudan, Kenya, Ghana, and the Ivory Coast. IRC is a big operation that often has several vacancies posted on its website (for international positions check online for the appropriate contact person). IRC also takes interns.

Robert F. Kennedy Memorial Center for Human Rights

1367 Connecticut Avenue, NW, Suite 200
Washington, DC 20036
(202) 463–7575
www.rfkmemorial.org/CENTER

The Robert F. Kennedy Memorial Center for Human Rights was established in 1988 to promote the work of the RFK Human Rights Award recipients. The center has helped gain the release of political prisoners in South Korea, supplied medical books and journals to Poland's first independent medical library, and contributed to the International Human Rights Law Group on the Chilean electoral process.

Project HOPE

People to People Health Foundation
255 Carter Hall Lane
Millwood, VA 22646
(800) 544–4673 or (540) 837–2100
www.projhope.org

Project HOPE (*H*ealth *O*pportunities for *P*eople *E*verywhere) began in 1958. Two years later, the world's first peacetime hospital ship, SS *Hope*, sailed on its maiden voyage, bringing a cargo of health educators to developing nations requesting HOPE's assistance. With the retiring of the ship, HOPE's objective focused on health-care education at home and abroad. Health personnel in the developing world are taught modern techniques of medicine, nursing, and dentistry. Among the countries now being served by HOPE are Barbados, Belize, Brazil, Chile, China, Costa Rica, Egypt, El Salvador, Grenada, Guatemala, Haiti, Honduras, Indonesia, Jamaica, Panama, Poland, Portugal, Swaziland, and the border area of the U.S. Southwest. It has an online application form for jobs and also produces a job opportunities newsletter.

Refugees International (RI)

1705 N Street, NW
Washington, DC 20036
(202) 828–0110
www.refintl.org

Refugees International was founded in 1979 to draw the world's attention to the terrible plight of Cambodian and Vietnamese refugees. Since then, RI has become the "refugees advocate" for more than 30 missions on behalf of war victims in Bosnia, and Africans fleeing war in Liberia, Ethiopia, Somalia, and Rwanda, to name several of its recent projects. It lists jobs, internships, and fellowship opportunities on its website.

Simon Wiesenthal Center

1399 South Roxbury Drive

Los Angeles, CA 90035

(310) 553–9036 or (800) 900–9036

www.wiesenthal.org

The Simon Wiesenthal Center was founded in 1977 to awaken the American people to the danger they faced from well-financed hate groups operating all over the country. It is dedicated to fighting anti-Semitism and bigotry around the world. To this effect, the center provides multimedia programs for interested parties. In order to teach young people how and why the Holocaust happened, the center conducts education programs for students in high schools and colleges and maintains an extensive library, film, and radio program. The center has international offices in Toronto, Paris, and Jerusalem.

World Concern

19303 Fremont Avenue North

Seattle, WA 98133

(800) 755–5022 or (206) 546–7201

www.worldconcern.org

World Concern is a Christian organization that rushes aid to disaster areas while stressing self-help in rehabilitating people. It has 85 fieldworkers on assignment in Africa, Asia, and Latin America. Specific projects include teaching self-reliance through food security, primary health care, literacy, and generating income. It only employs Christians; it advertises jobs online.

PEACE AND DEMOCRATIZATION

Nonprofit organizations dealing with peace and democratization have undergone a great deal of change over the last several years. With an emphasis on political and economic globalization and the formation of new democracies, many also tackle the issues of small arms control, electoral assistance, and the formation of civil society.

These organizations may be either research-driven or program-driven and occasionally both. Research-oriented groups have many traits in common with think tanks, although their subject matter is more specific to this particular field. Program-oriented nonprofits are similar in many ways to development organizations, involved in on-the-ground work in areas like election monitoring, conflict resolution, or the development of a strong civil society. Some of these organizations obtain funding from governments or international organizations, and others raise money from private donations and foundations.

Job seekers interested in this field should have a strong interest in political science, as even program-oriented work relies to some extent on political theory. For peace-related work, some background in international security is helpful, since you are often dealing with arms-related issues or regional conflicts. Like the other fields listed in this section, a master's degree is necessary for anything other than entry-level positions, which tend to be highly administrative. Familiarity with democratization theory and regional expertise are also highly recommended. If you are interested in program work, relevant field experience is often highly sought, and internships (here and abroad) can be an excellent way to begin building your resume.

America's Development Foundation (ADF)

101 North Union Street, Suite 200
Alexandria, VA 22314
(703) 836–2717
www.adfusa.org

America's Development Foundation is a U.S. nonprofit organization established in 1980 dedicated to the international development of democracy. By working with local and municipal governments, ADF helps civil society organizations strengthen democratic values, institutions, and processes in their countries and to develop their communities. ADF's programs encompass rule of law, local governance, human rights, advocacy, electoral processes, civil society development, and refugee return and reintegration. ADF operates programs in the Middle East, Central and Eastern Europe, Africa, Central America and the Caribbean, and Central Asia.

ADF regularly seeks experts relevant to the organization's program areas with extensive training and technical assistance experience. Foreign language skills, especially in French, Haitian Creole, Arabic, and Serbo-Croatian, are highly desirable. ADF posts job vacancies online.

Arms Control Association (ACA)

1726 M Street NW, Suite 201
Washington, DC 20036
(202) 463–8270
www.armscontrol.org

The Arms Control Association tries to promote public understanding of policies and programs with respect to arms control and disarmament. It aims to get public acceptance for limiting armaments and otherwise reducing international tensions. It puts out the monthly periodical *Arms Control Today,* a product of the research conducted by the association. Interns working at ACA may research and write about national security, defense, arms control, and communications issues or monitor arms issues on Capitol Hill. ACA posts job vacancies online.

Center for International Private Enterprise (CIPE)

1155 15th Street, NW, Suite 700
Washington, DC 20005
(202) 721–9200
www.cipe.org

The Center for International Private Enterprise is dedicated to building democratic institutions by strengthening corporate governance, fighting institutional corruption, supporting women entrepreneurs, and slashing red tape and the cost of doing business. By partnering with local organizations and companies, CIPE conducts programs in Africa, Asia, Eurasia, Latin America and the Caribbean, Central and Eastern Europe, and the Middle East that support market-oriented reforms. CIPE provides technical assistance and aims to connect reformers around the globe through conferences, publications, and a new electronic roundtable training tool. Its publications include the *National Business Agenda Guidebook*, a how-to guide for creating a business agenda, and the newsletter *Overseas Reports*. CIPE posts job vacancies online.

International Foundation for Election Systems (IFES)

1101 15th Street NW, Third Floor
Washington, DC 20005
(202) 828–8507
www.ifes.org

The International Foundation for Election Systems is a nonprofit NGO that supports elections, the rule of law, governance, and civil society. By working with civic and political leaders worldwide, IFES provides technical assistance in all areas of election administration and election management and supports other areas of democratic governance. IFES has been part of the electoral process in more than 100 countries. IFES also houses the F. Clifton White Resource Center and maintains a network of local Democracy Resource Centers that offer materials related to civil society and democracy building. Job and internship vacancies are posted on its website.

International Peace Academy (IPA)

777 UN Plaza, 4th Floor
New York, NY 10017–3521
(212) 687–4300
www.ipacademy.org

The International Peace Academy conducts policy research and concentrates on teaching basic practical skills associated with the achievement of peace: conflict analysis, mediation, negotiation, and the presence of an impartial third party to prevent or limit hostilities. It cooperates with NGOs, governments, and educational institutions throughout the world to organize courses on conflict resolution; conducts courses and seminars on its own; publishes material on peacekeeping; performs research to strengthen education and training for peace; and organizes new national committees. Interns working at IPA may research issues related to peacemaking, peacekeeping, and peacebuilding.

International Republican Institute (IRI)

1225 I Street, NW, Suite 700
Washington, DC 20005
(202) 408–9450
www.iri.org

The International Republican Institute is a private nonprofit organization that aims to promote democracy and strengthen free markets and the rule of law outside the United States. The institute aids emerging democracies by conducting nonpartisan programs in areas such as political organizing, campaign management, polling, parliamentary training, judicial reform, and election monitoring. IRI operates in Central and Eastern Europe, Eurasia, Africa, Asia,

Latin America and the Caribbean, and the Middle East. IRI posts job and internship vacancies online.

National Democratic Institute for International Affairs (NDI)

2030 M Street NW, Fifth Floor
Washington, DC 20036–3306
(202) 728–5500
www.ndi.org

The National Democratic Institute for International Affairs aims to promote and strengthen democratic institutions overseas. By working with civic and political leaders, NDI conducts nonpartisan programs to support democratic political development in new and emerging democracies. Areas of work include democratic governance, election and political processes, security sector reform, local government, political party development, citizen and women's participation, and information and communications technology. NDI operates in the Middle East, Africa, Latin America and the Caribbean, Central and Eastern Europe, Asia, Eurasia, and Northern Ireland. Interns at NDI may assist in administrative management or programmatic and functional skill areas. Job and internship vacancies are posted on its website.

National Endowment for Democracy (NED)

1101 15th Street, NW, Suite 700
Washington, DC 20005
(202) 293–9072
www.ned.org

Established by Congress in 1983 and subject to its oversight, the National Endowment for Democracy aims to strengthen democratic institutions around the world through nongovernmental efforts. NED funds projects that promote political and economic freedom, a strong civil society, independent media, human rights, and the rule of law. Project areas include: promoting workers' rights and responsible corporate governance; supporting the development of trade unions and political parties; fostering transparency and inclusive decisionmaking; and training journalists. NED encourages regional and international cooperation in promoting democracy. It also houses the Democracy Resource Center and publishes *Journal of Democracy*.

9

International Communications

A recent media student interned for CNBC both in Fort Lee, New Jersey, and in Hong Kong. While he often struggled to get substantive work at their headquarters, in Hong Kong he was an integral component on their *Business Asia* show. He credits his fluency in Mandarin Chinese and working in a smaller bureau with allowing him to gain much more responsibility.

Another student began her career in journalism, where she gained valuable experience in writing and reporting under deadlines. After focusing on international media and business during her master's program, coupled with several relevant internships, she landed a job with a prestigious New York–based public relations firm, dealing with both domestic and international accounts.

Yet another began his career freelancing. Rather than deal with the monotony of small town papers, he took off for Iran and developed a reputation for bravely reporting in difficult, conflict-ridden areas, in a region of the world where news and information were difficult to obtain. In just a few years, he was writing for the *Economist* and several other major publications as a stringer.

These three stories indicate the various ways one can break into the field of communications. And each anecdote has a common theme: paying your dues, planning a strategy, and gaining experience, backed with a substantive knowledge of media, politics, and economics, as well as good writing skills.

BREAKING INTO THE FIELD OF COMMUNICATIONS

Though it's often portrayed as a glamorous and high-profile industry, there is just as much tedium in a beginning communications career as in many others, and beginning salaries for undergraduates in media professions are low, generally between $18,000 and $25,000 a year. Salary depends on location; smaller cities and towns tend to pay lower salaries than places like New York, where a journalist with a few years of experience tends to command $35,000-$50,000. Job security has somewhat declined as more and more companies are relying on freelancers to complete projects. Combine that with stiff competition, long work schedules, and the fact that you may have to put your international training on the back burner during the initial stages of your career, and you may start to wonder if it is really the field for you. The good news is that newspapers, despite the downsizing in many news sections, are working hard to reinvent themselves and in many cases have created online versions for the Internet, which has also resulted in different job prospects. Journalists, advertising executives, marketing, public relations, and multimedia specialists have also found niches in the media side of the Internet.

So what's the best way to get ahead in this field? To prepare yourself academically for a career in international media, take a broad range of courses, from skill-based writing and reporting to economics, regional, and language courses. The majority of your journalism courses should be practical; they should include exercises for covering a story and then submitting your article for review under a deadline.

While your academic program is by no means irrelevant, most alumni and employers cite contacts and experience as the most important factors for getting a media-related job. A master's degree will help you advance more quickly and may offer useful background knowledge, but it is ultimately your experience and talent that determine your success.

Experience doesn't necessarily mean freelancing in five different countries. Interning during the school year and summer months can provide invaluable learning experiences and can help you accumulate a portfolio of clips. Whether you're working at CNN or the *Kalamazoo Gazette*, you'll gain a basic understanding of how news is gathered and produced. Sometimes, smaller is better in the communications industry because you're generally given more responsibility and will get more exposure to different aspects of the job. By working in a small advertising boutique rather than a top-ten ad agency, for example, you will be interacting with clients more quickly and will be able to begin writing and participating in the creative process without spending a lot of time paying your dues at the copier. On the other hand, it does matter where you've worked, and the names of big, respected companies on your resume will get you attention.

In addition to exposing you to the industry, internships also offer the chance to network and make contacts. Getting to know people in the business will help when it comes time to pass your resume around. The majority of my students hired for media positions had interned previously with the company or agency that eventually hired them. It seems that internships have basically become a prerequisite for employment. As an intern you'll often have access to the current job binders that post in-house job openings. And while assisting the organization by writing stories, editing tapes, or helping on ad campaigns or PR events, you'll also build a portfolio of your own work. These clips of your work are just as important as your resume and will set you apart from the hordes of recent communications graduates. Clips of well-written published articles are crucial if you want to work in print; a tape is very useful when applying for broadcast jobs, as are writing samples for script and production work.

In the land of bad pay and long hours, interns are no exception to the rule. Some coveted internships provide excellent salaries or housing benefits. As you may imagine, those internships are also the most competitive. Most media sectors, especially broadcast, offer only unpaid internships. If you're lucky, the company may spring for lunch or cover transportation costs. Thus, it's wise to save up, work part-time, or ask your parents for a loan. It's also a good idea to intern while enrolled in school because many of the large companies insist that you earn college or advanced degree credits for the internship.

JOURNALISM

Does covering the peace talks in Northern Ireland appeal to you? Do you hope to travel to the far ends of the globe to do an exposé on child labor conditions? Are you interested in analyzing an issue, interviewing several people, and writing a story about it, all before a 5 P.M. deadline? Such is often the life of an international journalist. The jobs are generally difficult to come by, the work environment is fast-paced, and the salary for entry-level to middle-level positions won't do much to help pay off your student loans. Newspapers tend to pay the lowest salaries, around $18,000–$24,000 for entry-level reporters, though this tends to be higher at larger papers. In new media—the hot area of Internet and World Wide Web technology—managers and reporters earn salaries comparable to those in print. Magazine reporters, especially the finance-oriented ones, earn about $35,000–$45,000 to start, but these jobs are fewer and harder to come by than newspaper positions. Salaries in broadcast vary widely. Everyone hears about Peter Jennings or Dan Rather commanding salaries in the millions, but there are very few star anchors. On-air talent (e.g., reporters, correspondents, and anchors) generally make more money than those involved in production (producers, production assistants, news directors, camera operators, and technical crews). Once again, it's difficult to gauge salaries because market size, experience, and job descriptions vary so much. But in television, your first job is likely to be either as a production assistant or assistant producer, and you'll earn a salary of between $18,000 and $28,000. Still, journalism careers offer freedom, ever-changing job descriptions, and an unorthodox way of life that few journalists would trade for a nine-to-five desk job.

In the case of journalism and broadcasting, international news is covered mainly by the large metropolitan dailies and broadcasting stations. Those interested in international journalism may work in international news organizations such as CNN or the *New York Times*, large metro dailies and broadcast news stations, national news magazines, Internet zines, or radio stations. Others may work as freelance reporters or stringers. Reporting jobs overseas with these organizations are practically nonexistent for the beginner. If upon graduation you apply to the *New York Times* or NBC, you will likely be advised to get a job with a small-town newspaper or broadcasting station and gain some real-world reporting experience before trying out for a major paper.

This initial job may be in obits, sports, or local news, but it is unlikely to be international. After a few years you may progress to a small metropolitan paper or station where your international background will still be of peripheral interest to your employer. It is only later—with five years or more of experience—that you will be considered for a reporting job with a large metropolitan paper or station. Even if you do land a job with the *New York Times* or the Associated Press (AP), for example, it doesn't mean you will soon be sent abroad as a foreign correspondent or even work in headquarters on international news. These jobs are usually reserved for those who have paid their dues and made names for themselves after some years in New York.

If you have command of a highly specialized language at a time when a news service is desperately in need of someone with that language fluency for an overseas office, you may be hired. It would be wise to recognize, however, that the chances of this happening are slim—but not impossible. It may be better to go overseas where your talents are needed rather than wade unknown through the myriad of editorial assistant and production assistant jobs in the metro cities. Some organizations, such as the *Economist* or *Wall Street Journal*, hire green reporters. If you're good, they'll send you abroad. If you are already there working for them, so much the better.

If you can't find a paid job and you intend to go abroad anyway, contact any of the wire services or major dailies to see if you can become a stringer. You will not be on the regular payroll, but you can submit stories and articles and get paid for those that are accepted. Chances of being a stringer are obviously better if the wire service or newspaper to which you are applying does not have a regular correspondent in the country where you plan to be. This background also adds strength to your resume. A useful guide for prospective freelancers is *The World on a String: How to Become a Freelance Foreign Correspondent* (by Alan Goodman and John Pollack, Henry Holt, 1997). It advises on such issues as contacting editors, choosing a home base, and other complications of working in foreign countries.

Much of the news generated abroad is covered by wire services who then deliver packages to newspapers, radio, and television stations across the United States and abroad. The major wire services are the Associated Press, Agence France-Presse, Bloomberg News, Deutsche Presse-Agentur, Dow Jones, and Reuters. As with other media-related career tracks, typical entry-level positions for wire services are editorial assistants and general news reporters. With the top wire services, you can expect to spend about five years working domestically and on the international desk before you're offered a position overseas. These positions often entail writing financial and business stories, so it's a good idea to combine financial or business-related coursework with writing courses. Courses in economics, finance, and business are most helpful, as few economists or computer specialists can make their sciences understandable to the general public. If you can write economic or technology-oriented stories that are informative and enjoyable, you may well find yourself in demand.

Still, there are many opportunities to position yourself as a local hire. The best way may be working as a freelance stringer or reporter and working abroad in the country of interest. Not only will you build up your clips, you may also be in the right place at the right time and find yourself stringing for AP in a country at the center of breaking international news. The downside is that a local hire is not officially considered part of the system and receives less pay and benefits than a full-time staff member. If a local hire wants to get a job full-time, he or she must then return to the United States and work domestically for about five years. Remember there are exceptions to every rule, and in journalism hard work, tenacity, and good writing skills can take one very far. Language skills are critical for working overseas for a wire service because, unlike newspapers that often provide translators for their reporters, wire service reporters generally need to communicate directly.

Another popular option is to go abroad and work for local English-language media. This has the advantage of familiarizing you with the country and quickly giving you experience and clips. Choose your publication carefully, though. Papers such as the *South China Morning Post* and *Bangkok Post* are well established and have good standards, but some expatriate newspapers are poorly managed and badly edited. Do your homework.

As in the other chapters, below we list only a few examples of newspapers, broadcasting stations, and new media. Directories and reference works with more detailed listing of newspapers, periodicals, and publishers are found in the Bibliography.

Wire Services

Agence France-Presse (AFP)
13, Place de la Bourse
75002 Paris
France
(33 1) 4041 4646; fax: (33 1) 4041 4632
e-mail: contact@afp.com
www.afp.com

North America:
1015 15th Street NW, 5th Floor
Washington, DC 20005
(202) 289 0700; fax: (202) 414 0525
e-mail: afp-us@afp.com

The world's oldest news agency, AFP was founded in 1835 by Charles-Louis Havas. Partly owned by the French government, the agency is headquartered in Paris, has regional centers in Washington, Hong Kong, Nicosia, and Montevideo, and maintains 110 bureaus. AFP has 2,000 staff, of which 900 work outside France. It distributes news and information in French, English, Arabic, German, Portuguese, Russian, and Spanish. In 1991, the agency launched AFX News (www.afxnews.com), an English-language subsidiary that provides economic and financial news; it later added AFX Asia. Other AFP subsidiaries include German-language service AFP GmbH (www.afp.com/deutsch), satellite data broadcaster Fileas (www.fileas.com), and Companynews (www.companynews.fr), which offers corporate press releases and financial statements in French.

Associated Press (AP)

50 Rockefeller Plaza
New York, NY 10020
(212) 621–1500
www.ap.org

The AP has grown since 1848 from a small domestic staff and one lone foreign correspondent in Nova Scotia to a cadre of 3,700 reporters, editors, photographers, and staff in the United States and abroad. It is not only the world's largest news-gathering organization, it is also the backbone of the world's information system, reaching more than 1 billion people a day through 15,000 new outlets around the globe. As Mark Twain once said, "There are only two forces that can carry light to all corners of the globe—the sun in the heavens and the Associated Press down here."

The AP has 242 bureaus worldwide, ranging in size from a single correspondent in Burma to a 120-person bureau in Washington, DC. For employment, contact the chief of the bureau nearest to you or the AP staffing department in New York. Those interested in radio or television should apply directly to the

AP Broadcast News Center (1825 K Street, NW, Washington, DC 20006–1253). The AP also sponsors a paid internship program, primarily for minority students in their last two years of college or graduate school. Contact the New York address for more information.

Bloomberg

499 Park Avenue
New York, NY 10022
(212) 318–2000; fax: (212) 980–4585
www.bloomberg.com or http://careers.bloomberg.com

Bloomberg L.P. is a privately owned information services, news, and media company founded by former Salomon Brothers trader Michael R. Bloomberg in 1981. It has career opportunities in broadcast, finance, research, news, operations, product sales, product training, and software development. Headquartered in New York City, Bloomberg has over 100 offices around the world and 8,000 employees. Its Bloomberg News division employs 1,200 reporters in 85 bureaus worldwide. Bloomberg's news content is almost entirely dedicated to business, economic, and financial information, which it distributes through leased terminals, online systems, and to newspapers worldwide.

The company also operates Bloomberg Television and Bloomberg Radio and publishes business and investment magazines in the United States, Britain, and Italy.

Deutsche Presse-Agentur (DPA)

Personnel Department
Mittelweg 38
D—20148 Hamburg
Germany
49 40 4113–2321; fax: 49 40 4113–2329
www.dpa.de

Germany's leading news agency, the Deutsche Presse-Agentur GmbH group of companies, is among the world's largest newsgathering organizations. It has 1,200 employees, including 900 editorial and reporting staff, plus thousands of freelance contributors. DPA has editorial offices in Washington, D.C.; Cork;

Buenos Aires; Madrid; Nicosia; and Bangkok. Correspondents report 24 hours a day from around the globe, providing news in German, English, Spanish, and Arabic.

Dow Jones & Company

200 Liberty Street
New York, NY 10281
(212) 416–2000
e-mail: djcareers@dowjones.com
www.dowjones.com

Dow Jones is a leading publisher of business news and information. Its flagship publication, the *Wall Street Journal*, is America's largest newspaper, with a circulation of 1.9 million. Dow Jones also provides real-time international market data, news, and technical analysis services through Dow Jones Newswires, publishes separate *Wall Street Journal* editions for Europe and Asia, as well as the magazines *SmartMoney*, *Barrons*, and *Far Eastern Economic Review*, owns 13 daily and 12 weekly community newspapers through its Ottaway Newspaper subsidiary, and produces TV news and information through an alliance with NBC. Established in 1882, Dow Jones employs 8,000 people in 100 countries. Many of its foreign bureaus are paired with AP bureaus. It also sponsors a newspaper foundation to encourage talented young people to enter news careers. Its programs serve the news industry by locating minority journalists and new editors, by encouraging excellence in journalism teaching at the high-school level, and by providing information about career opportunities in journalism.

Reuters

85 Fleet Street
London EC4P 4AJ
United Kingdom
44 207 250 1122; fax: 44 207 542 5411
www.reuters.com or http://about.reuters.com/careers

Reuters bills itself as the world's leading financial, media, and professional information company. It has 2,500 journalists, photographers, and TV-camera operators out of a total staff of 19,000. About 5,000 stringers also contribute data directly to Reuters. Founded in London in 1851, it has regional headquarters in New York, Geneva, and Hong Kong and maintains 230 bureaus. Reuters provides financial information; news and information on risk management and financial analysis; multimedia news; and professional briefing products for industry specialists and corporate executives. Career opportunities exist for those with backgrounds in journalism, technology, sales and marketing, human resources, finance, legal studies, and recruitment. For journalists, knowledge of economics and finance will prove very useful.

United Press International (UPI)

1510 H Street, NW
Washington, DC 20005
(202) 898–8000; fax: (202) 898–8057
www.upi.com

Founded by publisher E.W. Scripps in 1907, this wire service became United Press International in 1958 when UPI merged with Randolph Hearst's International News Service. In 2000, it was bought by the Reverend Sun Myung Moon's News World Communications (publisher of the *Washington Times*). Formerly a leading news service, UPI has struggled financially and dwindled in size and scope but continues with its two main tasks: reporting the news for subscribers in the United States and making sure that readers outside the United States have access to the news. Its divisions include UPI Radio, Business Wire and Financial News, Morning News, Religion, Spanish, and Sports. Its international World Desk has been renamed the Focus Desk. UPI recently merged with Meridian Emerging Markets to provide emerging market information on the Internet. UPI posts career opportunities online.

Newspapers and Magazines

Boston Globe

135 Morrissey Boulevard
P.O. Box 2378
Dorchester, MA 02107–2378
(617) 929–2000
www.boston.com/globe/ or
http://bostonglobe.com/aboutus/careeropps/index.stm

Owned by the New York Times Company, the *Boston Globe* has a daily circulation of over 450,000, with foreign bureaus in Hong Kong, Jerusalem, Berlin, Moscow, Mexico, and Quebec. Its related website (Boston.com) is one of the most visited regional portals in the world.

Christian Science Monitor

1 Norway Street
Boston, MA 02115
(617) 450–2000
www.csmonitor.com

Published by the First Church of Christ, Scientist, the *Christian Science Monitor* is a highly respected newspaper and does not produce religious propaganda. Rather, it publishes original and informative articles from its 13 bureaus around the world. The *Monitor* publishes not only daily North American editions but also a weekly international edition, which is printed in London and distributed worldwide. Unlike most American papers, the *Monitor* does not rely primarily on wire services for its international coverage, making it an ideal client for international freelancers. The *Monitor*'s international news bureaus are located in China, Germany, France, India, Israel, Japan, Kenya, Mexico, Russia, South America, the United Kingdom, and at the United Nations.

The Economist Group

The Economist Newspaper Group
Group Human Resources, North America
The Economist Building, 111 West 57th Street
New York, NY 10019
(212) 554–0662; fax: (212) 397–9438
e-mail: jobsny@economist.com
www.economistgroup.com

The Economist Group provides research and analysis on international business and world affairs. An international company, it employs 1,000 staff around the world, with offices in London; Frankfurt; Paris; Vienna; New York; Boston; Washington, D.C.; Hong Kong; mainland China; Singapore; and Tokyo. Its flagship publication is the *Economist*, a weekly magazine-format newspaper of news, ideas, opinion, and analysis edited in London since 1843. A highly respected and influential international magazine, it is published in six countries and on the Internet, and 80 percent of its over 830,000 circulation is outside the United Kingdom. It is partly owned by the *Financial Times*. Though focused primarily on business, finance, and politics, the *Economist* does not adhere to one particular ideology, and articles are rarely signed. Rather, articles are compilations of reports gathered from a worldwide network of stringers and staff correspondents abroad. The *Economist* often hires young talent to write for the magazine and thus is a good job prospect for those fresh out of school; however, while freelancing for the magazine is feasible, staff editorial openings remain few and far between. Most employees are British. The group also publishes *CFO* magazine and operates the Economist Intelligence Unit (www.eiu.com), which provides country and industry research through a variety of reports, websites, and publications. Its Pyramid Research division covers telecommunications and e-business. Catering to business decisionmakers, the Economist Intelligence Unit is more accessible to beginning journalists than the magazine.

Editor and Publisher

770 Broadway
New York, NY 10003–9595
(800) 336–4380; fax: (646) 654–5370
www.mediainfo.com/editorandpublisher

Editor and Publisher, the weekly newsmagazine of the newspaper industry, is often referred to as the newspaperman's newspaper. Its coverage includes activities of all departments of U.S. newspapers, including news and editorial, advertising, circulation, business, promotion, personnel, and public relations. *Editor and Publisher* also posts newspaper and new media job openings on its interactive classifieds.

Euromoney Institutional Investor PLC

225 Park Avenue South
New York, NY 10003
(212) 224–3730
www.institutionalinvestor.com

Founded in 1967, Institutional Investor (II) was acquired by Euromoney PLC in 1997. It is a leading international business-to-business publisher that targets readers at major financial institutions and governments. Euromoney

Institutional Investor produces 40 publications covering global business and finance, including *Institutional Investor* magazine in three editions (U.S., European, and Asian, with a combined circulation of 140,000), which is famous for its annual ranking of analysts. Other divisions include *Euromoney* magazine, several newsletters, financial news websites, and Internet Securities, Inc. (www.securities.com), which concentrates on emerging markets. Journalists working for II cover banking, brokerages, corporate finance, capital markets, money management, pension funds, mutual funds, institutional trading, alternative investments, derivatives, portfolio strategies, technology, real estate, and industry movers and shakers. Applicants should have knowledge of some of these areas together with writing and reporting skills.

Facts on File

132 West 31st Street, 17th Floor
New York, NY 10001
(800) 322–8755
factsonfile.com

Facts on File publishes reference books and CD-ROMs primarily for libraries and schools. One recent publication is the *Encyclopedia of the United Nations*. Facts on File's reference work of world happenings is updated by a staff of researchers whose functions are broken down into geographic areas. Much of the material is compiled from other journalism sources.

The Financial Times Group (FT Group)

Financial Times Newspaper (UK)
One Southwark Bridge
London, SE1 9HL
United Kingdom
44 20 7873 3000; www.ft.com or ftgroupjobs.ft.com

Financial Times Newspaper (U.S.)
1330 Avenue of the Americas
New York, NY 10019
(212) 641–6400

The London-based FT Group provides information, analysis, and business content for managers and investors around the world. Its flagship division is the *Financial Times* newspaper, which is printed on its distinctive pink paper in 19 cities and has a daily circulation of over 480,000 and global readership of 1.6 million. The company claims to devote "more resources to international business and economic stories than any other news organization" and employs over 500 journalists around the world. A division of Pearson PLC, FT has published an American edition since 1997 and maintains 10 U.S. bureaus with a staff of 70 journalists. Other business divisions include *FT Business,* which provides financial market intelligence and publishes industry magazines such as *Money Management* and *The Banker,* and business website FT.com, viewed by over 2.7 million people each month. The group also publishes *Les Echos* in France and *FT Deutschland* and owns a 50 percent stake in the *Economist.*

Forbes

60 Fifth Avenue
New York, NY 10011
(212) 620–2200
www.forbes.com

This major business and finance magazine publishes numerous stories about overseas business ventures and multinational corporations. *Forbes* has a print circulation of about 850,000 and also publishes numerous online versions of its magazine, including Forbes Digital Tool, its online version with original, interactive content; an online version of the print magazine; and *Forbes FYI,* a lighthearted look at leisure and culture. *Forbes ASAP,* which reported on the high-technology industry, was shut down in 2002. *Forbes* offers internships in each of the above areas. Since *Forbes* is primarily a business publication, it generally hires those with backgrounds in journalism, business, and finance.

Foreign Affairs

58 East 68th Street
New York, NY 10021
(212) 434–9400
www.foreignaffairs.org

Since its founding in 1922, the Council on Foreign Relations (see Chapter 8 on nonprofit organizations) has produced *Foreign Affairs.* Currently published

A	***A Staff Writer at Forbes***
DAY	
IN THE	
LIFE	

I awake at 7 A.M. to Bloomberg News blaring over my alarm clock/radio. Riding on the subway to work, I skim the business section of the *New York Times*. My first order of business in the office is reading the *Wall Street Journal* and figuring out what I want to accomplish for the day. Since *Forbes* is a biweekly business magazine, our schedule has peaks and valleys. On days when I'm not on deadline or visiting a company, I spend the morning phoning people for possible stories. Then I work on stories that are due for the next cycle. In the afternoon I often gather background materials for longer-term projects. The reporting involves both human sources—financial analysts, company executives, and other industry experts—and written material, such as news clippings and company documents. Late in the day I'll check out more company and industry reports for possible story ideas and catch up on other reading, such as the *Economist* and *Financial Times*. On deadline days, when my column goes to press, I meet with a fact checker to go over sources so that the article's facts can be verified. Then I have to proof my pages as they move through the editing and layout process. It's not uncommon for transmit days to run late into the evening. But that's a small price to pay for the freedom to explore undiscovered story ideas and create interesting, informative copy.

six times annually, it has about 185,000 readers. *Foreign Affairs* is a prestigious journal that contains articles from academics, researchers, and policy professionals in all areas of international affairs, with a famous book review section at the end of each edition. It has a small full-time staff but regularly takes interns. Vacancies are posted on its website. Pay is rather modest, and prospects for moving from a junior editorial position to becoming a contributor are slim.

Foreign Policy

1779 Massachusetts Avenue, NW
Washington, DC 20036
(202) 939–2230; fax: (202) 483–4430
www.foreignpolicy.com

A prestigious bimonthly journal on international affairs with circulation of 100,000, *Foreign Policy* is published by the Carnegie Endowment for International Peace (see Chapter 8 on Nonprofit organizations). The staff is small, but there is a well-known internship program that runs three times annually in winter, summer, and fall. Interns must have completed at least their junior year in college and have strong communication skills and a background in international affairs/politics. For more information, contact their Volunteer Internship Coordinator at the address above. Job openings, writers' guidelines and deadlines, and details on internships are posted on the website.

International Herald Tribune (IHT)

6 bis, rue des Graviers
92521 Neuilly Cedex
France
(33–1) 41 43 93 00
www.iht.com

A subsidiary of the New York Times Company, the *IHT* is an international daily newspaper printed at 20 sites with a circulation of over 260,000. Most of its content comes from *New York Times* reporters, but there are a few exclusive *IHT* correspondents and a small editorial staff based in Paris. The 115-year old newspaper began life as the *New York Herald Tribune*.

Knight Ridder Newspapers, Inc.

50 W. San Fernando Street
San Jose, CA 95113
(408) 938–7700
www.kri.com

Knight Ridder Digital
35 South Market Street
San Jose, CA 95113–2413
(408) 938–6000
www.knightridderdigital.com

Knight Ridder is an international information and communications company engaged in newspaper publishing, business news, information services, and cable TV. Knight Ridder's various information services reach more than 100 million people in 135 countries; its U.S. dailies have 8.5 million readers. The newspaper division has 32 daily newspapers located from coast to coast. Its range is from papers with close to half a million circulation (*Detroit Free Press, Miami Herald, Philadelphia Inquirer*) to those with less than 25,000 (*Boca Raton News*). Knight

Ridder has 16 foreign bureaus and representatives for the financial news bureau in 42 countries. It also produces the Real Cities network of 56 regional websites.

Knight Ridder publishes global job opportunities through its website in several different areas, including customer service, finance, technology, and marketing. It also sponsors a competitive internship program. Interns are generally placed with a daily newspaper and learn the ins and outs of newspaper publishing. Because most Knight Ridder newspapers maintain websites, there is a high demand for new media reporters and technicians.

Los Angeles Times

202 W. 1st Street
Los Angeles, CA 90012
(213) 237–5000
www.latimes.com; for jobs: www.tribjobs.com

The *Los Angeles Times* covers all major geographic areas and countries with its 23 foreign bureaus and 14 state and domestic bureaus. It is the fourth-largest newspaper in the United States, with daily circulation of over 1 million. Full-time foreign correspondents work in Beijing, Berlin, Bogota, Buenos Aires, Cairo, the Caribbean, Hong Kong, Jakarta, Jerusalem, Johannesburg, London, Mexico City, Moscow, Nairobi, New Delhi, Paris, Rome, Seoul, Shanghai, Tokyo, United Nations/Toronto, Vienna, and Warsaw. Its award-winning website also produces original interactive content. Job seekers can search positions available at the *Times* or link to other career resources online.

The *Los Angeles Times* is owned by the Tribune Company, which merged in 2000 with Times Mirror, a media and information company that owns numerous newspapers (including the *New York Newsday* and the *Baltimore Sun*), magazines (like *Field & Stream, Sporting News*), and cable TV stations.

The Nation

33 Irving Place
New York, New York 10003
(212) 209–5400; fax: (212) 982–9000
www.TheNation.com

Established in 1865 by a group of abolitionists, America's oldest weekly magazine still maintains a progressive stance on issues, politics, the arts, foreign and domestic policy, and civil liberties. Ralph Nader and Hunter S. Thompson published their first articles in *The Nation*. Owned by the nonprofit Nation Institute, it has a circulation of over 100,000. In addition to the magazine, the Nation Institute produces syndicated television and radio programs, conferences, and independent media projects in areas such as social justice, cultural politics, and peace and provides an internship program in conjunction with *The Nation*. Interns work full-time in either the New York or Washington bureaus as editorial or publishing assistants and also attend weekly seminars.

New York Daily News

450 West 33rd Street
New York, NY 10001
(212) 210–2100
http://nydailynews.com

The *Daily News* has only sporadic international coverage, but with over 700,000 copies distributed daily, it is America's sixth-largest newspaper. From time to time, it announces career openings for recent graduates as well as a limited number of summer internships for undergrads.

New York Times

229 West 43rd Street
New York, NY 10036
(212) 556–4080
www.nytimes.com; corporate: www.nytco.com

With more staff than any other newspaper (over 1,000 in newsrooms) and the second-largest network of foreign bureaus after the *Wall Street Journal*, the *New York Times* relies on its own foreign reporting far more than most newspapers. The *Times* has a daily circulation of more than 1.1 million and has expanded its brand in recent years to become a national newspaper with editions across the country. In 2002, it moved to buy out the *Washington Post*'s stake in the *International Herald Tribune*, a move expected to further expand the newspaper's global reach. The New York Times Company also publishes the *New York Times Magazine*, the *Boston Globe*, and 22 other newspapers; operates eight TV stations and two New York City radio stations; and engages in the worldwide syndication of news, features, photos, and graphics. New York

Times Digital operates Internet sites, including NYTimes.com, Boston.com, and NYToday.com.

As you may imagine, jobs and internships with the *New York Times* are highly sought positions. They are very difficult to obtain, especially for those just starting out. But don't be discouraged, because most journalists join a paper like the *New York Times* after several years of work experience; don't think of it as a first job but rather as a fourth or fifth. Each summer the *Times* offers paid full-time internships for young journalists with at least one full year of daily reporting experience. Although geared toward applicants of color, the program is open to anyone.

Newsweek

251 W. 57th Street
New York, NY 10019
(212) 445–4000
www.newsweek.com

One of the world's top weekly newsmagazines, *Newsweek* was established in 1933. In addition to the main U.S. edition, it publishes *Newsweek International* in four English editions and versions in Arabic, Korean, Japanese, Polish, and Spanish (a Russian edition was discontinued). All told, the magazine is read in 190 countries and has a circulation of 4.4 million. *Newsweek* has 60 correspondents spread between 22 bureaus in Atlanta; Boston; Chicago; Detroit; Los Angeles; Miami; New York; San Francisco; Washington, D.C.; and overseas in Beijing, Capetown, Frankfurt, Hong Kong, Jerusalem, London, Mexico City, Moscow, Paris, and Tokyo. Its Newsweek.MSNBC.com web presence is a combined venture with Microsoft, NBC, and the *Washington Post*. Newsweek has a paid 13-week summer internship program detailed on its website; the Washingtonpost.Newsweek Interactive division also takes interns. Hires tend to have a significant amount of previous reporting experience.

Time Inc.

Time & Life Building
Rockefeller Center
1271 Avenue of the Americas
New York, NY 10020

(212) 522–1212

www.time.com

Leading magazine company Time Inc. publishes 140 regular titles with 298 million readers. Its flagship *Time* newsmagazine claims to reach 24 million readers each week with over 4.2 million copies, including international editions in Europe, Asia, the Pacific, and Canada. If you are lucky enough to get a reporting job at *Time*, whether through long apprenticeships with small-town papers or through some fortuitous event upon graduation, you may not have to wait as long for an international assignment as you would with a newspaper. Your international background may even be crucial in your hiring and your apprenticeship at headquarters relatively short. Internationally, *Time* has ten domestic and 20 foreign bureaus, over 80 correspondents and 200 part-time reporters, and will parachute in a reporter to cover international events occurring outside the reach of its bureaus.

In addition to reporting and writing jobs, *Time* has a sizeable research staff that may be of interest. The magazine's research functions are broken down by geographic area, economics, and other functional subjects. Time's parent company, media and entertainment giant AOL Time Warner, also has hundreds of other jobs at its other magazine, Internet, and broadcast divisions. Some of its magazines, such as *Fortune, Money,* and *Business 2.0,* have international components to their reporting.

Tribune Company

435 North Michigan Avenue

Chicago, IL 60611

(312) 222–9100

www.tribjobs.com

A leading American media company, Tribune has broadcasting, publishing, and Internet subsidiaries, including 24 major-market television stations, 12 market-leading daily newspapers including the *Los Angeles Times* (see previous entry), the *Chicago Tribune* (circulation over 670,000), and *Newsday* (570,000), and 50 websites. Tribune Publishing employs over 4,500 journalists worldwide. The *Chicago Tribune* has more than ten full-time foreign correspondents based in Berlin, Moscow, London, and other cities. In addition, it uses part-time correspondents and stringers for coverage in other parts of the world. Journalists working on the award-winning website produce original content and often use digital audio, video, and graphic-design skills in addition to their reporting skills. Openings for all divisions are posted on the company's website, but hiring is handled locally.

Wall Street Journal

200 Liberty Street
New York, NY 10281
Tel: (212)416–2000
www.wsj.com
Mailing Address:
P. O. Box 300
Princeton, NJ 08543–0300

A division of Dow Jones and Company, the *Wall Street Journal* is the most widely read and scrutinized business and financial daily newspaper. The paper chronicles information about investing, money, technology, and politics. It also offers comprehensive overseas coverage through its bureaus and newswire services, located in more than 50 cities worldwide. About 1.9 million people read the *Wall Street Journal* daily in the United States alone. It is one of the few websites to charge a subscription fee *and* make a profit. The *Wall Street Journal* posts job vacancies online via the Dow Jones website. Because the paper is business-focused, those interested in a career here should have a strong financial and business background in addition to good research and writing skills.

Washington Post

1150 15 Street, NW
Washington, DC 22071–7300
(202) 334–6000
www.washingtonpost.com or www.washpost.com/employment

The *Washington Post* is America's fifth-largest daily, with a circulation over 700,000 and more than 1 million readers for its Sunday edition. It has 25 foreign correspondents located in Abidjan, Beijing, Berlin, Buenos Aires, Cairo, Hong Kong, Jerusalem, Johannesburg, London, Mexico City, Moscow, Nairobi, New Delhi, Paris, San Salvador, Tokyo, Toronto, Warsaw, and the United Nations. The Washington Post Company operates other news media including

Newsweek, TV and cable stations, Kaplan Prep Tests, and interactive production. It sold its stake in the *International Herald Tribune* to the New York Times Company in 2002. The *Washington Post* lists job vacancies online (journalists hired usually have several years of experience) and also sponsors a competitive internship program that places student interns in a variety of departments.

U.S. News and World Report

1050 Thomas Jefferson Street, NW
Washington, DC 20007
(202) 955–2000
www.usnews.com

A weekly national magazine with a circulation of 2 million, *U.S. News and World Report* publishes international, cultural, political, social, health, and science news and editorials. It has a staff of 250, five domestic bureaus, and foreign correspondents in Beijing, Moscow, and Latin America. Restructuring of the magazine has included a move toward public centered or civic journalism. Like other news organizations, *U.S. News and World Report* offers internships, generally in the Washington headquarters.

BROADCASTING

American Broadcasting Company (ABC)
ABC, Inc.
Human Resources Department
4151 Prospect Avenue
Los Angeles, CA 90067
or
77 West 66th Street, 13th Floor
New York, NY 10023
(212) 456–7777; fax: (212) 456–6850
www.abc.com

A subsidiary of the Walt Disney Company since 1996, ABC, Inc., has 20,000 full-time employees, a little more than half in broadcasting. The corporate staff amounts to about 270. Major news programs produced by ABC include *Good Morning America, World News Tonight, Nightline,* and *20/20.*

ABC has three major parts: The ABC-TV Network Group with 230 affiliates and 10 directly owned stations is divided into TV Stations East and West and Radio Stations Group 1 (in New York, Los Angeles, San Francisco, Detroit, Denver, and Providence) and Group 2 (Chicago, Forth Worth, Dallas, Atlanta, Minneapolis, Washington, D.C.), with 55 stations combined.

The Publishing Group includes Fairchild Publications and ABC Publishing. Newspapers include the *Kansas City Star-Times, Fort Worth Star-Telegram,* and the *Oakland Press.* Job openings are advertised through Disney online (http://disney.go.com/DisneyCareers). Internships for undergraduate students are offered in New York (use the above address) and in Los Angeles (write to Internship Program, 500 S. Buena Vista Street, Burbank, CA 91521–4391).

BBC World Service

BBC Recruitment
P.O. Box 7000
London, W1A 8GJ
United Kingdom
0870 333 1330
e-mail: Recruitment@bbc.co.uk
www.bbc.co.uk/worldservice; jobs: www.bbc.co.uk/jobs

The BBC World Service is the international section of the government-funded British Broadcasting Corporation (BBC). Since its inception in 1922, the BBC has become legendary for its editorial independence and commitment to impartiality. The World Service provides international news, analysis, and information in English and 42 other languages to 153 million listeners each week and is available via FM radio in 120 capital cities. BBC World Service Television was launched via satellite in 1991 and was relaunched in 1995 as BBC WORLD (offering 24-hour news) and BBC PRIME (entertainment) within BBC Worldwide, the BBC's commercial division. Other divisions with international elements are BBC News Online, the service's popular website, and BBC Monitoring, which scans the world's media in over 150 languages and 100 countries.

Recruiting is done centrally by the BBC, which has positions in business support and management, journalism, new media, programming, specialist technical and design services, and technology. Jobs are listed by type rather than BBC department; World Service positions usually can be found under location listings for London or central London. As one of the largest foreign-language broadcasters, the BBC will be of interest to journalists with fluency in other languages. The BBC runs a number of internship and training programs, including the BBC Broadcast Journalist Trainee Scheme. They are open only to UK nationals or those with proper work authorization. Details can be found online.

Cable News Network (CNN)

1 CNN Center
Atlanta, GA 30303
(404) 827–1500
www.cnn.com; jobs: www.turner.com/jobs

Since its inception in 1980, CNN has evolved into one of the most influential sources of breaking news stories and world events. A subsidiary of Turner Broadcasting, which in turn is owned by AOL Time Warner, the CNN news group is the largest and most profitable 24-hour news and information company in the world. It includes CNN, CNN Headline News, CNN International, CNNfn, CNN/SI, and CNN en Espanol, three private networks, two radio networks, three websites, and a syndicated news service, CNN Newsource. Its website (CNN.com) is one of the Internet's top news sites. The News Group has 31 bureaus and 600 broadcast affiliates around the world. Turner Broadcasting System (TBS) distributes news and entertainment products. In addition to the CNN Newsgroup, its network includes the Cartoon Network, Turner Classic Movies, the Atlanta Braves, Castle Rock Entertainment, New Line Cinemas, Turner Pictures, and a management company.

CNN seems to prefer journalists with international experience and degrees in international affairs in addition to writing and broadcast experience. CNN sponsors unpaid for-credit internships for college and graduate students. Interns may be placed in a variety of offices, depending on interest and experience. Starting salaries are quite low for CNN (low to middle $20s).

Columbia Broadcasting System (CBS)

524 West 57th Street
New York, NY 10019
(212) 975–4321
www.cbs.com or www.cbsnews.com

CBS began as a radio broadcasting service in 1928 and today operates one of the nation's top commercial TV networks, 14 TV stations, a nationwide radio network, and 77 AM and FM radio stations.

Now owned by media conglomerate Viacom, Inc., CBS sold its magazine publishing and recorded music business in 1987. Since then it has focused entirely on its historic core business of broadcasting. CBS News operates 14 news bureaus and offices around the world in addition to its headquarters in New York. Shows with an international element include *60 Minutes,* the *Early Show, Face the Nation,* and *CBS Evening News.* CBS Radio News provides hourly newscasts, breaking stories, special reports, and updates to over 2,000 radio stations. It also produces shows including *World News Roundup,* the longest-running news presentation in broadcasting history, and *World Tonight.* Like the other major networks, CBS offers unpaid internships during the school year and summer months to aspiring journalists. For internship information contact CBS News (524 West 57th Street, New York, NY 10019 or [212] 975–2114).

American Women in Radio and Television (AWRT)

1595 Spring Hill Road, Suite 330
Vienna, VA 22182
(703) 506–3290; fax: (703) 506–3266
www.awrt.org

AWRT is a nonprofit organization of professional women in the broadcast industry and allied fields. The goals of the organization are to provide a medium of communication and exchange of ideas, to promote the advancement of women in broadcasting, and to try to improve the quality of radio and TV. It is an excellent way to network and meet professionals in the field, get advice, and learn about professional trends.

Corporation for Public Broadcasting (CPB)

401 9th Street, NW
Washington, DC 20004–2129
(202) 879–9600
www.cpb.org

The Corporation for Public Broadcasting is a private organization established by Congress in 1967 and is still largely supported by federal funds. It also receives foundation and corporate funding. Its mission is to help develop an American noncommercial public radio and TV system that will inform, enlighten, entertain, and enrich the lives of people. CPB, in turn, created PBS in 1969 and National Public Radio (NPR) in 1970 (both are described in greater detail below). It lists national job and internship openings on its website.

Among CPB's responsibilities are to stimulate diversity, excellence, and innovation in programs; to advance the technology and application of delivery systems; to safeguard the independence of local licensees (it operates through nearly 1,000 local radio and TV stations); and to act as trustee for funds appropriated by Congress or contributed to CPB by other sources. CPB is also responsible for determining the potential audience's priority needs and interests.

Fox News Channel

Department of Human Resources
1211 Avenue of the Americas
New York, NY 10036
(212) 575–4670; fax: (212) 301–8588
e-mail: Resume@foxnews.com
www.foxnews.com

Fox News Channel is a 24-hour news channel that was launched in 1996 as a rival to CNN. It is a division of the Fox Entertainment Group, which is in turn 85 percent owned by the News Corporation. Fox News reaches about 80 million U.S. households through its cable affiliate stations. It provides international news, commentary, analysis, and shows such as *The O'Reilly Factor*, *The World*, and *On the Record*. For job openings or internship opportunities, apply to the address above.

National Broadcasting Company (NBC)

30 Rockefeller Plaza
New York, NY 10020
(212) 664–4444
www.nbc.com; jobs: www.nbcjobs.com

Employing over 7,000 worldwide, NBC reaches viewers in more than 100 countries. The scramble for jobs in NBC parallels that in ABC and CBS. Even those with a master's degree sometimes start as production or desk assistants

| A DAY IN THE LIFE | ***A Reporter at CNBC*** |

I usually begin my workday reading the newspapers—the *New York Times* and *Wall Street Journal*—and the news service wires—Associated Press and Reuters. That often gives me a good idea of the story I may be assigned or a story that I may suggest to work on that day.

When I have received my assignment or find a story for the day (sometimes it may be something I have been working on for a few days), I begin making phone calls to sources to find out more information and locate someone who is willing to be interviewed on camera. That part is much more challenging than reporting for print media because often people will tell you much more over the phone than they are willing to say with a camera stuck in their face.

I may try to schedule a couple of interviews in one area, or sometimes I find someone in Los Angeles, Chicago, or Boston and will interview them via an NBC affiliate in that area. Meanwhile I may ask the assignment desk to send a photographer to shoot some video for the story or call our tape library to gather footage for my story. When I have completed the interviews and have an idea of how I will approach the story, I will write my "stand up" or the short part of the story in which I appear on camera—summing up or adding a final thought or bridging together two different ideas within the story.

I'll finish writing the story and send the script on to my assignment editor, who checks for grammatical errors and, of course, makes sure it makes sense. Then I'll "track" it, or read the parts in which my voice appears over the video, and go into a room with a tape editor who puts the audio and video together to make a story.

When the story is finished I will often sit on the set with the anchor and introduce the story and may discuss it a little with the anchor afterward—trying to give the viewer as much information as possible in less than three minutes.

and then get in line for higher-level jobs as they open. The progression is usually from page or desk assistant to research, and from there to news writing and production. In 1986, General Electric purchased RCA, the owner of NBC, making it a giant in the entertainment industry. NBC broadcasts programming to nearly 200 countries. Its 24-hour cable news divisions CNBC and MSNBC offer numerous internship and job opportunities. MSNBC, the joint venture between Microsoft and NBC, is found both on the Internet and television. Its headquarters are in Secaucus, New Jersey, though much of its Internet programming is produced in Washington. CNBC, headquartered in Fort Lee, New Jersey, focuses on business news. In 2002, NBC acquired Telemundo, the second-largest U.S. Spanish-language TV network. NBC offers unpaid internships year-round as well as a paid and highly competitive news associates program for recent graduates. Details are available online.

National Public Radio (NPR)

635 Massachusetts Avenue, NW

Washington, DC 20001

(202) 513–2000; fax: (202) 513–3329

www.npr.org

National Public Radio produces and distributes programming nationwide through 680 member stations using a state-of-the-art satellite system. Over 20 million people listen daily to popular shows such as *Morning Edition, All Things Considered*, and *Talk of the Nation*. Although NPR concentrates on programs with national content, it does have some international programming, including *Living on Earth* and *The Thistle and the Shamrock*. NPR has many correspondents stationed abroad. It also receives reports from BBC correspondents. NPR offers internships in a variety of areas such as news and cultural programming, finance, development, communication, human resources, and information technology. NPR posts job openings online.

Public Broadcasting Service (PBS)

1320 Braddock Place

Alexandria, Virginia 22314

(703) 739–5000

www.pbs.org

PBS is the nation's noncommercial, educational, informational, cultural, and entertainment TV broadcasting agency. PBS is funded by member stations, educational institutions, and the Corporation for Public Broadcasting. Its 349 member stations produce TV programs for national broadcast on PBS affiliates around the country. A few of the more innovative and bigger PBS affiliates are WNET in New York (www.wnet.org), WETA in Washington, and WGBH in Boston (www.boston.com/wgbh). PBS.org is the most visited such website in the world. Internship and career opportunities at headquarters are posted online; other positions are available at affiliate stations on programs and websites.

Public Radio International (PRI)

100 North Sixth Street, Suite 900A

Minneapolis, MN 55403

(612) 338–5000; fax: 612.330.9222

www.pri.org

Similar in nature to NPR and one of its fastest-growing competitors, Public Radio International is a public radio producer providing educational, informational, and educational programming. PRI's noncommercial format is broadcast to 715 affiliates around the country, reaching over 13 million listeners each week. PRI, the BBC World Service, and WGBH Boston broadcast *America One*, a public radio program in Europe. PRI also produces international programming including *The World*, a global news program, and *Marketplace*, a global business and economics show. PRI lists job vacancies online.

NEW MEDIA

Almost every company, organization, or group has a website. That's good news for those interested in interactive communications. This field, which often combines knowledge of technology with a love or art or words, offers a myriad of opportunities for writers, graphic designers, market researchers, advertisers, and web designers. While the dot-com fallout rattled countless business ventures, news and information sites continue to thrive and search for new talent. The majority of organizations listed in this book have websites and maintain a staff whose responsibilities lie solely with web maintenance and development. Many media-related sites produce original content for the Internet. This often means equipping a reporter with a digital camera and tape recorder so that he or she can produce a multimedia story for the site. There are numerous zines (magazines published solely on the web) that cover a wide spectrum of interests from music to culture to politics.

The digital revolution is an international one. Although it only takes a modem, data line, and computer to transmit your message to any point on the globe, the majority of new media services in America are concentrated in several cities. Silicon Valley in California manufactures much of the technology, while Silicon Alley in Manhattan actually implements the technology and much of the new media content. Bill Gates's Microsoft complex in Redmond, Washington, is another big new media center along with Austin, Texas, and Portland, Oregon.

What are employers looking for? According to John Pavlik, professor and executive director of the Center for New Media at Columbia University, "Skills needed for those interested in the new media marketplace are of three types: (1) talent for and interest in adaptability — the new media industry is in a great, dynamic, and continuous state of change, (2) facility with new technology, especially telecommunications and computing, and (3) excellent communications capability, both written and visual."

Desktop publishing and the Internet have made it possible for anyone with an idea and a computer to create a zine on the Web. There are thousands of sites concerning just as many specialized issues, so it is highly likely that if you have a story to tell, someone is willing to give you the space to say it. That said, there are not many zines dealing with international issues. Most will cover an international issue if the topic is in the news but international news is not their focus.

Here are some sources of information for the new media:

Center for New Media (www.ccnmtl.columbia.edu). Based at Columbia University, the center works to advance the use of new media and digital technologies in education. It has information about the new media community and its uses in the field of education.

The Cole Pages (www.colegroup.com). A resource that focuses on the nexus between technology, newspapers, and publishing.

The Media Lab (www.media.mit.edu). Based at MIT, the Media Lab builds bridges between academics and industry to explore the relationship between technology and the everyday world.

The following are a few webzines:

Ananova (www.ananova.com). A British website providing news, sports, and entertainment information.

Slate magazine (slate.msn.com). *Slate* is an interactive magazine of politics and culture from Microsoft. It offers news, analysis, political insight, and cultural criticism.

Salon (www.salon.com). *Salon* is an Internet journal that maintains a network of sites titled News, Politics, Technology & Business, Arts & Entertainment, Books, Sex, Life, People, Comics, and Salon Audio.

News.com (news.com.com). Winner of the 1998 Webby Award for best news, CNET's News.com is a comprehensive technology news site. It is updated throughout the day, offers features, and is sorted into useful categories like The Net, Intranets, and Business and Computing.

Internet Resources for Journalism Jobs

Websites that list newspapers and other media around the world:

> www.refdesk.com/paper.html
> www.newspapers.com
> www.thepaperboy.com.au
> http://library.uncg.edu/news/
> www.journalistexpress.com/
> www.escapeartist.com/media/media.htm

Journalism Job Sites

JournalismJobs (www.journalismjobs.com)

Mediabistro (http://mediabistro.com)

JournalismNext (www.journalismnext.com)

JournalistUSA (www.journalistusa.com)

American Society of Newspaper Editors—careers (www.asne.org/kiosk/careers/index.htm)

Berkeley Graduate School of Journalism jobs board (www.journalism.berkeley.edu/jobs)

Investigative Reporters and Editors job center (www.ire.org/jobs)

Journalism Job Resources (http://bailiwick.lib.uiowa.edu/journalism/jobs.html)

Editor & Publisher online classifieds (www.editorandpublisher.com/editorandpublisher/classifieds/index.jsp)

Detroit Free Press Journalism Job Tools (www.freep.com/jobspage/toolkit/index.htm)

The Poynter Institute (www.poynter.org)

dot Journalism (www.journalism.co.uk)

Jeff Gaulin's Canadian Journalism Job Board (www.jeffgaulin.com)

ADVERTISING

As borders blur and commerce crosses borders, the advertising industry has found itself at the forefront of the globalization trend. Cable and international advertising produce special programming and national identity commercials for foreign broadcast or for segmented audiences within a city and market products or services to a foreign market. But ad agencies do much more than create a Coca-Cola commercial that will be well received worldwide. The creative department conceives of an ad campaign, writes and designs the ads, and works with production companies to produce the advertisements. The media department develops the marketing strategy and buys air time, print, or billboard space. The account services staff studies a client's company and its competitors and is the business side of the agency. Aspiring advertising executives can choose to work either in house or as a freelancer in any of these departments.

Much like other media-related fields, advertising is full of deadlines, long hours, stress, and job insecurity. The ability to be flexible, work long hours, and start at the bottom are often cited as key success factors for careers in advertising. This is especially true when working on international accounts, as you are dealing with different time zones and cultures. Additionally, awareness of different cultural norms and styles of communication is critical to ensure that a product or service is marketed in a culturally appropriate way.

Competition is stiff, and a botched or lost account could result in pink slips for those involved. Those in the industry are constantly moving from agency to agency or crossing over to the client side, hoping to better their reputations and their salaries. It has been said that in this competitive industry—like most media industries—moving over means moving up: After a certain point in your career, you often need to change companies in order to get a raise or promotion. Starting salaries are not high, but there is opportunity for rapid advancement. In agencies, "creatives" make the most money, followed by the account staff, then the media staff. Generally, you can expect to make anywhere from the high $10s to mid-$20s when you accept an entry-level position with a B.A. degree. Top executives and directors often earn six figures, but this also varies by agency size and location. In-house agencies are similar to pure ad agencies but are staffed by company employees and develop advertising and promotion strategies only for that company's products or services. In addition to opportunities for advancement, there are also chances to work on international accounts or abroad.

Often, because starting salaries are low, many individuals enter the field straight out of college. Many firms have structured summer internship programs, which can be researched through their websites (see the large organization profiles below). You might also consider developing your own internship or volunteering for a local community or nonprofit organization. Most organizations or professional associations have marketing or outreach committees, which can be great places to test the waters and see if you enjoy the skills involved. Thus, your initial work doesn't have to be international; like most communications jobs, it is important to get hands-on experience writing, creating, and conceptualizing campaigns. Chambers of Commerce are other good places to explore for possible internships.

Coursework in advertising, marketing, and public relations is helpful, but internships are the best way to get your foot in the door, make contacts, and gain an understanding of the industry from the inside. Web-related experience is also important, both on the account and creative sides. It's also a good idea to work at several agencies, both large and small—perhaps even an in-house agency—to get a variety of experiences and perspectives. The majority of advertising agencies are still in New York City, though Chicago, Los Angeles, Detroit, and San Francisco also have large advertising centers. While many large firms have a global presence, their offices abroad are staffed largely with nationals from that particular country or region, with just a handful of expatriates in more senior positions.

For more information on the advertising field and job possibilities, explore:

Advertising Age (www.adage.com). A major periodical for advertising professionals that also has a job bank.
Adweek (www.adweek.com). Another major industry publication that has a career and job classified section.
Fristoe & Carlton Executive Search and Recruiting (www.adjob.com). This website also has great tips for breaking into the field of advertising.

The following are some big advertising agencies with international clients:

J. Walter Thompson Company
466 Lexington Avenue
New York, NY 10017
(212) 210–7000
www.jwtworld.com

J. Walter Thompson is a global brand communications agency, which means it works to make products brands or household names. It pioneered the studies of consumer lifestyle as opposed to traditional demographics. With 250 offices in 88 countries, J. Walter Thompson's international clients include Citibank, De-Beers, Eastman Kodak, Ford, Kraft, Nestlé, Nike, and Sprint. It also offers marketing services such as direct consumer communications, loyalty creation, and market segmenting. The company has over 9,000 employees around the world and posts job vacancies online.

BBDO Worldwide

1285 Avenue of the Americas
New York, NY
(212) 459–5000 or (212) 459-JOBS
e-mail: nyhrmanagerrecruiting@bbdo.com
www.bbdo.com

Number three worldwide with 345 offices in 76 countries, advertising agency BBDO is part of the Omnicom Group. It focuses on brand identity, aiming to "create and communicate relationships between products or services and users." BBDO prides itself on winning awards for advertising campaigns for international clients. Clients include Bayer, Apple Computers, Pizza-Hut, Pepsi-Cola, and Wella. It has over 20,500 staff. Hiring is done by regional offices, with contact details available online.

Bozell Worldwide

40 West 23rd Street
New York, NY 10010
(212) 727–5000
e-mail: bozellhr@newyork.bozell.com
www.bozell.com

Bozell Worldwide, a unit of True North Communications, Inc., is the world's eleventh-largest U.S. advertising agency, earning $2.9 billion annually. Part of advertising conglomerate Interpublic Group, it has about 460 employees. Bozell is responsible for the widely popular "Got Milk?" campaign, which features celebrities from film, television, and politics, each with his or her own milk mustache. Other clients include multinationals such as Pepsi-Cola, AT&T, American Express, and Maxwell House Coffee. Bozell is known for being innovative and for its flexibility and client commitment.

Ogilvy & Mather Worldwide

309 W. 49th Street
New York, NY 10019
(212) 237–4000
www.ogilvy.com

Ogilvy & Mather is a worldwide marketing communications company that has been in existence since 1948. It launched Dove Soap and created the first Pepperidge Farm commercial in 1956. A subsidiary of the WPP Group (which also owns J. Walter Thompson), it is the sixth-largest agency network in the world, having developed alliances with a number of respected foreign advertising companies. Among the first to enter the former Soviet Union in 1989, Ogilvy & Mather has 15,000 employees at 450 offices in 100 countries. Divisions include Ogilvy Public Relations Worldwide, OgilvyOne, which provides direct marketing to individual consumers, and Ogilvy Interactive. It lists career opportunities on its website.

Saatchi & Saatchi

375 Hudson Street
New York, NY
(212) 463–2000
www.saatchi.com

Billing itself as an "ideas company," Saatchi & Saatchi focuses not only on promoting a product or service but also on the people who purchase such products—a very consumer-oriented approach, which pleases clients such as Tide, Delta Airlines, Toyota, and Hewlett Packard. It has a worldwide network of 138 offices in 82 countries employing over 7,000 people. Saatchi & Saatchi's website has links to its many partners around the globe. The agency was acquired by Paris-based Publicis in 2000 and moved its headquarters to New York, where any job inquiries should be directed.

PUBLIC RELATIONS

Public relations (PR) has rapidly become a global industry as companies and organizations work to communicate their messages across borders in a culturally appropriate way. Thus, opportunities abound in many areas to work on international public relations campaigns or issues, from pharmaceuticals to antilandmine campaigns. Public relations specialists enhance, maintain, and promote the image of their client, be they individuals, corporations, or nations. Instead of buying commercial space or time, PR professionals work closely with the media, disseminating information to the public through stories, staged events, or conferences. PR specialists do their work in a variety of ways, from setting up press conferences to sending out press releases to serving as the liaison between the media and their clients. Nonprofit organizations, especially, rely on PR specialists to get their message out, to assist with fundraising, and to promote events, as they rarely have an advertising budget.

Still, there is a lot of competition and movement as people search for higher salaries and more experience. Once again, internships are the springboard to a career in public relations. Strong writing skills are also coveted in this field because a large component of the job requires strong verbal and written communication skills. Creativity, a thick skin, and an ability to work under pressure are also important qualities of a successful PR specialist.

Because public relations is such a client-centered business, it has a strong service orientation. Any evidence of your ability to work with clients in such a way is valued. Successful professionals learn quickly how to listen closely to clients' needs and desires through communication with them via e-mail, telephone, meetings, or other correspondence. Then, often under deadline, they must devise a creative strategy to transmit the clients' desired message—this involves the creation of a comprehensive communications strategy to deliver the message to intended recipients—through outreach, events, third-party media, and website development.

Those interested in public relations may choose to work with an agency or in house in the public information departments of corporations, foundations, nonprofits, and international organizations. Some organizations mainly recruit entry-level professionals and promote from within, whereas others are more open to considering individuals with other backgrounds; this will be an important part of your job research. Starting salaries are comparable to those in advertising (generally fairly low), however, they can rise fairly quickly and become lucrative in middle to senior positions. Corporate positions generally pay better than agencies, and agencies pay better than government or nonprofit PR departments. Most of the top firms are in New York, Chicago, Los Angeles, and Washington, D.C., though smaller agencies abound. A small agency may specialize in a particular niche or market (for example, the Latin market or a functional area like telecommunications).

Recommended public relations websites:

Public Relations Society of America (www.prsa.org). This site has a tremendous amount of resources, including excellent publications, jobs, professional development opportunities, and links to continue your research.

Public Affairs Council (www.pac.org).

PR Week (www.prweek.com). This site has international and regional editions, so it's a great way to keep abreast of trends.

The following are several of the top public relations agencies. Note that the advertising agencies listed previously also have PR divisions, as do most major companies and international organizations.

Burson-Marsteller

230 Park Avenue South
New York, NY 10003
(212) 614–4000
www.bm.com

Owned by the WPP Group and a leader in commercial communications and counseling, Burson-Marsteller is at the forefront of global perception management. *Perception management* is an industry buzzword that essentially means overseeing how someone or something is perceived and attempting to portray it in a favorable light. Among its industry and practice specialties are the fields of health, consumer products, and high-tech and in public affairs, government relations, crisis communications, investor relations, and the environment. It has 2,000 employees and accounts or offices in 30 countries across the Asia-Pacific region, Europe, Latin America, and North America. The firm is especially big in the emerging markets area, with operations everywhere from Uganda to Russia to Chile and Indonesia. Burson-Marsteller posts job openings and internship opportunities on its website.

Edelman

200 East Randolph Drive, 63rd Floor

Chicago, IL 60601

(312) 240–3000

www.edelman.com

Started in 1952, Edelman (the firm dropped "Public Relations Worldwide" from its name in 2002) is the largest independent public relations firm in the world and ranks sixth overall. It specializes in health care, technology, corporate finance, consumer and public affairs, tourism, and crisis communications. Edelman has 1,900 employees, 38 offices, and 60 affiliates around the world. It recruits online and also offers a paid, full-time internship program for college juniors and seniors.

Hill and Knowlton

466 Lexington Avenue, 8th Floor

New York, NY 10017

   (212) 885–0300

   www.hillandknowlton.com

Another firm that's part of advertising juggernaut WPP, Hill and Knowlton has 70 offices in 36 countries and over 2,000 employees. Its PR specialists work in corporate communications, media relations, financial relations, crisis management, consumer and business-to-business marketing, public affairs, advanced technology, reputation management, lobbying, and health care. Hill and Knowlton may be best known for specializing in political campaigns and issue advocacy. The company has a three-track career system that streams hires into general management, practice management, or global account management. You can apply online for positions and internships.

Ruder Finn

301 East 57th Street

New York, NY 10022

(212) 593–6423

e-mail: careers@ruderfinn.com.

www.ruderfinn.com

A family-owned company, Ruder Finn bills itself as a complete public relations, marketing, and advertising company. Its PR specialists work in a variety of fields, including health care, technology, engineering, and the environment.

Other specialties are corporate relations, public and government affairs, high-technology, visual technology, travel, and international hospitality. It has over 600 employees. The New York headquarters is the second largest in the city, and the firm also has major offices in Washington, Chicago, Los Angeles, Raleigh, Paris, London, and the Pacific Rim. Ruder Finn sponsors an executive development program for qualified undergraduate and graduate students. Less than 10 percent of the 500–600 applicants are chosen for the four-month training program. Ruder Finn also offers an unpaid summer internship program for college juniors; you can find details online.

Professional Associations in the Field of Media and Journalism

American Society of Journalism and Authors/Society of Professional Journalists: (212) 997–0947 or (317) 927–8000; www.asja.org or www.spj.org

Investigative Reporters and Editors/The American Society of Newspaper Editors: (573) 882–2042 or (703) 453–1122; www.ire.org or www.asne.org

Women in Communications/National Press Club: (703) 920–5555, (212) 983–4655, or (202) 662–7505; www.WOMCOM.org or http://npc.press.org

10

Teaching Abroad

TEACHING ABROAD is an excellent way to experience another culture and learn a local language, and it is relatively easy to do without significant specialized training, unlike many other options in this book. Many students who enter a graduate school in international affairs have taught abroad prior to applying. Many times, teaching schedules are flexible so that you might pursue a part-time internship in another field (international development, business, etc.) while earning money to live in your country of choice.

You can find a diverse array of opportunities to teach overseas, both structured (with formal application deadlines) and unstructured (that you create yourself, or are offered in a more ad hoc way) in all regions of the world. A bachelor's degree is necessary in most cases, though not always required. Teaching experience at home is also very helpful; if you do not have formal teaching experience, volunteer group or individual tutoring experience will facilitate obtaining a position. The background needed to teach abroad varies depending on individual institutions or organizations.

The main sources of teaching jobs overseas vary widely; opportunities exist within the federal government, through foreign governments, or with private institutions and nonprofit organizations. Teaching positions abroad generally require a commitment of one or two years, often on a one-year renewable contract. In general, proficiency in a particular foreign language is not required.

FEDERAL GOVERNMENT

Overseas American Schools/U.S. Department of State
Office of Overseas Schools

Establishing a Credentials File

When you are being seriously considered for a job, your potential employer may ask for a copy of your dossier or "credentials file"—consisting of transcripts, letters of recommendation, and the like. Therefore, before you start looking for a job, establish such a file; arrange to have transcripts and letters of recommendation on file at your college career services office, or in your own possession. It is often acceptable to send the material yourself to an overseas school, but it may be easier to let your college or university handle such administrative responsibilities. Thus, if your college provides such a service, it is worth the nominal fee usually charged. Check with your undergraduate career office for information.

Department of State

www.state.gov/m/a/os

The State Department does not employ teachers directly; however, the above website links to several excellent organizations that hire teachers to work abroad. Simply click on "Teaching Overseas" to find multiple programs. You will also find information about the 180-plus American International Schools currently in existence, as well as helpful links to a variety of teacher resources and educational associations. These schools have either binational or international student bodies. Qualifications to work in American International Schools include a background in education and international affairs; foreign languages and regional knowledge is definitely helpful.

The Department of Defense Education Activity (DoDEA)

www.odedodea.edu

The Department of Defense Education Activity is a civilian agency under the U.S. Department of Defense. It is headquartered in Arlington, Virginia, and operates schools in 14 foreign countries, seven US states, Guam, and Puerto Rico. Approximately 8,800 educators work with over 100,000 DoDEA students—all dependents of U.S. military and defense personnel. Student teachers and qualified educators are eligible. For hiring information about any DoDEA school, go to the website noted above; click on "Personnel" and then "Employment" for information on current vacancies and application procedures.

Peace Corps

1990 K Street, NW

Washington, DC 20526

(202) 606–3886

www.peacecorps.gov

The Peace Corps hires teachers with experience in a wide range of areas, from English to math and science and special education. It maintains programs in Africa, Asia, and Latin America. See Chapter 5 on the federal government for more information on the Peace Corps.

Peace Corps: One Student's Experience

HERMENCE AREGBA (PCV TOGO)

During my senior year of college, I decided that if I wanted to get hands-on experience in my international affairs major, I had to leave the United States and move to a country where I could use all the skills I had acquired. I joined the Peace Corps as a Girls' Education & Empowerment Volunteer in Togo, West Africa. The thought of working with young girls and women while learning a culture different from mine thrilled me. Once I arrived to Togo, I underwent an extensive three-month training course that prepared me for the education and empowering that I would do with Togolese girls and women precisely in Kabou, a Muslim village north of the capital, Lomé.

I arrived in Kabou very excited but at the same time worried that the community didn't know exactly why I was there. Soon after my arrival, Mr. Fofana, the director of Kabou's most popular junior high school, quickly confirmed my worries. After a warm welcome, Mr. Fofana announced that he was thrilled I was his English teacher. I bowed my head in bewilderment, scratched it, looked at Mr. Fofana, smiled, and spoke in my best French.

"Non!" I said, and explained that I was in Kabou to educate the village on the importance of girls' education and HIV/AIDS prevention and awareness—not to teach English. At this, Mr. Fofana laughed, heartily slapped me on the back, and told me to bathe and change my clothes, since the students were expecting me. He walked out of the house leaving the doors wide open and me standing wide-eyed, all flustered, and puzzled.

Mr. Fofana's plan for me not only disregarded my three months of training, but it also challenged me to rethink my own plans. How was I going to educate students and the community on the importance of girls' education and empowerment and HIV/AIDS prevention and awareness while teaching English?

After a warm shower, I rode my mountain bike down the dusty crowded road to Kabou Ouest Junior High School. At the school, Mr. Fofana declared in French, "Here is your new English teacher . . . and girls educator." Although he had not clearly explained what educating girls would entail, I was content with his introduction. At the sound of the rusted tin bell, all the students entered their respective classrooms, and I followed the director into a large brick room.

To my astonishment, I was facing 119 students, standing at attention military-style, ready to salute the new teacher. Noticing my trepidation, Mr. Fofana slapped me on the back, told me everything was going to be fine, and left.

Making sure he was out of sight, I placed my book bag on the floor and climbed on top of the instructor's table. I placed my hands on my hip and scanned the classroom from left to right. Before I realized what my action might have looked like to a bunch of teenagers, the class filled with laughter, which I couldn't help joining in. After the laughter resided, a young boy looked up at me and asked in an English I slightly understood if I would teach them English songs and games. I happily obliged and with my arms raised up high, right foot tapping the table, I counted one, two, three—and the singing began.

When the school bell rang and the students cleared the classroom, I knew the solution to my problem. I needed to integrate girls' education and empowerment and STD and HIV/AIDS prevention and awareness into my English lessons with the help of songs, games, and learning activities. My English classes became my medium. For the remainder of the school year I had my students write their own short stories in English depicting their lives in Kabou. They created lists of vocabulary words and found corresponding words in English. My students wrote songs to educate the community about STD and HIV/AIDS prevention and awareness.

As a Peace Corps Volunteer, I not only met the needs of the community by teaching English, but I also applied my training to implement my original mission, all the while adapting to unsuspected change and need. Upon joining the Peace Corps my expectations and goals were very clear: I would move to a country I had never known, use all the knowledge I learned in college to help the people of that country, and experience a new culture and lifestyle. But now I know all too well that I should have had only one expectation: to be prepared for change. Change in my assignment, change in work methods, change in how I view others in the world, change in how others view me, and—most of all—change in me. I came back to the United States knowing that I was no longer the same young college graduate who joined the Peace Corps. I was a better and changed person. I was educated and empowered!

OTHER OPPORTUNITIES

European Council of International Schools (ECIS)

www.ecis.org (for contact information for its four regional offices)

The European Council of International Schools, founded in 1965, is the largest membership organization of international schools in the world, maintaining offices on three continents. Among its many other missions, ECIS works with individual schools and teachers interested in teaching and administrative posts abroad. See www.ecis.org/staffing/jobs.htm for more information, including criteria for teaching and administrative candidates. ECIS holds recruitment fairs in London, Vancouver, and occasionally in cities around Australia; you must register in advance for such fairs (see the website for details). Internships are available in some schools for teachers in their first year of certification. Global vacancies are posted on their website, and they offer information on seminars and teacher exchanges. Take advantage of this excellent resource!

International Schools Services (ISS)

15 Roszel Road, Box 5910
Princeton, NJ 08543–5910
(609) 452–0990
www.iss.org

International Schools Services provides educational services for American and international schools overseas. Among these services are recruitment assistance of teachers, school supply procurement, curricular guidance, liaison responsibilities between overseas schools and American educational resources, and consultative visits to overseas schools. More than 700 schools are affiliated with ISS in Africa, Europe, Central and South America, the Middle East, and Asia. ISS runs three annual recruitment fairs in the United States; to attend, you must both register and create a credentials file with ISS prior to attending. Applicants should have a bachelor's degree, at least two years of teaching experience at the primary or secondary level, advanced degrees for guidance counselor positions or higher administration work, and overseas living or work experience. Most contracts are for two years, but times and necessary teacher certification vary. Contact ISS directly about specific recruitment fair (dates and locations) and be sure to review the website carefully for application and credentials file information. You may apply online.

WorldTeach

c/o Center for International Development
Harvard University
79 John F. Kennedy Street
Cambridge MA 02138 USA
(800) 4-TEACH–0 (483–2240) or (617) 495–5527

e-mail: info@worldteach.org

www.worldteach.org

WorldTeach is an independent nonprofit organization founded in 1986 that provides opportunities for individuals to make a meaningful contribution to international education by living and working as teachers in developing countries. WorldTeach offers voluntary teaching positions in developing countries. Most volunteers teach English, though in some country programs WorldTeach volunteers teach computer skills, science, math, environmental education, or HIV/AIDS awareness. No formal teaching experience is required to apply to the programs, although participants must complete 25 hours of Teaching English as a Foreign/Second Language before departing for their program. A bachelor's degree (in any subject), or equivalent professional experience, is required for participation in the yearlong programs. Summer programs are open to undergraduate students and anyone over the age of 18 with a demonstrated interest in teaching and service. Applicants do not need to be U.S. citizens but should be fluent in English. Applications are accepted on a rolling basis; instructions and the application form are available on the website at www.worldteach.org.

Volunteers can teach for one year in Costa Rica, Ecuador, Namibia, or the Marshall Islands or for six months in China. Six-month Nature Guide Training Programs are offered in various locations, usually in Central America. Shorter two-month summer programs are offered in Namibia, China, Ecuador, and Costa Rica.

Participants pay a fee prior to departure to cover costs of transportation, visa, teaching placement, health insurance, field staff support, and an in-country orientation and training program. Fees are $3,990 for the summer programs and $4,990–$5,990 for longer-term programs. Many volunteers raise the fee through fundraising in their home community. Volunteers receive housing (often with a host family) and, in the longer-term programs, a modest monthly stipend from their host school. For more information, go to www.worldteach.org or call the WorldTeach office.

TEACHING ENGLISH OVERSEAS

Many individuals teach English abroad; in countries where English is a second language, there is often much demand. This is particularly true in Asia, though there is also demand in Latin America and Africa. If you are interested in teaching English as a second language, begin your research by contacting Teachers of English to Speakers of Other Languages (www.tesol.org/index.html), which offers a wealth of information about teacher certification opportunities, professional development opportunities, publications, and the field in general. Additionally, the Center for Applied Linguistics has information on teaching of English as a second or foreign language. Visit its website (www.cal.org) to find important links to other associations in the field, resources and publications, and job listings.

WHERE ARE THE JOBS?

Asia currently has the highest demand for English teachers. You will therefore find several well-established programs that can help you get situated in this part of the world. According to a former graduate student at Columbia, the most lucrative teaching jobs in Asia are in Japan, where you also find the best working conditions, although recently it has gotten more difficult to find employment due to increased competition coupled with the difficulties some of the regional economies are experiencing. Many teaching opportunities are becoming available in Thailand, Korea, and Vietnam (although salaries are considerably less).

Three excellent resources for teaching in Asia:

Volunteers in Asia (www.volasia.org). This site has information on teaching and volunteering in China, as well as other Asian countries.

Princeton in Asia (www/[romcetpm/edu/~pia). This site offers two different types of internships: teaching and nonteaching. This is an excellent program to explore; opportunities exist for teachers in a wide array of South and East Asian countries; nonteaching internships range from community development to business and media.

Jobs in Thailand (www.escati.com/thaijobs.htm). This site offers tips for those interested in teaching in Thailand.

Japan

Japan Exchange and Teaching Program (JET)

JET recruits several thousand Americans annually to teach English in Japanese schools and colleges as well as municipal and prefectural offices in Japan. Established in 1987, JET quickly developed an excellent reputation for its structure and orientation/training. The program is for one year, though it is usually possible to extend for two. Housing fees and facilities will vary widely depending on location. Most of the participants in the JET program work in middle or high schools and may work at several schools. Those interested should get an application through the JET website, which has extensive information about the program as well as stories from JET alumni at www.mofa.go.jp/j_info/visit/jet/index.html.

Teaching experience, though helpful, is not necessary for JET. International experience and motivation for work abroad are usually more important. Completed applications and required documentation are screened at the Japanese Embassy, and selected candidates are interviewed for final selection at the embassy or consulate general.

AEON

www.aeonet.com

AEON employs 250–300 people from around the world to teach conversational English to elementary through university students, businesspeople, and other adults. It also has a program for individuals who wish to teach children. Applicants must send a resume and one-page personal statement about "Why I want to live and work in Japan." Applicants need neither teaching experience nor knowledge of Japanese.

In the United States, applicants should check out www.aeonet.com or contact one of the AEON U.S. recruiting offices below:

Los Angeles
Aeon Inter-Cultural USA
1960 East Grand Avenue
El Segundo, CA 90245
(213) 414–1515

New York
Aeon Inter-Cultural USA
230 Park Avenue
New York, NY 10169

A
DAY
IN THE
LIFE

An English Teacher at a Japanese Middle School/JET Program

At 7 A.M., with the frogs already croaking in the rice field behind my apartment build-ing, I wake, wash my hair in a basin of water, then sprint out the door to ride my bicy-cle to school. As I squeeze in the backdoor to the teacher's room and slip on my "school shoes," the vice principal is getting ready to start the morning meeting. Every-one stands up and bows to each other. As usual, the meeting lasts fifteen minutes, then, after a short break, first period begins. This is a class of Terao-sensei's thirteen-year-old first-year students. Terao-sensei and I always teach this group as a pair, playing off one another's jokes, so by the time we were ready to start the first English game on this particular day, the students were already overcome with giggles. The next class was comprised of forty third-year students. The days left before their high school entrance exams were rapidly ticking away, and the ten-sion in the room was palpable. We had covered a few grammar points, practiced pronuncia-tion, and made it halfway through a short game of twenty questions before we could get the students to crack a smile.

After one more class and a free period, it was time for lunch. I had promised to eat with Fuji-sensei's second-years, and when I went to her room with my school lunch, I brought my old high school pictures. Most of the lunch period was spent bent over the photos fielding ques-tions about the strange customs of American high schools. As lunch period ended a group of boys from the adjacent classroom poked their heads in and asked if I would play volleyball with them during recess. We played, and then, when the buzzer sounded, stayed together to pull weeds during the school's "cleaning time."

Two more periods were left—another first-year class and then a free period. When cleaning time was over, I sprinted inside, brushed the dust off my slacks, and downed a quick cup of coffee with the gym teachers. Classes ended at 2:30; twenty minutes later, afternoon home-room let out. For an hour, I corrected English essays with Fuji-sensei, then went off to practice with the basketball team.

That particular night, I had to go to dinner with a group from the board of education and then work on a speech for the PTA the next week. With this in mind, at 5:00 I went to tell the principal that I would be leaving and, after saying goodbye to the rows of teachers in the teach-ers room, slipped out the door and grabbed my bicycle for the ride home.

(212) 808–3080

Chicago
AEON Inter-Cultural USA
203 North LaSalle Street, Suite 2100
Chicago, IL 60601
(312) 251–0900

China

In China the need for English language teachers is particularly great. Millions of Chinese want to learn English, but the few Chinese qualified to teach it complain of small salaries compared to what they could earn in other occupations. Despite the communist slogan "A teacher is a candle, giving light to others while burning itself," few Chinese are attracted. As a result, opportunities exist for others qualified to teach English.

Here are some good websites for teaching English in China (note that the websites for teaching in Asia listed above also have China programs):

Teaching English and Living in China (www.tealic.com). Provides resources, articles, and information on teaching English and living in China.
Council on International Educational Exchange (www.councilexchanges.org). Has a program on teaching in China.
Colorado China Council (www.asiacouncil.org). Offers yearlong opportunities to teach English in China.

Middle East

American-Mideast Educational and Training Services (AMIDEAST)
1730 M Street, NW, Suite 1100
Washington, DC 20036–4505
(202) 776–9600
ww.amideast.org

America-Mideast Educational and Training Services, Inc., is a private non-profit organization promoting cooperation and understanding between Americans and the people of the Middle East and North Africa through education,

---

The Fulbright Teacher and Administrator Exchange Program

The Fulbright Teacher Exchange Program has placed teachers and educational administrators overseas since 1946. Application deadlines are in mid-October each year. For information on the program, application instructions, frequently asked questions, and alumni stories, visit their website at grad.usda.gov/International/ftep/html.

information, and development assistance programs. Headquartered in Washington, D.C., AMIDEAST has a network of offices in Bahrain, Egypt, Jordan, Kuwait, Lebanon, Morocco, Syria, Tunisia, the United Arab Emirates, the West Bank/Gaza Strip, and Yemen. Internships, consultancy positions, and full-time positions in their Washington office and in the countries in which they operate are advertised through their website.

TEACHING AT HOME

If you wish to teach international subjects at home, you will need to decide at which level you'd like to teach. On the high school level, certification will depend on the state in which you reside. If you are interested in community colleges, you generally need at least a master's degree, although in some cases a doctorate will be required. Opportunities may be available in political science, international economics, languages, area studies, or history.

Obviously, for professorships in four-year colleges and universities, a doctorate is essential. Occasionally, adjunct practitioner positions are available, particularly in professional schools, for middle-level to senior professionals with a master's degree and relevant work experience. For information on pursuing an academic career, it is a good idea to check relevant professional associations in your field of study, like the American Political Science Association, various Area Studies associations, and the like. Visit the American Political Science Association website (www.apsanet.org/jobplc) for information on political science careers, relevant articles, a video, and links to other resources about teaching at the community college and university level. There are also publications on pursuing an academic

---

United Nations International School

24–50 East River Drive
New York, NY 10010

The UN International School is for students whose parents are associated with the United Nations and have come to New York from abroad. It is a day school, beginning with the five-year-old level and continuing through preparation for college and university. It has two locations: on the East River south of UN Headquarters, and in Queens (an elementary branch). Qualifications include teaching experience, regional expertise, and languages.

career in the bibliography of this text; one popular one is *The Academic Job Search Handbook* by Mary Morris Heiberger and Julia Miller Vick.

For additional information in your job search for teaching positions in the United States, visit the website of the American Federation of Teachers (www.aft.org) or the National Education Association (www.nea.org).

HELPFUL RESOURCES

For a list of agencies that assist overseas placement, or for specific job opportunities under U.S. government and foreign government programs, see the website for the Institute of International Education (www.iie.org). A booklet with information on agencies and organizations in almost a hundred countries that are concerned in one way or another with recruiting teaching staff may be obtained through UNESCO (www.education.unesco.org).

Additional websites:

Dave's ESL Café (www.eslcafe.com)
English Language Education in Japan (www.ling.lancs.ac.uk)
Best Bets for Teaching Abroad (www.cie.uci.edu/iop/teaching.html)
Teach Abroad.com (www.teachabroad.com)

11

International Law

WITH COUNTRIES increasingly linked through international trade and finance, and subject to international regulation though agencies such as the International Criminal Court and the World Trade Organization, the importance of international law is growing. International corporate law and positions in firms that deal with international financial transactions are on the rise. Human rights organizations are gaining prominence, and the field, albeit competitive, is growing. Work in the area of democracy and governance, and better policing, requires legal expertise. Collective efforts around environmental issues, narcotics control, immigration, and trade all require international legal experts to work in a variety of capacities.

For any job in this field—whether it be with a small nonprofit organization or a prestigious private firm—analytical ability and good research and writing skills are essential. It is also helpful to be familiar with the basic differences in the world's legal systems, as well as the political and cultural contexts in which those systems operate, according to a current international lawyer.

A JOINT DEGREE: JURIS DOCTOR AND A MASTER OF INTERNATIONAL AFFAIRS

There is an increasing trend to pursue both a degree in law and a master's in international affairs simultaneously, known as a joint degree. Usually, a law degree takes three years and a master of international affairs two. However, many international affairs schools have joint degree programs with their law schools that grant the juris doctor and the master of international affairs in a total of four years. This is seen as a real benefit to many, particularly those who want additional training beyond what a law degree offers, for example, in human rights or international economics and business.

If you are interested in pursuing a legal career, which degree is more important? Of the two degrees (law and international affairs), a law degree is definitely of paramount importance in the job hunt. Thus, experts recommend first developing your legal knowledge and skills through internships and clerkships. If those are used strategically, you can further gain important experience in your areas of international interest, be they immigration, finance, trade, or something similar. Beyond a J.D., an international degree, even though it will not guarantee you work that is global in scope, will put you on the inside track for such jobs as they develop within your firm or organization. Language skills in Japanese, Mandarin, Korean, Spanish, German, or French, as well as overseas experience, are also helpful for a career in international law.

For international legal work in banks or law firms, courses such as finance and economics will be valuable when pursuing your law degree. As one senior vice president and general counsel of a major Japanese corporation who received both a master's degree in international affairs and a law degree put it,

> Students should focus their MA on the coursework that best supplements the legal skills one attains in law school for the type of international job they want. For example, if you are interested in corporate law, focus your master's coursework in business and finance. If you are interested in environmental law, your master's degree should encompass environmental science, environmental economics, and policy, along with regulatory courses.
>
> Additionally, students should get experience in the Jessup moot court competition and become an active member of their international law journal in law school. Writing a "note" on an important subject can often be a ticket to success, as it demonstrates writing skills, commitment, and an expertise in the issue at hand.

The best law schools with specializations in international law, according to *U.S. News and World Report* 2003:

1. New York University
2. Columbia University

3. Harvard University
4. Georgetown University
5. Yale University

A WORLD OF OPPORTUNITIES

Federal Government

All of the agencies of the U.S. government have legal divisions or general counsel offices that would find, in certain cases, a background in international law of particular interest. Initially, out of law school or a different area of law, you may be assigned to domestic legal issues. Be flexible: It is a great foot in the door, and if you have international training and interests and you make these known, you can apply for vacancies that demand international expertise or request an expansion of duties to include international cases or policy issues. International legal positions are extremely competitive on the federal level and usually are not entry level. However, the number of agencies that hire international lawyers is growing, notes Sushan Demirjian at the section on international law and practice of the American Bar Association. Such agencies include the International Trade Administration at Commerce, Department of the Treasury, Department of Justice, Environmental Protection Agency, Department of Energy, and Federal Communications Commission. Federal government salaries are good and have excellent benefits but are obviously not as high as those in top law firms. Competition for government jobs, accordingly, may be less keen than in the private sector but potentially more interesting. See Chapter 5 on the federal government for more specific information about each agency and its mission.

Businesses and Banks

Multinational corporations and financial institutions often have their own legal division or general counsel. Other companies place their legal work in the hands of retained law firms—often large firms that have a strong global presence and reputation. Where businesses and banks are heavily engaged in international work, a background in international law will make you a competitive candidate, particularly if you have some economics or financial coursework under your belt *after* a few years of experience in a private law firm. This is because most corporate, or in-house, attorneys first refine their skills in law firms; it is rare for a law school graduate to be offered a position in a company directly upon graduation.

Many U.S. corporations with extensive overseas activities maintain legal staffs abroad. Members of such staffs represent their corporations in negotiations with foreign governments, as well as with nationals of such countries. They will also deal with immigration problems of corporate employees, employment contracts, and other matters. Rarely will members of the legal staffs of such corporations be permitted to argue in the courts of the foreign country. Generally, it is the headquarters legal staff of a corporation that will supervise its legal staff abroad. If the corporation does not have an overseas legal staff, members of headquarters staff may travel abroad to represent the corporation.

As noted above, these departments tend to hire more experienced lawyers. They don't have a lot of time to train, and thus hire, lawyers after they have developed an expertise through several years in a law firm. As Karen Monroe, former assistant director of career services at Columbia Law School, stated, "In my seven years at Columbia, I have seen only two individual students go directly to an in-house position."

United Nations

Jobs are few and highly competitive in the Office of Legal Affairs at the UN Secretariat as the United Nations remains under pressure to cut costs and streamline operations. Because most specialized agencies in the UN structure have their own legal staffs, these should also be included among your targets. Note, however, that much of this work is extremely specialized, and thus rarely will there be an opening for someone without significant work experience and credentials. Remember, too, that nationality quotas are in effect, so your competition is global. That being said, there may be some wonderful internships available for law and graduate students.

Individuals who are hired by the United Nations to work in the field of international law have a wide range of specializations. Attorneys might be involved in interpreting the United Nations Charter and the rules of international law, providing advice on commercial matters, or responding to member states as they work through legal, political, economic, scientific, technical, and environmental aspects of the law of the sea. Lawyers at the United Nations also may have the exciting opportunity to represent the Secretary-General before the International Court of Justice and in the settlements of claims.

These responsibilities could place you in the Office of the General Counsel, where you could work generally on contracts and claims, or codification and the legal issues described above.

Communications

The largest wire services, broadcast networks, and publishers either have their own legal staffs or contract for legal services from outside firms. A combined background in law and media is a decided plus.

Similar to the banks and businesses described above, attorneys rarely obtain such a position directly out of law school. It is more common to first gain government experience at an organization like the Federal Communications Commission or a private firm with a practice group dealing with the communications industry. Many of the most well known of these firms are in New York or Washington, D.C., because of their proximity to federal legislation and the top communications companies. After gaining three to five years of experience in the field, you become much more attractive to the actual communications firms themselves. This is because you not only know the issues but also have a network in the government and in firms that may help you to better represent their interests and negotiate more effectively on their behalf.

Nonprofit Organizations and Foundations

There are opportunities for international legal work in nonprofit organizations specializing in the fields of human rights, democracy and governance, and the environment. An interesting development, notes Sushan Demirjian, is "the growing area of technical legal assistance" to developing countries as they reform their legal systems. The experience needed varies by project and country, but certain international living experience, language skills, and familiarity with the region of interest are helpful to have in addition to a legal background.

Only the largest of these organizations in the international field have legal staffs. The majority obtain outside legal help from private firms. Just as with banks and businesses, nonprofits do not have time to train lawyers fresh out of law school and thus also follow the trend of hiring individuals with previous

The American Bar Association has a Central Eastern European Law Initiative (CEELI). It allows attorneys to become involved in pro bono (no-charge) projects in the areas of international development and democratization. If you have an interest in this region, look into this option, which allows for work abroad on a wide range of legal projects in the areas of legal assistance, developing new legal structures and systems, and providing technical advice to country governments. See www.abanet.org/ceeli/home.html for more information.

experience in government or a private firm. The field is small, particularly in human rights; most candidates are midcareer, either having worked in another capacity in the human rights field (with a juris doctor, of course), or with the federal government, international organizations, or a private law firm.

According to Steven Marks, a well-known international lawyer in the field of human rights who has worked extensively with the United Nations, four ingredients—beyond a knowledge of international law—make you stand out to a human rights organization: internships with human rights organizations (to gain experience and develop a network of contacts); languages; a joint degree; and a publication of some sort—anything from an op-ed in a newspaper to a note in a law journal.

Private Law Firms

With an interest in the nexus between international affairs and law, it makes sense to explore law firms with special international interests or corporations with extensive overseas activities. The legal work you do will generally be in the field of private international law, rather than public international law, which is intergovernmental in nature. In a private firm, you will probably gain experience in joint ventures or project and structured finance, generally corporate in nature.

Early years at an international law firm generally bring very long hours (12-hour days are not uncommon). You may have exposure to many high-profile firms and cases, and the opportunity to travel is definitely a possibility, particularly as you move up the ladder. Pressure can be great but so can rewards; salaries are generally in the three-figure range, especially in the New York and Washington law firms. Days can be stressful, since you are often juggling multiple cases and potentially working with multiple attorneys. As one attorney told me:

The truth is, there is no real organization to my day. It just doesn't exist. I spend some time each day learning about the facts of a given case, some time researching and reading about the relevant law and some time writing memoranda to partners at the firm telling them the results of my research. As part of learning the facts, I often spend time sifting through documents (contracts, correspondence, etc.) that the client has sent. The cases I work on tend to be very long and drawn out.

The American Bar Association: A Window to a World of Opportunity

The American Bar Association's International Legal Exchange Program is an excellent opportunity for attorneys who are working domestically and would like to experience a stint abroad. The ABA accepts U.S. lawyers who want to work abroad and non-U.S. attorneys who wish to work in the States; it helps them to connect with short-term placements or seminar opportunities abroad. Information on this program is available at the ABA's website (www.abanet.org; click on "International," then "International Law and Practice"). This sort of experience is a terrific way to build your resume, particularly for those interested in a career change into the global arena.

Major U.S. Law Firms with International Practices

Typically, the majority of U.S. law firms involved in international legal practices are located in New York; Washington, D.C.; Los Angeles; Chicago; and Miami. In international corporate practice, lawyers represent a global client base in a variety of areas. *Careers in International Law* (published by the American Bar Association) names a few: intellectual property rights, taxation, labor and employment law, distribution and sale of goods, and governmental regulation. Other areas can include financial transactions, securities and merchant banking, mergers and acquisitions, joint ventures, private finance, leveraged leasing, project finance, privatization, and bankruptcy and corporate reorganizations.

You will, as a rule, be permitted to practice law only in the courts to whose bars you have been admitted to practice. Normally, you will not be allowed to work in the courts of a foreign jurisdiction. U.S. law firms practicing in the fields of maritime law (admiralty), aviation law, trademark law, copyright and patent law, and licensing often represent foreign clients that are subject to the jurisdiction of courts in the United States.

Many of the cases litigated in the United States arise abroad and require investigation outside the United States, knowledge of foreign law, and travel abroad to confer with clients and investigate the facts. A number of U.S. law firms have branch offices abroad to represent their U.S. clients and maintain liaisons with their foreign clientele. In certain types of practice, such as maritime law, aviation law, copyright law, and others, there are international networks of specialty law firms that engage one another in the handling of cases. Even relatively small firms in these specialties often provide opportunities for travel and involvement with foreign law firms.

Below is a sampling of some law firms:

Baker & McKenzie

1 Prudential Plaza
130 East Randolph Drive, Suite 2500
Chicago, IL 60601
(312) 861–8800; fax: (312) 861–8823
www.bakernet.com/BakerNet/default.htm

One of the largest and most international of U.S. law firms is this Chicago-based firm, founded in 1949. A network of more than 64 offices in 35 jurisdictions makes Baker & McKenzie a truly international law firm. More than 3,000 lawyers provide local, regional, and international expertise at offices in major business and commercial centers around the world. Lawyers at Baker & McKenzie possess multinational legal training and experience in both civil and common law. Many are admitted to practice in several jurisdictions and are multilingual.

Davis, Polk, and Wardwell

Director of Recruiting
450 Lexington Avenue
New York, NY 10017
(212) 450–4144; fax: (212) 450–5548
www.dpw.com

Davis, Polk is a medium-sized law firm with about 660 lawyers in offices in New York; Menlo Park; Washington, D.C.; London; Paris; Frankfurt; Madrid; Tokyo; and Hong Kong. Associates in the firm's New York and Washington offices may seek assignments to a foreign office for periods of approximately two years. Unassigned associates are frequently sent to work in the London office for periods of up to six months.

The London office, the firm's largest outside the United States, has 10 partners and 33 associates. The Paris office has one counsel and two associates. The Tokyo office has two partners, one counsel, nine associates, one summer associate, and two legal assistants. The U.S. legal staffs of these foreign offices are among the largest American law firms in these cities.

In projects involving the London and New York offices, Davis, Polk has been involved in numerous securities offerings by U.K. companies in the United States. The Paris and New York offices of Davis, Polk have participated in the privatization of several French companies. The Tokyo office worked on the financing of Bridgestone's tender offer for Firestone, one of the largest U.S. acquisitions made by a Japanese company

Jones Day

North Point
901 Lakeside Avenue
Cleveland, OH 44114
(216) 586–3939; fax: (216) 579–0212
www1.jonesday.com

Jones Day is an international law firm with offices located in 12 U.S. cities (Atlanta, Chicago, Cleveland, Columbus, Dallas, Houston, Irvine, Los Angeles, Menlo Park, New York, Pittsburgh, and Washington, D.C.), 6 European cities (Brussels, Frankfurt, London, Madrid, Milan, and Paris), and 6 in Asia (Hong Kong, Shanghai, Singapore, Sydney, Taipei, and Tokyo).

With more than 1,600 lawyers, Jones Day is one of the largest law firms in the world. Its international operations span the firm's five practice groups: corporate, government regulation, litigation, real estate/construction, and tax.

Opportunities for Students to Intern Abroad

If you are enrolled in law school and would like to explore the possibility of a summer internship abroad, contact the American Bar Association's Law Student Division. Join as a student and receive a reduced membership fee. Annually, this division compiles and publishes a list of summer programs outside the

United States, which can be ordered through their service center by calling (312) 988–5522.

Opportunities for Students and Legal Professionals to Go Overseas

The Fulbright Scholar Program, though quite competitive, allows individuals with legal backgrounds to go overseas for up to one year. There are opportunities for those with strong research interests that are more academic in nature, but also for individuals with applied professional backgrounds. Application information is available at the Council for International Exchange of Scholars (www.cies.org).

Other Major Law Firms with International Practices

Akin, Gump, Strauss, Hauer & Feld, LLP, Washington, D.C. (www.akingump.com)
Allen & Overy, London (www.allenovery.com)
Arnold & Porter, Washington, D.C. (www.arnoldporter.com)
Clifford Chance, London (www.cliffordchance.com)
Coudert Brothers, New York (www.coudert.com)
Shearman & Sterling, New York (www.shearman.com)
White & Case, New York (www.whitecase.com)

HELPFUL RESOURCES

International law–related websites:

American Bar Association (www.abanet.org; lick on "International")
International Law Institute (www.ili.org)
Eattorney (www.eattorney.com)
Social Law Library: International Law (www.socialaw.com/irg/il.html)
International Law Students Association (www.2.magmacom.com/~dbell)
The Counsel Network (www.headhunt.com/contactus.htm)
World Intellectual Property Organization, vacancies (www.wipo.int/hr/en/vacancy/index.htm)
EscapeArtist—Legal Jobs (http:// jobs.escapeartist.com/Openings/Law-Legal)
Euromoney Legal Media Group (www.lawmoney.com)
The CIA's Office of General Counsel (www.cia.gov/ogc/best.htm)

Vault.com resources on law jobs (www.vault.com)

Looking for internationally oriented jobs:

1. Consult directories of law firms such as *Martindale-Hubbell's* to ascertain names of firms with international practices.
2. The *International Career Employment Newsletter* publishes international jobs in a variety of fields including international law.
3. The *National and Federal Legal Employment Report* offers individual subscriptions.

Publications:

International Trade in Legal Services: Regulation of Lawyers and Firms in Global Practice, by Sydney M. Cone III (Little, Brown, 1996).

Directory of American Firms Operating in Foreign Countries, 14th ed., 3 vols. (Uniworld Business Publications, 1996).

Directory of Opportunities in International Law, put out by the University of Virginia School of Law. The cost is $7 for students of the University of Virginia, $10 for other students, and $20 for the general public. Checks, made payable to John Basset Moore Society of International Law, should be sent to the society at the University of Virginia School of Law, Charlottesville, VA 22901.

America's Greatest Places to Work with a Law Degree and How to Make the Most of Any Job, No Matter Where It Is, by Kimm Alayne Walton, 1st ed. (Harcourt Brace Legal and Professional, 1998).

The Official Guide to Legal Specialties: An Insider's Guide to Every Major Practice Area, by Lisa L. Abrams, J.D. (Harcourt Legal and Professional, 2000).

Guerrilla Tactics for Getting the Legal Job of Your Dreams, by Kimm Alayne Walton, J.D. (Harcourt Brace Legal and Professional, 1999).

Jobs for Lawyers, by Hillary Jane Mantis and Kathleen Brady (Impact Publications, 1996).

RECOMMENDED READING

CAREER DEVELOPMENT, THE JOB SEARCH, AND WORKPLACE ISSUES
(INCLUDING GENDER, RELOCATION, AND DIVERSITY)

Bastress, Frances. *The New Relocating Spouse's Guide to Employment*. Manassas Park, VA: Impact Publications, 1993.

Boldt, Laurence. *Zen and the Art of Making a Living*. New York: Arkana/Penguin Group, 1999.

Bolles, Richard. *The 2002 What Color Is Your Parachute? A Practical Manual for Job Hunters and Career Changers*. Berkeley: Ten Speed Press, 2002.

Earning a PhD in Political Science. Washington, DC: American Political Science Association, 1999.

Jackson, Tom. *The New Perfect Resume*, rev. ed. New York: Doubleday Press, 1996.

Kaltreider, Nancy, ed. *Dilemmas of a Double Life: Women Balancing Careers and Relationships*. New York: Jason Aronson, 1997.

Karl, Shannon, and Arthur Karl. *How to Get Your Dream Job Using the Web*. Coriolos Group Books, 1997.

Krannich, Ronald, and Cheryl Krannich. *The Directory of Websites for International Jobs*. Manassas Park, VA: Impact Publications, 2002.

Kruempelman, Elizabeth. *The Global Citizen: A Complete Guide to Creating a Global Life and Career*. Berkeley: Ten Speed Press, 2002.

Passport to Opportunity: U.S. Women in Global Business. New York: Catalyst, 2000.

Sher, Barbara. *I Could Do Anything If I Only Knew What It Was*. New York: Dell, 1995.

Tayeb, Munir H. *The Management of a Multicultural Workforce*. New York: John Wiley and Sons, 1998.

Thompson, Mary Anne. *The Global Resume and CV Guide*. New York: John Wiley and Sons, 2000.

Tullier, Michelle, and L.I. Lishing. *Cover Letters*. New York: Princeton Review Press, 1997.

Yate, Martin. *Cover Letters That Knock 'Em Dead*. Holbrook, MA: Adams Media, 2002.

GOVERNMENT

Banarjee, Dillon. *So You Want to Join the Peace Corps: What to Know Before You Go*. Berkeley: Ten Speed Press, 2000.

Congressional Directory. Washington, D.C.: U.S. Government Printing Office.

Washington Information Directory. Washington, DC: Congressional Quarterly, 2002–2003.

NONPROFIT ORGANIZATIONS/ASSOCIATIONS

Alternatives to the Peace Corps: A Directory of Third World and U.S. Volunteer Opportunities, 9th ed. San Francisco: Food First, 2001.

Doyle, Kevin. *The Complete Guide to Environmental Careers in the 21st Century*. Cambridge, MA: Environmental Careers Organization, 1998.

Encyclopedia of Associations. Denise Akey, ed. Farmington Hills, MI: Gale Research, 1998.

Everett, Melissa. *Making a Living While Making a Difference.* Gabriola Island, BC (Canada): New Society Publishers, 1999.

Olson, Stan, ed. *Foundation Directory*, 24th ed. New York: Foundation Center, Columbia University Press, 2002.

Pybus, Victoria. *The International Directory of Volunteer Work.* Oxford, UK: Vacation Work Publishers, 2003.

BUSINESSES AND BANKS

Capela, John J., and Stephen W. Hartman. *Dictionary of International Business Terms.* Hauppage, NY: Barron's Educational Series, 2000.

Directory of American Firms Operating in Foreign Countries. New York: World Trade Academy Press, 2001.

Directory of Foreign Firms Operating in the United States. New York: Uniworld Business Publications, 2002.

Dun and Bradstreet Exporter's Encyclopedia (World Marketing Guide). New York: Dun and Bradstreet International, annual.

Fortune 500: Top 50 Exporters. Annual list and information on top U.S. exporters, published by *Fortune* magazine.

Japanese External Trade Organization. Available online at www.jetro.go.jp (many publications on doing business with Japan).

Liu, Ying, ed. *Harvard Business School Career Guide to Finance.* Cambridge, MA: Harvard Business School Press, 2002.

Standard and Poor's Register of Corporations, Directors, and Executives, 2 vols. New York: Standard and Poor's, annual.

MANAGEMENT CONSULTING

Association of Management Consulting Firms—Directory of Members. New York: Association of Management Consulting Firms, annual.

Directory of Management Consultants. Peterborough, NH: Kennedy Information, 2003.

Harvard Business School Guide: Management Consulting. Maggie Lu, ed. Cambridge, MA: Harvard Business School Press, 2002.

Parkinson, John. *"Where do we go from here?" The Future of Management Consulting—"Strategic Predictions on the Effects of 9/11 on the Management Consulting Industry."* New York: Association of Management Consulting Firms, 2002.

Your Career in Management Consulting. New York: Association of Management Consulting Firms.

INTERNATIONAL MEDIA AND COMMUNICATIONS

Editor and Publisher International Yearbook: The Encyclopedia of the Newspaper Industry. New York: Editor and Publisher, 2000.

Goodman, Al, and John Pollack. *The World on a String: How to Become a Freelance Foreign Correspondent.* New York: Henry Holt, 1997.

National Register Publishing Editorial Staff, eds. *Standard Directory of International Advertisers & Agencies, 2003: The International Red Book*. New Providence, NJ: National Register Publishing, 2003.

Yudkin, Marcia. *Freelance Writing for Magazines and Newspapers: Breaking in without Selling Out*. New York: HarperCollins, 1993.

LAW

Bell, Susan J. *Full Disclosure: Do You Really Want to Be a Lawyer?*, 2nd ed. Peterson's Guides, 1992.

Federal Careers for Attorneys, 2nd ed. Federal Reports, 1997.

Guide to Education and Career Development in International Law, International Law Students Association.

Herman, Richard L. and Linda P. Sutherland. *The Insider's Guide to Private/NonProfit Legal Employers in the Washington, D.C., Metro Area*. Federal Reports, 1997.

Janis, Mark W. and Salli Swartz eds. *Careers in International Law*, 2nd ed. American Bar Association Publishing, 2001. The ABA website has links to a wide variety of global legal associations, from the International Court of Justice to Indiana International Environmental Law Sources.

Law Firms Yellow Book. Leadership Directories, 1997.

Mantis, Hillary. *Alternative Careers for Lawyers*. Princeton Review Publishing, 2000.

Muneke, Gary A. *The Legal Career Guide: From Law Student to Lawyer*. American Bar Association, 1992..

Turnicky, Ann. *How to Get a Job You Want in a Law Firm*. John Wiley and Sons, 1997.

INDEX